The ImpactAssets Handbook for Investors

The ImpactAssets Handbook for Investors

Generating Social and Environmental Value through Capital Investing

EDITED BY
JED EMERSON

ANTHEM PRESS

Anthem Press
An imprint of Wimbledon Publishing Company
www.anthempress.com

This edition first published in UK and USA 2017
by ANTHEM PRESS
75–76 Blackfriars Road, London SE1 8HA, UK
or PO Box 9779, London SW19 7ZG, UK
and
244 Madison Ave #116, New York, NY 10016, USA

British Library Cataloguing-in-Publication Data
A catalogue record for this book is available from the British Library.

ISBN-13: 978-1-78308-729-7 (Hbk)
ISBN-10: 1-78308-729-3 (Hbk)

This title is also available as an e-book.

We would like to dedicate this book to all those social entre-preneurs and impact investors around the world who have spent their lives creating the knowledge and experience we each now build upon.

While many entering the field of impact investing mis-takenly believe it to be new or untested, in truth there are many who have paved the path upon which those coming to the practice now walk.

We thank you for your good efforts, for taking early risks to pioneer best practices in impact investing and for teaching us there is more to investing capital well than simply mak-ing money.

Contents

Contributors

Jed Emerson
Senior Fellow, ImpactAssets
Edition Editor

Tim Freundlich
President, ImpactAssets

Brad Harrison
Director, Threshold Group

Amy Hartzler
Founder, Do Good Better

Jennifer Kenning
Co-founder, Align

Sara Olsen
Founder, SVT Group

Sandra Osborne
Investments Director, ImpactAssets

Kris Putnam-Walkerly
Founder, Putnam Consulting Group

Stephanie Cohn-Rupp
Managing Director, Threshold Group

Lindsay Smalling
Producer Curator, SOCAP

Matthew Weatherly-White
Partner, The CAPROCK Group

Introduction

Jed Emerson

Your picking up this book is a reflection of the fact that while we all may acknowledge many of the incredible, positive effects finance and capital have had upon our world—lifting millions out of poverty, bringing electricity (increasingly solar generated) into formerly dark places and improving housing options for great numbers of people—the reality is many of our planet's most critical challenges remain. Accessible primary health care and secondary education are beyond reach for many, affordable housing is an issue in both developed and developing nations and the diverse effects of climate change are now making their presence felt around the globe. These are not issues government or nonprofits can address alone. While the role of philanthropy and public funding will continue to be key, the reality is you cannot donate your way out of poverty or back to a green planet. There is a direct and meaningful role to be played by business in working with other sectors to drive positive change in our world. And whether we're talking about mission-driven for-profits or nonprofit social enterprise, the fuel of business is capital.

Traditional, mainstream investing has been built on the belief that investing and consideration of social or environmental issues are two distinct worlds—and that if you include considerations of social or environmental factors within your investing, you will underperform financially. The reality is investing currently creates impacts—both negative and positive—in our world. But today we have the opportunity for investors, both large and small, to work

1

to minimize negative impacts and optimize positive ones through the intentional and strategic deployment of their capital. And in recent years investment strategies that seek to generate various levels of financial return as well as the creation of positive social and environmental impacts have come together under the broad banner of impact investing.

This process has occurred because we now know that not only may we invest to create a better world, but we may do this and at the same time provide for ourselves, our families and our community. We can be financially responsible and advance a more just, sustainable planet. The goal of this book is to help you begin to do just that—to invest your financial capital with positive impact or, if you're an advisor to investors looking to align their assets with their values and life goals, perhaps to refine your approach to helping others engage in impact investing. While it isn't as easy as just giving your money to someone else to manage for you in order to make more money and it may at times be more challenging than writing a check to someone else to do good in your name, impact investing is a lot easier, engaging, and meaningful than you might ever imagine!

Our audience for this book is, first and foremost, those who are looking to manage their investment capital—whether for retirement or for a lifetime—in a way that takes the best ideas of impact investing and puts them to work. Second, we're interested in helping those who are currently investment advisors understand what impact investing is all about in order to more effectively meet the needs of their clients. And, third, we're keen on helping those who are generally interested in impact investing to understand what impact investing is, how it works in practice and what cautions we should all keep in mind as we approach this work.

With that in mind, it's important to remember the following: impact investing is not about "checklist investing" where if you just follow a concise list of "how to's" you'll meet with success. This is not a book of simple answers, but rather considerations, questions and ideas for you to keep in mind as you develop and execute your own strategic approach to managing your money for more than simply financial returns. In the pages of this book, we've gathered a group of professionals who've been active in impact investing for many years and asked them to offer you their best thoughts on how to think about the assets you have to invest, how to approach a process to structure those assets and how to understand how those investments are generating financial returns with social and environmental impacts. Impact investing is a practice, process and journey. And we have complimented their insights with refreshed versions of a few of ImpactAssets' best Issue Briefs. We're glad you've decided to take the initial step of researching this field of work and look forward to helping you continue on your way!

This book will help you understand the following:

- What are the opportunities within impact investing?
- How might you think strategically from a portfolio level to optimize the deployment and performance of your capital for the returns you seek?
- How to find the most current advice, best advisor for you, and relevant resources you should draw upon as you develop your impact investing strategy?
- How can you best anticipate some of the challenges you may encounter on your path?
- How to develop and assess the best metrics and strategies to communicate your approach and its impact?
- How best to manage your expectations for what is possible today as opposed to what you'll be able to do tomorrow?

But before we turn our attention to the tools, approaches and practices to help you invest with meaning (as we say at ImpactAssets), let's get a few things out of the way right up front by outlining some initial considerations!

First, these are *not* new, untested concepts—impact investing, in various forms, has evolved over a good number of years.

While growing numbers of traditional investors and wealth managers are coming into the field of impact investing and these may be new practices to them, the idea that one can invest with consideration of more than financial value creation is not new. In fact, you may be surprised to learn that the very first company to broadly offer equity shares to outside investors—the Dutch East India Company founded in Holland in 1604—had investors who objected to how the company was being managed and organized a campaign to change corporate governance practices. There were also other investors in that same company who, after speaking out against the fact the company was engaging in mercenary practices (actually, uh, piracy!), sold their shares in protest.[1] Since those ever so early days, investors have been exploring how best to manage their investments in a responsible, ethical and impactful manner. Indeed, in many ways the idea that one's values should be a part of one's investing is as old as capitalism itself.

Second, impact investing is *diverse* with a variety of names and approaches to explore.

We will go into the details of the various types of impact investing over the following chapters, but at the start it is important you understand that since impact investing has evolved out of a number of related areas of investing and business activity, it can go by many different names, with its various practices being called different things by different actors. For example, you may hear people refer to:

Socially Responsible Investing (SRI) (referring to screening out companies an investor does not want to have in his or her portfolio, such as companies selling weapons or alcohol);

Environmental, Social and Governance (ESG) Integration (referring to the idea that if you are not thinking about how "extrafinancial" factors such as climate change, pandemics or access to water may affect companies you're invested in, these and other issues could represent "off balance sheet" risk to your portfolio and threaten its financial performance—much less, not advance a more sustainable planet. And, conversely, ESG Integration also asks one to look for investment opportunities that may provide answers to some of today's key challenges—and become opportunities for forward thinking investors with vision);

Mission-Related Investing (referring to a philanthropic foundation using its assets to invest in a way that promotes its mission to combat poverty, help create a more just and equitable world or protect the environment);

Microfinance (referring to investments or loans made to small or "micro" enterprises initially employing a small number of people, often within low-income communities or targeted populations); and

Direct Impact Investing (referring to investors who make direct investments in mission-driven companies and entrepreneurs at an early or growth stage of development).

And any number of other terms that have evolved over the years—many of which have now come to be viewed as falling under the broad umbrella of impact investing. The important thing to remember is these are *all* tools in the impact investing tool kit.

But don't let these various terms confuse you or scare you away! If it walks like a duck and quacks like a duck, I assure you, it *is* a duck! Whether you want to call it a Mallard or a Pintail or a Black Bellied Whistling Duck (truly—that is the name of a type of duck!), the only way you can really tell the difference is if you're positioned right in there, down in the reeds, as it were, and can pick out the differences between the various ducks. If you care only about one kind of impact duck, then yes, you need to pay close attention and over time, even if you only care about ducks in general you will learn to tell them apart to find just the one you want, but for now simply know it's all good; the broad field of practice called impact investing includes a number of specific types of strategy and practice—which is great!—but at the end of the day, when you're sitting there, watching these different ducks and trying to sort them all out, remember, they are all just … ducks!

Third, this is *not* a discussion about trade-offs.

In a traditional, bifurcated approach to investing and philanthropy, it is quite normal to ask, "How much do you want to give up in order to do good?" This question is based on the idea that investing is a zero sum game where you either make money, lose money or you give it away. In contrast, impact investing asks,

What is the purpose of your capital; what levels of financial return do you need to generate along with what types/nature of impact?

More specifically, impact investing is not about sacrificing financial return for some ill-conceived notion of "doing good." Rather, it is about understanding the type and form of total, blended value you want to create in the course of your life through your investment of capital and then structuring your investments to achieve your goals as a citizen investor.

Fourth, different investments create different types of impact.

This handbook introduces you to the concept of Total Portfolio Management and within such an approach we understand different investment opportunities offer the promise* of various levels of financial return together with different types of social and environmental impact. Just as you don't expect to get the same amount of financial return from two investments in differing asset classes—say a bond note versus a private equity investment—you shouldn't expect to get the same type of impact from all types of impact investments. This is neither good nor bad; it is just the nature of both impact and investing.

We will explore this in detail later in this book, but for now what is important to understand is that your definition of impact and your objectives as an investor will differ from the person sitting next to you on the bus or in a bar, much less in a capital market. And that is a good thing! It means you can pursue various levels and forms of social/environmental returns in the same way you'll pursue various levels of financial return—all of which combines into giving you the total performance of your portfolio.

Let's state this again: Simply because one investment may offer deep, community level impact and another investment broad market-level impact isn't necessarily either a good thing or a bad thing. It simply is. The important thing is that you be clear with regard to the nature of the impact *you* are interested in creating and how best to structure your capital to position you to attain your goals as an impact investor.

Fifth, if you want to have big impact, you do *not* need to have big bucks!

Now, of course, as is also the case with traditional investing, if you have many millions of dollars to invest you will have more opportunities, more options for hiring advisors to tailor strategies to fit your needs and more people banging on your door asking you to participate in the latest and greatest impact investing strategies. That said, as we will discuss in the following pages, investors

* Remember: as is true of *all* investing, past performance is no guarantee of future returns!

at *all* levels have options for investing with impact; with a growing number of investment products and strategies coming to market targeting investors with smaller amounts of capital to invest and with the specific intent of "democratizing" impact investing. You may have to work a little harder to find and secure good opportunities that fit your needs, and (depending upon your interests) you may not be able to go fully 100 percent impact with your portfolio today, but there are more and more opportunities to do just that.

With all that in mind, if you are a smaller investor with fewer assets, some of the opportunities you will hear about—direct investment in new companies or fund investments in innovative, new strategies—may actually *not* be good investments for you, regardless of whether or not you are an impact investor. Investors with a lot of money have more money to potentially lose and more money they can *afford* to lose. Investors with less money have less money to lose and should be very careful about taking on more risk than they should—regardless of whether or not you're engaging in impact investing. Remember: Impact investing isn't about ignoring sound, fundamental investing principles—it is about augmenting those principles with consideration of social and environmental impact potential. As you move from your savings account to your retirement account to your direct investing funds, a good rule of thumb is that if you cannot ride the ups and downs of investing—and if you cannot handle the loss of your funds entirely—then you need to be in a "safer" investment strategy, regardless of the level and nature of impact you would like to have. Which leads us nicely to our next point ...

Remember: Doing good does *not* automatically translate to your doing well!

While it is certainly ignorant to think impact investing is good people doing bad deals, the inverse is also not true: Just because you're trying to do good does not mean you will do well! As you move through the impact investing ecosystem to explore the variety of actors and opportunities out there, the good impact intent of you as an investor or the entrepreneurs and fund managers you will encounter does *not* take the place of sound investment practice and business acumen. Impact investing is built upon taking the *best* investing practices and applying them to create community level or global change. Entrepreneurs (regardless of whether they are traditional or socially oriented) are by nature optimists who focus on the potential and possibilities they see before them. The upside of this is their enthusiasm is what will get them through tough times; the downside is they may overestimate the investment opportunity and underestimate potential challenges and hidden pitfalls. This may mean they don't recognize or fully appreciate either their own weaknesses or those of their team and business strategy. Regardless of your great vision and passion for a cause, the key practices of good financial planning, market analysis and management execution will be central to your success. As you assess business plans and listen to well-honed pitches from charismatic entrepreneurs and fund managers, always keep this rule of thumb in mind: whatever estimates you hear for timelines and budgets, it will often take twice as long and cost twice as much to execute the strategies you are investing in. If that turns out not to be the case, good for you—the impact gods have smiled on you and you're all the better for it! But if not, you need to be prepared and aware since, as we all know, nothing in life ever goes according to plan.

The fact you're investing for a better planet and community has nothing to do with the reality that assumptions need to be continuously revised, market opportunities shift and the cost of operations could rise from X to 10X. So, sharpen your pencil, hone your skills and build your network for success. The fact you want to do more than simply make money and are also seeking to create positive value in the world actually makes your task more challenging than it is for investors focused only upon making as much money for themselves as they can, however they are able. You can be an effective and successful impact investor, but that doesn't mean you can ignore the proven practices of good management and fundamental investing.

Seventh, if you're going to attempt to have an impact upon the world, it would be good to hear the voices of those whose lives you seek to impact.

Much of the discussion and practice of impact investing—indeed, the general focus of this book as well—takes the perspective of the investor, asking questions having to do with intent and purpose, portfolio construction, performance metrics and so on. While on the one hand understandable, within the context of impact investing the point is to effect change in the world and the world is made up of people with their own ambitions, values, goals and agenda; indeed, people with their own agency as human beings

Never forget: the reason you are doing this is not to advance your own interests apart from those of others or their communities; it is to advance your interests together and in partnership with those communities. Groups such as Transform Finance, RSF Finance and Resource Generation are raising significant and profound questions concerning power, wealth and equity. As you move along your path, however most appropriate for your investing strategy and capacity, always ask,

"Who is directly and indirectly effected through this strategy and how can I ensure I'm hearing their perspective, concerns and ideas?"

Sustained impact means more than simply generating a return to investors; it also means creating changed communities and potentially a transformed society. Be sure to keep that top of mind in your reflections regarding what you seek to do in the world with your capital, how you assess investment opportunities and how you may best be engaged as a collaborator *with* those whose lives you hope to connect your capital for the benefit of you, these stakeholders and the planet.

Finally, impact investing is dynamic, evolving and growing!

Depending upon when you start the clock, it has taken traditional "Western" investing somewhere on the order of 400 years—and through many booms and busts—to evolve its current set of operating practices, standards, terms of investment, performance metrics, advisor ecosystem, operating infrastructure and so on. And how we traditionally invest in the market is markedly different from how and in what we invested even 20 years ago. Within this larger capital marketplace, impact investing is also growing, changing and undergoing significant development. As David Blood, formerly of Goldman Sachs and presently managing partner of Generation Investment Management, recently observed at an impact investing conference hosted by *The Economist* magazine, investing for social impact is not a 5 percent niche anymore—it's more like

20–30 percent of the market and it's clear many major investors are increasingly focused on sustainability.[2]

While this is great to see, it is also true that, depending upon the asset class or investment strategy you're interested in, impact investors may not have as many investment options or products as one would find in the capital market mainstream. That is okay, however, since impact investing, while building upon traditional investment practices, is not the same as traditional investing. As new investible opportunities are brought to market over coming years (as they have now been developed and brought to market in years past) investors will only have more and better options to select from in the future. Today is the day to begin educating yourself about these emerging strategies and developing the skills and understanding you will need to be successful not only as an investor, but as an investor who may join with others to leave a legacy of impact in our world.

With these opening thoughts in mind, let's dial our focus in a little tighter:

- What, exactly, is impact investing?
- How big is the market opportunity for impact investing?
- What kind of financial performance have investors had to date?

And perhaps most importantly for our conversation, since this is about impact investing and not simply traditional investing:

- What kind of impact returns have investors seen and how are those returns measured, tracked and valued?

While different, discrete strategies within impact investing will define it differently, for our purposes we define impact investing as follows:

> *The investment of philanthropic, near-market and market-rate capital in pursuit of various levels of financial return together with the generation of social and environmental impact.*

Within this definition, investors should consider not only their market-rate capital as a form of investment, but *all* their capital as part of a single, Total Portfolio of investible assets to be managed and deployed through a defined strategy and viewed as part of the overall resources available to create not simply financial returns but the overall impact returns you seek to generate over the course of your life. Since this is an important concept to understand, the first chapter of this book presents the idea in greater detail.

It may strike you as odd that we include philanthropic capital in this definition. Since this is the first idea some may find "different" about impact investing, it is worth our taking a minute to discuss. From our perspective, all capital creates impact and all capital has potential to generate various levels of financial value—philanthropic capital is not only charitable, but also has economic value and should be considered together with how we think about the management of our other forms of capital.

Think about it this way:

If you give your money away through a direct, charitable gift or if you create a donor advised fund (DAF) (don't worry—we have a whole chapter on those!) or if you set up a family foundation, you receive a tax benefit from the government. Naturally, this differs depending on your country of residency and the amounts involved, but generally speaking in many countries when you engage in charitable giving, you receive a tax benefit of some type.

This is just one form of financial return you receive—and we're not even talking about the financial value that nonprofits and nongovernmental organizations create in the course of doing their work to pursue their charitable mission. According to Elizabeth Boris, PhD, director of the Center on Nonprofits and Philanthropy at the US-based Urban Institute, the nonprofit sector in the United States contributed 5.5 percent to GDP, had revenues of 2.1 trillion dollars, paid \$576.9 billion in wages—which is 9 percent of the total wages paid out in the nation—and employed 13.7 million Americans.[3] If one applies a Social Return on Investment calculation to this investment of charitable dollars, the financial returns to society alone are in the trillions of dollars.

As will be explored in later chapters, philanthropy—whether traditional or venture philanthropy—is society's risk capital, and it supports research, inquiry and early stage development of not only nonprofit but for-profit ventures. In addition, charitable foundations may make use of something called a Program

Related Investment (a low-interest, higher risk loan) that, again, is technically drawing upon charitable "giving" dollars, but that—depending upon how it is structured—can generate not only interest rate returns, but equity returns to investors as well. In these and other ways, philanthropy has economic value and can create financial returns.

One other thing we should point out before moving on to our discussion of the size of the impact investing capital market:

While definitions of impact investing often include a reference to the need to measure the impact one seeks to have, you may notice that—in contrast to that traditional definition of impact investing—we did not include reference to metrics and measurement in our definition. We fully acknowledge the critical importance of metrics and measurement of financial and extrafinancial performance of capital and organizations. In fact, we think it is so important we have a whole chapter of this book devoted to the topic and have spent much of our professional life promoting innovative measurement practices.

That said, we would expect many of those who are long-time impact investors, academics who study the development of the evaluation field within impact investing and those who promote practices of measurement may strenuously object to our exclusion of any reference to metrics in our definition. Dear reader, prepare yourself for seeing impact investing folks rallying with pitchforks and burning this book on the town hall stairs!

Let us explain . . .

We are not including a commitment to metrics and measurement within our definition of impact investing because we feel it is redundant. When you invest, you invest to create value and returns. If one claims to be interested in investing, you have to have a way to understand whether and in what ways you have achieved your performance goals. Therefore, it goes without saying those deploying capital should already be committed to making use of the appropriate metrics to inform not only investors with regard to assessing the returns on their capital, but more importantly entrepreneurs and managers who claim to be operating their ventures in order to generate impact returns. Indeed, if you are considering investing in an impact opportunity that does *not* have meaningful metrics as a part of their performance management, tracking and reporting process, that should be your first red flag for "impact washing" or at least an indication that whatever impact is being created may differ from your own understanding of "impact."

Impact measurement and metrics are key to engaging in investing. Period. Today, if all you do is seek financial returns and you are not managing your assets with consideration of social and environmental risk factors, we would argue you are not only facing the possibility of underperforming financially, but may also be in violation of your fiduciary duty—regardless of the type of assets you are responsible for and how you define "returns." Furthermore, if you are an impact investor who feels consideration of social and environmental factors are material to the performance of your investment strategy, how could you not make use of the most appropriate metrics by which to manage your investments, much less engage in a discussion of what metrics are the best fit to assess the total performance of your particular strategy?

Finally, we fear the various and sundry debates regarding what are the "best" and "most appropriate" metrics threaten to take the impact investing field down a rabbit hole. The point is not having the right and perfectly groomed metrics but investing in impact returns that are most relevant to the entrepreneur, community and asset owner. While many of us have been committed to advancing the best possible approach to metrics, we must not let the perfect be the enemy of the good. Yes, you must work with others to create and apply the best metrics practices that integrate social and environmental with financial reporting. But we must also recognize efforts to do so are only several decades old, while our approach to assessing financial performance is—again, depending upon when you start the clock—many centuries old.

As a possible newcomer to the conversation, know this:

Measuring and assessing the extrafinancial value of your investments is critical. And every asset class—every type of capital—will approach it differently, have different ways to think about it and will be able to generate metrics with various levels of confidence with regard to their integrity and relevance to your investment thesis. Therefore, read our chapter on metrics and measurement, research which types of metric practices are most important to the type of investing you will be engaging in and the type of performance you seek to create and then track only those things that matter to you and for the types of investments you're making.

And know that when you go to your first impact investing conference—which we would encourage you to do as part of your process of becoming an impact investor—you will be able to generate a firestorm from the floor when you announce yourself as an impact investor yet pronounce your indifference to the metrics debates in which others will be deeply engaged with diverse and heated passions![4]

Alright, so great ... with all that said and done, one of the first questions many ask about impact investing is just how big is the impact investing arena today? People want to know this to help them understand how many other investors are making use of this approach and, of course, the more people engaging in impact investing, the easier it is for you to buy and sell your investment positions, the more options for investment products you will have to help manage your risk and, overall, the easier it will be for you to find the types of opportunities that best reflect your interests and strategy.

In light of the previous discussion, you should not be surprised to learn that one's definition of the size of the impact investing market depends on the type of investing you consider "impact," the type of capital you are interested in deploying and the type of "duck" you're wanting to go birding after. With all that in mind, here are a few figures that should get your attention.

The Report on US Sustainable, Responsible and Impact Investing Trends 2016 stated thus:

- Overall, the field experienced 135% growth from 2012 to 2016
- $8.10 trillion in US domiciled assets at the outset of 2016 held by 477 institutional investors, 300 money managers and 1,043 community investing financial institutions to which various ESG criteria are applied in investment analysis and portfolio selection, and
- $2.56 trillion in US domiciled assets at the start of 2016 held by 225 institutional investors or money managers that filed or co-filed shareholder resolutions on ESG issues from 2014 through 2016.

- These two segments of assets, after eliminating double counting for assets involved in both strategies and for assets managed by money managers on behalf of institutional investors, yield the overall total of $8.72 trillion, a 33 percent increase over the $6.57 trillion that the US SIF Foundation identified in sustainable investing strategies at the outset of 2014.[5]

Or consider Dennis Price, writing for ImpactAlpha, who states that:

- The latest tally of socially responsible investment shows growth in fixed-income and retail investing. The Global Sustainable Investment Alliance, which rolls up regional and national surveys from a half-dozen partners, casts a wide net, including negatively and positively screened public equities, green bonds and impact and community investments.
- Screened investments that exclude sectors like tobacco and firearms, still makes up the largest segment, with $15 trillion in assets.
- Bonds, including climate-aligned bonds, made up 64 percent of Socially Responsible Assets, up from 40 percent in 2014, partly driven by the growth of green bonds.
- European investors account for more than half of global SRI assets, compared with 38 percent for the U.S. The portion of SRI assets owned by retail investors doubled to 26 percent.
- From a small base, impact and community investing grew by 146 percent to $258 billion.[6]

How does all that compare to the size of traditional capital markets? Interestingly enough, that sector also suffers from an inability to agree upon the right metrics and definitions of just what all should be considered a part of mainstream capital markets (which must be what we mean when we say that impact investing is really just investing ...) in that estimates of the size of traditional capital markets vary from between $118 trillion,[7] to $294 trillion[8] depending upon the time frame and constellation of assets taken into account.

Adoption of impact and sustainable investment practices by traditional, mainstream asset managers is also an indication of the degree to which these ideas have migrated from the fringe to the mainstream. Morgan Stanley and Bloomberg News conducted a survey in 2016 that found that 64 percent of asset managers state that they apply some form of sustainable investing within their practice.[9] We can discuss exactly what practices are being executed under "sustainable investing" and how these managers define sustainable investing—yet the fact a majority of managers are aware of and believe themselves to be engaged in sustainable investing in one form or another is a significant tipping point in our efforts to advance impact throughout mainstream capital markets.

Of perhaps greater importance than discussions regarding the size of impact investing markets relative to traditionally managed capital markets is the financial performance of current impact investors. After all, a key part of this conversation is the notion that we may do well *and* good; namely, that we may attain financial returns competitive with traditional investing, but that also generate various types and levels of "impact" (however we may each define that impact). Again, if one's understanding of impact is moving X number of people from a dollar a day to two dollars a day income, investing in global public equities may be a long road to impact. If, however, you seek to invest in a diverse portfolio of conforming investment products and strategies that offer market-rate returns (meaning, financial returns competitive with those of other investors like you ...), but with various levels of social and environmental value creation, then you need to understand this is not only possible, but a completely realistic expectation.

Speaking from personal experience, over the past seven years I've worked with five families investing all their assets on a Total Portfolio Management basis (totaling, in aggregate, approximately $1.2 billion in assets). None of those families has generated financial returns that were less than expected due to the impact aspect of their investing. And our experience is consistent with the larger market as reflected by the following:

> A 2015 study from the Institute for Sustainable Investing examined performance data from 10,228 open-end mutual funds and 2,874 separately managed accounts (SMAs) over seven years and found that investing in sustainability has usually met, and often exceeded, the performance of comparable traditional investments, both on

an absolute and a risk-adjusted basis, across asset classes and over time. The study also showed lower median volatility for the funds and SMAs studied since companies that score well on ESG also tend to be less vulnerable to negative headline risks, large-scale lawsuits or environmental risks.[10]

And years of academic research also validate the notion that while one cannot guarantee outperformance relative to traditional investing strategies and, of course, one may still find and invest in "bad" managers regardless of whether or not they are "impact" investment managers, the general consensus and actual demonstrated experience has been that impact and sustainable investing strategies do *not* financially underperform the market relative to traditional investing strategies.

Mic drop.

Okay, so let's get going ...

How does one "do" impact investing?

What follows is not an answer book or outline for attaining guaranteed riches with impact, but rather a set of reflections, lessons learned and best practices of a wide array of impact investors and professionals involved in the impact investing community. This book is not a simple "five step, how to" book. Investing is by definition a process of taking on some level of risk in exchange for projected financial, and in this case, impact returns. At this point in the field's evolution and our own professional development, what is included here are some of our best ideas and perspectives with regard to how to "do" impact investing in a responsible manner. We intend to share as many tips and insights with you as possible.

And we will do that in the following way:

Chapter One presents an overview of Total Portfolio Management—the idea that all your assets should be managed on an impact basis and the best way to be successful in life and investing is by stepping back from your capital to reflect upon what you're ultimately trying to achieve as an investor—and then develop an investment approach that reflects the total, integrated and blended value you seek to create over the course of your life.

Chapter Two takes the Total Portfolio Management idea to a deeper level with a discussion by Matthew Weatherly-White of The

CAPROCK Group on how they take those ideas and put them into practice with their clients.

Chapter Three, authored by Tim Freundlich, Jed Emerson and Lindsay Smalling, is a brief exploration of seed stage impact investing. This area of investing is tough and higher risk, so we urge caution—but also encourage impact investors interested in working closely with the next "impact Facebook" to take a hard look at how best to become active in this dynamic area of focus.

Chapter Four, coauthored by Brad Harrison and Stephanie Cohn-Rupp of Threshold Group, talks about the steps asset owners may take to understand the type of investment advisor best suited to their needs and how to go about the process of identifying and vetting possible advisors to assist you in your impact investment process.

Chapter Five moves across the capital continuum with a look at how investors may make use of the philanthropic vehicle of a DAF to engage in both philanthropic and impact investing. Coauthored by the senior teams of ImpactAssets, RSF Social Finance and Tides Network each of these institutions executes strategies to catalyze community and enterprise impact by more effective structuring of philanthropy *through* impact investing.

Given the fear some impact investors have at being confused with philanthropy, some might wonder why a book on impact investing would offer a lengthy discussion on best practices *in* philanthropy. As explored elsewhere in these pages, philanthropy is one of the types of capital we view as making up the Total Portfolio of asset owners and is therefore worthy of inclusion on that merit alone. But perhaps more importantly, while one often hears folks unfamiliar with modern approaches to philanthropic and nonprofit management make vacuous comments about the need for nonprofits to become more business-like, in point of fact, many investors and business people have a great deal to learn from philanthropy, nonprofit managers and social entrepreneurs. This is not simply a question of learning how to "look beyond the numbers" (as positive a step as that might be for many "expert" investors!), but also speaks to the fact that sound philanthropic practice and principles actually mirror many of the better approaches to skilled investing. Chapter Six, contributed by philanthropic advisor Kris Putnam-Walkerly, examines fundamental aspects of effective philanthropy and how those approaches to charitable giving may be augmented by an investment mindset. In reviewing this chapter, the reader is encouraged to reflect upon how what Kris has to share might inform your own approach to managing your impact investing activities.

Chapter Seven moves the discussion from strategy and portfolio construction to execution; namely, how does one identify, assess and engage in due diligence of possible investments? Director of Investments for ImpactAssets Sandra Osborne shares her approach and pointers for investors looking to bring greater discipline to their process of impact investing.

With a strategy in place, due diligence conducted and investments being made, a common challenge for many impact investors is understanding how to best assess and document the impact they have created—and by extension, how to understand the way funds and social entrepreneurs generate impact through the management of their entity. In Chapter Eight, Sara Olsen, founder of SVT Group, a leading metrics and measurement advisory firm, explores issues and practices in applying appropriate metrics to impact investing practice.

Chapter Nine describes the challenge of then communicating impact—as well as, from the investor perspective, understanding how those communicating impact to *you* may be viewing that challenge. Amy Hartzler, founder of the communications consulting group Do Good Better, shares her insights on communicating impact and how best to think about the various audiences one needs to consider when creating a communications strategy.

Finally, we understand many of those reading this book will want to get down to it and engage in impact investing as soon as possible. For those folks, we offer reflections from Jennifer Kenning, a former institutional markets investor who came over to impact, discussing the four key steps to impact as she views them based upon her journey. Her lessons are then followed by our closing chapter, Getting to Impact, that discusses immediate options you may explore to get going today to deploy impact capital—at various levels of financial minimums and, of course, after you have conducted your own diligence!

We conclude the guidebook with a set of final considerations offered to you by Tim Freundlich, President of ImpactAssets and myself. We feel these are important points to bear in mind as you continue your journey, explore what impact investing means for you and develop a strategy to guide your investing over coming years.

Impact investing is a promising and exciting area for you to engage. There are emerging best practices and approaches you may build upon, and new approaches for you to explore. While impact investing develops out of the experiences of past years, the amount of innovation and opportunity that lies ahead of us is truly exciting. We welcome you into this process and wish you all the best as you continue your journey from success to significance and beyond!

Notes

1 Niall Ferguson, *The Ascent of Money: A Financial History of the World* (Penguin Books Group: New York City, 2008), p. 132.

2 Published February 22, 2017, Accessed March 27, 2017, http://nextbillion. net/mainstreaming-impact-investing-12-takeaways-from-the-economist-event/.

3 Elizabeth Boris Presentation, Accessed April 3, 2017, https://philanthro-pynewyork.org/sites/default/files/resources/The%20Nonprofit%20 Sector%20in%20the%20United%20States%20Size%20and%20Scope.PDF.

4 For more reflections on metrics, please see: Jed Emerson, *The Metrics Myth: Why Quantitative Presentation of Qualitative Value Matters,* February 10, 2015, Accessed April 3, 2017, http://www.blendedvalue.org/the-metrics-myth/.

5 Accessed March 27, 2017, http://www.ussif.org/files/Trends/US%20 SIF%202016%20Trends%20Overview.pdf

6 Published March 29, 2017, Accessed March 29, 2017, http://impactalpha. com/global-sustainable-investment-assets-hit-23-trillion-up-25-percent-in-two-years/.

7 Accessed April 3, 2017, https://www.google.com/search?q=total+size+of+glo bal+capital+markets&ie=utf-8&oe=utf-8.

8 Accessed April 3, 2017, http://www.marketwatch.com/story/global-stock-market-cap-has-doubled-since-qes-start-2015-02-12.

9 Morgan Stanley and Bloomberg Survey Finds Sustainable Investing Has Gone Mainstream; Published November 2016, Accessed April 20, 2017, https://www.morganstanley.com/press-releases/morgan-stanley-and-bloomberg-survey-finds-sustainable-investing-.

10 "Millenials Democratizing Impact Investing," Published March 6, 2016, Accessed April 3, 2017, Blog Post from Morgan Stanley, https://www. morganstanley.com/ideas/millennial-sustainable-investing.

1

Construction of an Impact Portfolio: Total Portfolio Management for Multiple Returns

Jed Emerson and Lindsay Smalling

Introduction

Despite the growing media coverage of impact investing, and that coverage's increasingly sophisticated character, there continues to exist a widespread misperception that impact investing is a single type of investing and not a broad approach. It is easy for those considering impact investing to conclude it is similar to, say, venture capital investing—direct, volatile, high risk and a strategy available only to high net worth individuals. This perception was underscored when influential organizations initially made the mistake of labeling impact investing as an "emerging asset class," implying that impact cannot be achieved across all asset classes.

While understandable as a "way into" a discussion of how capital may be invested for financial return with the generation of social/environmental impacts, such an approach initially segregated impact investing within a single category of capital as opposed to laying the foundation for exploring how investors might manage all their assets for impact across an entire portfolio. In point of fact, impact investing is broad and nuanced. One may look at impact investing as both a "sleeve," which is to say as a discrete strategy within a larger portfolio of investments, or as a "lens" through which one looks at an entire portfolio. For the purposes of this chapter, we will operate at a portfolio level and take the "lens" approach. When adopting such a total portfolio perspective, impact investors seek to achieve an appropriate financial return for any given investment instrument, fund or strategy under consideration within their portfolio while simultaneously asking,

> *What is the best way to think about the nature of impact within this particular investment or asset class?*

When one takes this perspective, impact may be pursued across an *entire* portfolio with appropriate consideration of various risk, impact and financial return objectives for the allocation of philanthropic, near-market and market-rate capital. Developing this understanding of how best to incorporate impact within portfolio construction is especially timely for individual investors interested in taking a more holistic approach to their investment strategy as well as financial advisors who receive growing numbers of client requests to consider the social and environmental impacts of their portfolio as well as structure capital investments to advance positive impact.

Regardless of how much money you may have to invest, and while specific strategies may differ, it is increasingly possible to achieve positive impact across all one's capital investments. And every month sees investment products being brought to market that make impact investments available at lower minimums to a broad cross-section of investors at different levels of wealth. While not yet an "off-the-shelf" approach, impact investing is a growing option for many investors. This chapter is offered as an introductory guide to help investors and advisors construct portfolios that integrate impact appropriately across asset classes. We refer to this practice as Total Portfolio Management.[1] Within such a Total Portfolio Management approach, all capital—philanthropic, near-market and market-rate—is managed to optimize financial performance across asset classes while maximizing the impact potential of each asset class you are invested within.

Emerging Practices of Total Portfolio Management

For financial advisors, engaging with a client in the process of portfolio construction offers an opportunity to understand and strategically respond to that investor's personal financial priorities and objectives. And for individual investors operating without an advisor, the process of exploring and identifying what investment options are available in which asset classes can be one of discovery and real excitement. As your investment objectives evolve to include social and environmental impact, the conversation between investors and advisors must weave considerations of impact throughout the portfolio construction process. Total Portfolio Management is an approach that seeks to optimize diversified financial returns while maximizing impact as appropriate for any given investment asset class. It is not reductive (asking, *What do we remove from consideration from the investment universe?*) but rather additive (asking, *How do we take traditional investment practices and augment them with enhanced analytics and perspective to allow for consideration of both off balance sheet risk and impact investment opportunities?*). In this way, when engaging in Total Portfolio Management, the fundamentals of traditional investment management still apply.[2]

As discussed below, it is important to understand that Total Portfolio Management considers the full array of capital being deployed by asset owners: philanthropic, near-market and market-rate. Such an approach acknowledges charitable giving—by providing donors with tax benefits and other considerations—offers financial value while generating social and environmental returns. In this way, asset owners may bring a holistic approach to their consideration of how best to manage all their capital to pursue the full, blended value they seek to create as they manage and deploy their capital resources.

This chapter offers an introductory overview of these ideas and suggests some initial steps investors may take to envision, create and execute an investment approach that integrates financial considerations with social and environmental concerns.

Step One: Establish Goals and Objectives

As every skilled investor knows, the first step in professionally managing assets is to define your core goals and objectives. These typically cover such issues as:

- date of future retirement,
- potential college or other education expenses, and
- wealth preservation for future generations

and so on. The next step is to take stock of the unique cash flow needs, risk tolerance and time horizon of the individual asset owner. All of this information is taken into account when engaging in a traditional investment approach or crafting the asset allocation, investment policy statement (IPS) and investment portfolio in a more customized manner.

These factors are considered when developing a traditionally managed portfolio of investments and are equally important for effectively constructing an impact portfolio. However, in addition to standard "financial only" discussions that inform the creation of an investor's profile, the process of creating an impact portfolio also includes simultaneous exploration of the investor's expectations and objectives with regard to the generation of social and environmental impact.

It is important to understand the "right" answer as to what should constitute the impact agenda of any given portfolio differs for each and every investor. For example, one family may be generally interested in making sure they are not invested in "bad" companies while having a broad interest in issues related to women and girls. Another investor may be spending her professional career focused on combating climate change or protecting the environment, and so will most likely not feel comfortable with financial returns generated largely from significant investments in fossil fuel production. And yet another investor may have a deep connection to his community or region and find tremendous value in identifying investment opportunities in regionally specific local food systems or area affordable housing.

Regardless of the ultimate goal and set of investment strategies, exploring your core values and expectations is critical to attaining a broader understanding of your definition of the purpose of your capital in order to create a strategy that best advances toward your goals.

Step Two: The Investment Policy Statement

The Investment Policy Statement (IPS) is a document that outlines the overall vision and goals for the investment strategy. For those working with an investment advisor, the IPS outlines how the client's investments will be managed over the course of a year or more. The reader will find this topic referenced in the following two chapters as well, from the perspective of investment advisors. However, even if you are not working with an advisor, having a single memo outlining your vision, goals and objectives as well as detailing how you want to allocate your investment dollars across various strategies and asset classes is a good document to have. Either way, the IPS serves as a guide star for family members, advisors and, if you have one, your investment committee—even if it consists only of you and your partner or pooch!

While important for all types of investing, for clients seeking to intentionally integrate impact across their entire portfolio the IPS is critical. Ad hoc impact divestment or investment is not a sustainable strategy for impact. The IPS provides a framework for evaluating current holdings, exiting investments that are not consistent with the evolved investment strategy and assessing new investment opportunities. It is the framework to be used in evaluating the total performance of a portfolio that seeks to generate financial returns with social and environmental impact.

Crafting an IPS with consideration of impact can be a challenge for advisors taking their first step into impact investing with a client. Although there is substantial evidence to support the position that impact investments may deliver market-rate returns for any given asset class, many financial advisors and investment committees are resistant to change, mistakenly believing investing with an impact orientation might threaten the fulfillment of their financial fiduciary responsibilities. Since the IPS is the foundational agreement between an advisor and client, explicit goals and practices outlined in the IPS should address investment committee concerns, detailing how any given asset owner defines their fundamental fiduciary obligations.

It should also be understood that the IPS is not a static document but rather a dynamic one that should be revisited annually, with its assumptions reaffirmed or modified based upon any number of factors. Such factors might include significant shifting of the overall market context or evolving investor intent—but should not be revised in efforts to try to "time the market." At the same time, while any changes to the IPS should certainly not be undertaken lightly, the IPS offers "guard rails" to guide and direct investment practice, not "train tracks" to lock in an investment committee regardless of where the train appears to be headed!

The Portfolio Carve-Out

A Possible "On Ramp" to Total Portfolio Management

While the focus of this chapter is on a holistic, Total Portfolio Management approach to investing, we acknowledge that some individuals begin their impact journey by taking a portion of their investment portfolio and designating that allocation to be managed on an impact basis. Within this approach, the advisor and client agree to carve out a portion of the portfolio to be dedicated to specific impact investments, themes or strategies. Accordingly, this capital may be invested in a single asset class or distributed across asset classes with specific impact themes.

Such initially incremental approaches to impact investing may be necessary to help investment committees and fiduciaries become more comfortable with the idea and practices of aligning capital with ultimate investor intent. And for many asset owners new to the concepts of impact investing, taking a staged approach to exploring and deploying impact investment strategies may make the most sense. Such an approach may also be required in order to best manage investment lock-ups or tax considerations. With that understanding in mind, two points should be considered.

First, all capital has impact of one form or another. For foundations or families concerned with advancing "the greater good" of society as well as fulfilling their fiduciary responsibilities, assuming one's investments do not have impacts upon the world (whether positive or negative) is increasingly being called into question.

Second, while in the past there may have been challenges in executing impact investing that helped justify taking a multiyear, incremental approach to deploying investment capital, more recently a significant increase in the availability of impact investing product—and the ever growing successful track record of managing that product—makes it possible for many impact investors to deploy capital across an array of conforming, competitive investment products, funds and managers. Regardless, identifying and then investing in new, impact investing approaches may take one to three years, and all investors should recognize executing these ideas might take a certain amount of time, discovery and planning. Even those investors seeking to go "all in" will find it is not a process that takes a quarter but rather a year or more.

It comes as no surprise that various investors will handle the specifics of this investment process differently, but it is in the IPS where investors outline what is referred to as an impact thesis. This will entail drafting of an investor-specific understanding of impact and broadly defining how you view the integration of impact and financial performance. Some investors will feel it important to include several pages of narrative on how they understand the nature of the impact they seek to create through their portfolio while others will simply address it in a few paragraphs or sharply stated sentences. Either way, it is critical the IPS explore this question with enough definition to guide both the individual investor operating on her own, as well as an investment committee and/ or wealth advisor who may be working with individuals with larger portfolios and assisting the asset owner in their decision-making process.

Setting a leading example, The F. B. Heron Foundation wrote their IPS to reflect the "intent to balance the social and financial return on all assets, and to select opportunities for deploying capital, whether as grants or as investments, so as to maximize the combination of both kinds of return within each."* You will find their full IPS on their website and other examples may be found in the web pages included in the resources section of this handbook.

Step Three: Asset Allocation

With an understanding of your financial and impact performance objectives, as well as risk tolerance and time horizon, investors should now establish the initial structure of the portfolio; this is done through a process of asset allocation. Since each asset class has its own risk, return and impact profile, investors may customize a portfolio to fit their specific objectives by varying the level of. investment in each asset class.

For example, additional risk taken on in private equity may be balanced by a larger fixed-income allocation. There are sophisticated asset allocation strategies used to optimize the classic risk-return trade-off upon which traditional portfolio construction is based, and these strategies may be adapted to include consideration of impact across asset classes. An investor or advisor who

---

* Across this volume, any quoted matter from organizations/companies have been taken from their website and readers can look up the sources for more information.

seeks to thoughtfully integrate impact within a portfolio will evaluate where impact is redundant, complementary, or catalytic in relation to the ultimate objectives of the investor as needs to be expressed through your portfolio.

When taken together, each of the specific investment allocations contributes to the Total Performance of the portfolio, generating financial and impact returns across various asset classes, including philanthropic. Accordingly, the impact goals sought through any given investment should be appropriate to that investment opportunity just as the financial returns expected of any strategy will differ based on the investment approach of that particular asset class. Said another way, one should not expect microloan impact from a socially responsible mutual fund, just as one does not expect private equity returns from a fixed-income product. In this way, impact and financial returns may differ across individual asset classes within any given portfolio, but you should seek to structure the total portfolio to best manage your capital in a manner that seeks to generate financial and impact returns in alignment with your specific goals.

Manager Search, Due Diligence and Selection

After the asset allocation is established, the process of you and your advisor researching managers, conducting due diligence on those managers and selecting possible investments for consideration may begin. Chapter Seven of this handbook explores various aspects of due diligence in greater detail, but for now you should know a good starting place for your research are the socially responsible and impact investing communities that have compiled resources for identifying investment products with social and environmental criteria. Refer to our appendix sections for more on this information.

As with all other investment products, specific diligence requirements differ with asset class or deal structure. However, it is always important to take a close look at the background and experience of the people managing the investments, the philosophy behind their approach, the process they use for selecting investments and the total performance (meaning assessment of both impact and financial returns) they have achieved over time.

The evaluation of performance for an investment in an impact portfolio includes measurable, demonstrated and reported impact that is aligned or complementary to the portfolio objectives. Therefore, it is critical those considering various managers analyze their impact reporting capacity and practices as well as their traditional financial management and reporting practices.

If you find you're especially interested in an investment that doesn't quite fit the agreed upon criteria for that asset class, this can be thoughtfully accommodated by taking a Total Portfolio Management approach. For example, you may want to pursue an investment that takes on greater risk in relation to the expected financial return because it generates a particular type of demonstrated impact. Alternatively, an investor may choose to unconventionally risk-balance a portfolio to permit pursuit of high-innovation impact opportunities that offer an elevated probability of failure not due to their impact DNA but simply due to their innovative structure. And as discussed below, savvy portfolio construction may compensate for many different forms of risk—execution, liquidity, credit, innovation, start-up, and so forth—through complementary investments within each asset class, shifting your own monitoring and engagement practices or by adjusting the overall asset allocation.

Key Concept: Know Your Risk Tolerance

When considering your approach to *any* investment strategy, it is critical you be realistic when it comes to the risk you are willing to assume as an investor. If you have a significant amount of assets, a good number of years experience managing your investment process and an investment team to help you engage in deep due diligence then, depending upon your specific investment goals, you may be in a position to take on any number of higher risk direct or fund investments. However, if you are an individual investing on your own, with limited investment capital and managing your assets in order to fund your long-term retirement, it may well be inappropriate for you to take on various higher risk, direct or fund impact investments. Many people are attracted to impact investing because they want to draw as straight a line as possible between their investment dollars and community, family or individual impact. While admirable, the reality is that the risk of such investments can be much greater and even though you may have access to such deals through crowdfunding and other platforms or via networks and word of mouth, if you are an investor of more limited means there may be a number of reasons why you should *not* engage in higher risk investing—whether or not they are intentional impact investments. Be cautious! Do not invest simply because you "like" an individual or a cause; do not invest simply because someone tells you they have done their homework and you can trust them! Remember: If you can't afford to lose your money, don't take on investment risk—regardless of whether it is an impact or traditional investment opportunity!—that might entail your having to lose your investment funds! There are various other ways you can invest with impact (by keeping your cash in a local, FDIC-insured community bank or regional credit union, for example) where you can feel you're contributing to your local community without taking on greater risk.

Step Four: Performance Monitoring

A best practice for any portfolio, and especially for a portfolio that is actively designed to generate positive impact, is regular monitoring and evaluation. Chapter Eight of this handbook goes into this topic in greater detail, but for now it's important to understand that in alignment with your IPS, benchmarks and/or performance goals should be set for both financial and impact performance. Periodic review of portfolio performance against these benchmarks will indicate necessary revisions to the investment strategy as well as provide an opportunity to adjust investment strategy based upon new factors such as changing client circumstances or market conditions. By taking a formative approach to portfolio monitoring, the comparison of actual outcomes to expected outcomes highlights both the strengths and weaknesses of an investment strategy. These insights inform potential revisions that need to be made to the portfolio strategy over time in order to best meet your objectives. For those making use of investment advisors, this is a unique opportunity to create value within the investment relationship by engaging with a financial advisor and an opportunity to strengthen the relationship between a client and advisor based on a more complete understanding of client values.

The Bondage of Benchmarks and the Investor as "Market"

Comparing any given investment strategy with a complimentary benchmark is the bread and butter of traditional investing. However, the use of benchmarks can be a limiting practice for both traditional and impact investors, having the effect of constricting one's expectations of return and limiting one's understanding of how any given strategy may be executed within a dynamic market. The portfolio profile of an investor may not conform to that of other investors in the market at a similar level of wealth—yet if the total performance objective of the investor is being attained, the financial performance of an underlying benchmark may be completely irrelevant. In this sense, the investor is the "market," defining what financial returns and impact are acceptable for the goals she is pursuing.

When choosing to make use of benchmarks to assess performance, the first question one must ask is whether the comparison benchmark is, in fact, truly comparable. Perhaps of equal importance is the fact that every investor should consider whether an outside benchmark would be effective for assessing performance—whether at the portfolio or individual investment level. For example, if an investor's objective is to use capital to sustain the planet, they may opt to invest in a Real Asset[†] allocation that could increase their exposure to long-term, ill-liquid investments for which the "exit" is decades away.

Or if an investor is committed to placing their capital within a specific geographic region, investing in global equities may not be relevant to or advance their ultimate, long-term investment goals. In either case, what "the market" does or does not deliver in terms of performance may be irrelevant to the goals of the individual investor.

[†] Real Assets refers to such "hard" assets as real estate, forestry, ranch land and so on, but may also include "hard infrastructure" such as solar panels or wind turbines.

Regardless of the final decision investors and advisers may make with regard to how best to assess comparable performance, as Mathew Weatherly-White of The CAPROCK Group (and author of the following chapter on impact investing) has declared, "We should seek to liberate our clients from the tyranny of the benchmarks!"

Defining Impact Across Asset Classes

Whereas the earliest examples of impact investing were easily classified into alternative investment strategies creating what could be thought of as "direct impact," the evolution of the field has enabled a Total Portfolio Management approach to impact that wasn't possible even 15 years ago. While there are still some gaps in product and strategy offerings, today there are credible impact options across many asset classes and investors are being offered an increasing number of options every year. And there is also a growing body of case studies profiling leading impact investors who have demonstrated how Total Portfolio Management works in action generating various types of impact across various types of investment strategies. The resources section of this book offers several websites and networks that provide extensive examples of impact investments available in various asset classes. The examples listed here are only for illustration and are but a few options among many. Those looking to invest for impact should engage in their own process of due diligence and inquiry; furthermore, please note these examples are not offered as investment guidance or advice.

Cash and Cash Equivalents

Easily overlooked, moving cash to community institutions is low hanging fruit for providing impact alternatives to individuals at any asset level. By moving deposits from a multinational bank to a community development bank, regional bank or local credit union, investor assets are supporting small businesses, affordable housing, and other community banking activities that have positive social impact in low-income communities. Mobile and online banking have made many of these alternative banks as accessible as major financial institutions.

Several networks within this asset class offer resources for investors to learn more about cash investment opportunities, including the National Federation of Community Development Credit Unions and the Global Alliance for Banking on Values.

Private and Public Fixed Income

Making impact investments through fixed-income products is also widely accessible and may be directed toward a range of social and environmental issues. One fixed-income example is green bonds that address carbon footprint reduction while advancing energy efficiency in emerging markets. One diversified fixed-income mutual fund invests in corporate bonds in clean technology and sustainability, as well as project focused muni bonds, real estate, and international development that address environmental challenges. Advisors can also help clients to directly invest in municipal and corporate bonds that finance projects with social or environmental impacts. Also worth considering is a first-of-its-kind impact-rated bond portfolio, which provides investors with a quantified assessment of the impact realized by their investments. Finally, one well-known nonprofit focused on environmental preservation offers fixed-income options to impact investors interested in financing critical habitats around the world—while receiving a financial return competitive with other offerings in the fixed-income arena.

As increasing numbers of bond products are introduced, investors must continue to call for real transparency and objective analysis of the degree to which such products actually invest in sustainable impact as opposed to simply finance new, traditionally conceived development projects. Over years to come, many new offerings will claim impact and sustainability—and it will be up to the market to track their total performance relative to their claimed intent to be "green," "sustainable" or "impact."

With a more social objective, nonprofit loan funds are additional options within a fixed-income allocation. Since nonprofits and cooperatives often cannot take equity capital, exploring ways to support these organizations with long-term debt financing, such as loans or loan guarantees, can provide necessary capital for program expansion.

Fixed-income investments in microfinance are primarily made through private debt funds available only to accredited investors. There are many private debt funds being deployed for issues beyond microfinance, including sustainable agriculture, community development, and clean energy. One starting place for getting an overview of impact funds presently active across various thematic areas is the Impact Assets 50—known as the "I.A.50." This is not an investible index or "top 10" list of the best funds, but rather offers you an introduction to the types of funds out there and the way they are structured to generate financial return with impact. Another database of impact funds will be found at ImpactBase and is worth exploring as well.

Product innovation plays a role as some private debt fund structures target greater liquidity, lower minimums and the ability to be held in brokerage accounts. As discussed in the closing chapter of this book, Getting to Impact, with some notes, investors may invest in a strategy for as little as $2,000.

Public Equity and Debt

Many investors deploy their capital in public equities through mutual funds or separately managed accounts. In separately managed accounts, the advisor has more control to develop customized screens based on a client's values. There are also firms that specialize in hyper-customized, separately managed accounts and accommodate a wide variety of impact screens. This level of customization has high minimum investment levels, but wealth advisors may be able to pool client assets at their firm to provide access to public equity impact strategies through separately managed accounts. The screens available in mutual funds tend to be more general in part because they are based on popular interest.

There are three primary ways you, as an investor, may pursue impact through public equities, regardless of the vehicle. Divesting from stocks that have negative impact, such a fossil fuels or sin stocks (alcohol, tobacco, firearms), was one of the first efforts in the socially responsible investment arena, and many managers have been profitably investing with negative screens for many decades. While a traditional approach to investing would assume that any limit placed upon investments open for consideration would constrict the investible universe and thereby result in financial returns below those generated by investment strategies without such restrictions, many years of research indicate these strategies actually perform in line with—and may even exceed—traditional benchmarks.[‡]

The second approach is by integrating environmental, social and governance (ESG) criteria into the selection and due diligence process. This can be a more proactive approach to promoting sustainable practices within corporations. Several fund families have mutual funds across multiple investment styles that all apply ESG criteria in their selection of holdings. In many cases, applying ESG criteria has actually been shown to outperform the benchmark by capturing value that is not widely taken into account by the larger capital market.

The negative screening practices of Responsible Investing are often augmented with a third approach to creating impact through public equities: shareholder activism and engagement. Mission-aligned managers generally will vote proxies on behalf of clients to advance responsible governance and other practices. There are also organizations such as As You Sow and Sum of Us that organize and activate share holders to hold corporations accountable for negative environmental or social practices, such as fair pay, diversity, or transparency. And investors may contract with organizations such as Proxy Impact to ensure their proxy votes are consistently exercised in accordance with their impact agenda.

Private Investing

The landscape of private equity impact investment managers is increasingly diverse, across geographies and issue areas. The previously mentioned ImpactAssets 50 and ImpactBase[§] are centralized resources for identifying and learning more about established

---

[‡] http://www.ussif.org/performance

[§] The Global Impact Investing Network (GIIN) published ImpactBase Snapshot in March 2015, a comprehensive analysis of the 300+ impact investment strategies on ImpactBase.

impact managers in private debt and equity. Because these impact fund managers are directly investing in ventures that advance social and/or environmental impact as they grow, this is a very targeted approach to addressing impact challenges.

Impact investors comfortable with the risk, illiquidity, time and cost requirements of direct investment frequently identify individual deals to support social entrepreneurs directly advancing the issues they care most about. Direct investments in impact ventures can be made using private debt, equity, or convertible debt (a debt/equity hybrid). Transaction costs for direct investments may be high and require specialized expertise, but there is constant demand for early and expansion stage capital to scale organizations with demonstrated impact. Networks such as Toniic and Investors' Circle facilitate direct investments by coordinating member efforts to source potential investments, perform due diligence, and gather best practices across transactions.

Real Assets

This category has tremendous opportunity for impact and appeals to many investors because of the tangible nature of the investment. Within the category of real estate development, there are several leading mission-based, green real estate policy, development, project management and investment firms that have demonstrated an integrated approach to development can have significant social and environmental impact, alongside consistent financial returns. Sustainable real asset strategies have been used for decades in farmland, ranchland, and timber but some have not explicitly identified their funds as impact investments. These funds tend to be long term (7–10 years or beyond), and may provide the potential for consistent returns, although as with any investment one should be cautious in predicting ultimate exit valuations.

Program Related Investments

Asset owners interested in using their philanthropic portfolio to make impact investments may catalyze impact through the use of program related investments (PRIs). This means you would need to have established a private or family foundation or have created a donor advised fund (DAF). Chapters Five and Six explore philanthropic impact investing in greater detail. For now, you should know PRIs come directly out of the investment pool of a charitable vehicle such as a DAF or foundation. These investments may take the form of private equity, but are more frequently structured as low-interest, yet higher risk, loans. Still widely underutilized, PRIs may count toward the 5 percent annual charitable distribution requirement and may be invested in both nonprofit and for-profit corporations.

The guidelines set by the IRS require these investments be made in alignment with the charitable purpose of the foundation or DAF and that its sole purpose cannot be to produce financial return. Since investors are accustomed to evaluating investments based upon their projected market-rate return and evaluating their philanthropic options by social and environmental impact there is a wide middle ground of opportunity for investing in below market-rate impact opportunities that has remained largely underexplored. However, the capital returned from PRIs may then be utilized to generate additional impact in the future.

Mission Investors Exchange published a helpful primer on PRIs in 2012 and in 2013 the Rockefeller Foundation funded an independent evaluation, conducted by Arabella Advisors, of 12 years of PRIs made both domestically and internationally. Impact investments that take on exceptional risk or are expected to produce concessionary returns are ideal for PRIs and have impact potential beyond the specific individual investment. These catalytic investments may also be used as a tool to support development of an emerging market opportunity or attract traditional capital sources by being placed in a subordinate position in the "capital stack." Importantly, an advisor who wishes to support a client's PRI desires should become reasonably well versed in the intricacies of PRI regulations before embracing this potentially powerful tool.

Grants, Gifts and Related Philanthropic Investment Capital

Investors and advisors have traditionally managed their philanthropic grantmaking entirely separate from their financial investments. Within a Total Portfolio Management approach, grants are an effective tool to achieve the overall objectives of a unified portfolio. Grant capital may be used to provide technical assistance to accelerate social ventures to investment readiness, can subsidize transaction costs for due diligence or deal structuring, and can fund high-impact programming to extend the work of an existing investment. Organizations such as The Eleos Foundation and The Grassroots Business Fund, among others, offer good examples of this type of approach. These are just two examples of how grant capital and investment capital can work hand in hand to achieve greater impact than either one might achieve alone. It should also be noted that impact investors should exercise caution when executing these approaches, but syndication structures and other vehicles may be used to appropriately respect rules regarding self-dealing that might arise when making both philanthropic and market-rate investments in proximity to each other.

Risk, Return and Impact

Constructing an impact portfolio necessitates engaging in an integrated evaluation of risk, return and impact, a theme explored in Impact Assets Issue Brief #2, by that same name and released in 2010. The notion of "three degree performance" has now gone mainstream with a recent report on impact investing published by the G7 proclaiming,

> This [impact investing] requires a paradigm shift in capital market thinking, from two-dimensions to three. By bringing a third dimension, impact, to the 20th century capital market dimensions of risk and return, impact investing has the potential to transform our ability to build a better society for all.[3]

This is no small task as there may be additional kinds of risk to evaluate for an impact investment and multiple levels of impact to consider along the range of financial return. This makes a holistic Total Portfolio Management approach especially valuable for those interested in impact investing. For an investor to achieve their overall objectives, the risk, return and impact options are evaluated not in isolation but as complements to each other and as essential components of a larger whole.

Types of Risk

Understanding risk within impact investments, and subsequently designing a portfolio with appropriate risk for the investor, can position impact investors to see market opportunities overlooked or misunderstood by traditional investors. To begin with, impact investors consider all the same initial risk elements as traditional investors. These may include, but are not limited to:

- first fund risk,
- manager risk,
- specific aspects of market risk, and
- other traditional forms of risk consideration.

Again, it is important to remember that impact investing simply takes traditional investment practice and augments it with considerations of social and environmental value creation. When considering risk and return, impact investors may allocate risk across a portfolio in the same way as traditional investors.

With that idea in mind, it is also important to understand that "impact risk" may take some effort to define and manage in light of individual investor perspective and appetite. Specifically, in the past the perception of risk, whether real or imagined, has been a hurdle for the growth of impact investing. Various reports have attempted to explore and address the multiple dimensions of risk to unlock additional impact investments. For some traditional investors and advisors, the fact that something is new to them means they view it as having greater risk than it may actually carry. For example, microfinance debt has provided many impact investors with low volatility and uncorrelated, consistent returns for many years. While these investors are quite comfortable allocating a portion of their portfolio to such funds, to mainstream investors unfamiliar with this category microfinance may still carry the aura of a "nonconforming" investment opportunity and may be viewed as quite risky. As discussed further below, investors not familiar with that segment of the market may "misprice" the risk of such investments and, in the process, miss out on viable invest-ment opportunities impact investors seek to capture. In this way, it is interesting to observe that within certain areas of traditional investing (venture capital, for example) the ability to take greater risk in favor of potential future returns is lauded, while those same traditional investors unfamiliar with how to assess risk within impact investments such as sustainable agriculture or microcredit may wrongly view impact investing as carrying too great a risk in exchange for the financial returns one might project.

The Bridges Ventures report *Shifting the Lens: A De-risking Toolkit for Impact Investing*, released in 2014, includes an analysis of the five types of risk most relevant to impact investing, along with tools to mitigate or "de-risk" each type of risk. Of course, risk varies depending on investor expectations and the individual investment, but the tools to de-risk an investment may be more accessible than tools to boost financial returns. Types of risk iden-tified in the report are:

- Capital Risk (loss of principal capital),
- Exit Risk,
- Unidentifiable Risk,
- Impact Risk, and
- Transaction Cost Risk.

From the opposite angle, many investors have made the case that ESG and impact investing actually *reduce* or mitigate investment risk. For example, some ESG strategies seek to manage risk by investing in sustainable management in companies that face less regulatory risk in the face of impending climate change regulations and less reputational risk due to corrupt or unjust business practices.

It is also interesting to note impact investments in emerging markets, especially in private debt and equity, may be largely uncorrelated to developed global markets and may therefore pro-vide risk mitigation in times of a financial meltdown such as the crisis of 2008.[4] Furthermore, for many impact investors the risks of permanently destroying our environment; rising social and economic inequality and other looming social and environmen-tal challenges pose far too great a risk to not address with the assets they have available. For those investors, engaging in impact investing strategies of various types is in and of itself a type of risk management.

Types of Impact

Much of the foundational work for Total Portfolio Management has focused on the development of frameworks to consider multiple layers of potential impact. Often visualized as a bull's-eye or capital investment spectrum, these frameworks allow categorization of investment options by their expected impact. At one end, there are investments that are contrary to mission. When transitioning a traditional portfolio to an impact portfolio there may be existing assets that fall in this category that are important to identify and create a plan for reallocation. Next, there is a category of investments that produce no material benefit or harm in relation to investor objectives. This is generally an investment category where some negatively screened funds might be placed—especially those that do not engage in any type of shareholder advocacy or proxy voting campaigns asking the company's managers to improve sustainability or worker rights practices.

Moving into general benefit, this category of investments may apply general ESG criteria or broadly promote economic development or environmental sustainability.

The category of relevant benefit begins to narrow the lens to the specific objectives of the individual investor but still takes a relatively broad view of the investment options that have a relevant impact. For example, an investor that has a specific objective of supporting women and girls may make investments into affordable housing and health that do not specifically target women, but clearly support the intended impact of the overall portfolio.

Moving to the direct impact categories, while it is not necessary to concede financial return for impact, and in fact the relationship between impact and financial return offers demonstrably low correlation, some impact investors intentionally choose to make investments that may be concessionary in some way to achieve elevated, broader or deeper impact. These are often categorized separately from direct impact investments that are expected to deliver attractive risk-adjusted financial returns. This distinction is made so that the expected versus actual financial and impact returns may be appropriately evaluated for different types of direct impact investments.

Some believe asset owners may achieve the most direct and targeted impact through philanthropic investments. And, as previously mentioned, grantmaking is important to include on the capital spectrum of how we consider all the capital one may deploy since it can be a valuable tool for reducing risk, increasing impact and even increasing return within a holistic portfolio approach. That said, significant and direct impact may still be achieved in other, nonphilanthropic categories of investing. Therefore, as stated earlier, when considering "impact" across a variety of asset classes within a portfolio, many investors take a blended approach by asking,

What is the comparative financial return this investment category offers
and
what is the best way to think about the nature of the impact it creates?

Remember that, especially for impact investors in the United States, while philanthropic capital may not provide a direct financial return to the asset owner in the future, charitable gifts to a donor advised fund, family foundation or nonprofit entity do provide financial benefit to the donor and in that way offer financial "returns" to impact investors making use of one or more of those vehicles as part of an overall approach to investing capital for impact.

Metrics and Ongoing Evaluation

For many years, the general question of metrics and how best to apply them within an impact investing strategy has been the subject of much debate and deliberation. Because of the additional complexity of constructing a portfolio that considers risk, return and impact, metrics and ongoing evaluation play an important role in achieving client objectives and is the focus of Chapter Eight of this handbook.

Within traditional investing, metrics have been largely refined for financial risk and return but are still being developed for measuring impact, which is critical work for the integration of impact into investment performance evaluation. Impact expectations and criteria should be established within each asset class, along with the process and tools for collecting, organizing, evaluating and reporting specific, measurable metrics. If some investments do not report their impact, it is still important to identify criteria for evaluation that connects investments to the impact thesis and objectives laid out in the IPS.

The most relevant metrics are those allowing the investor and advisor to evaluate whether the total performance of the portfolio is in line with the investor's objectives. Some standard financial and impact metrics will be appropriate, and in many cases the impact metrics will need to be customized in order to inform ongoing evaluation and portfolio management. In other cases, even if a particular investment offers lower financial returns, it may outperform with respect to its intended impact, and vice versa. Depending on the objective of the portfolio, the allocation to such an investment may need to be reweighted or reconsidered in relation to total performance of the portfolio.

Ongoing evaluation is an opportunity to reassess risk, better understand the nature of returns, and course-correct for sustainable impact. So too is portfolio construction not a one-time exercise to set the course, but rather an iterative process of trying, evaluating, learning, and adjusting one's mix of investments over time.

Conclusion

Investors are increasingly aware of both the positive and negative impacts that may be generated through the investment of financial capital. A growing community of investors, as well as a robust body of research, does not accept the notion that investors must accept a trade-off between financial return, risk management and social/environmental impact. The Toniic Network, a global network of impact investors, recently published a report documenting the strategies and experiences of some of their members in executing Total Portfolio Management approaches. Entitled *T100: Insights from the Frontiers of Impact Investing*, the report profiles over 50 impact investors with assets ranging from $2 million to over $100 million and describes their experience in executing "100% Impact" investment strategies.⁵ Review this report as well as the various profiles of impact investors one can find online to have a better understanding of how others are approaching the construction of their portfolios.

Total Portfolio Management provides a powerful set of tools for aligning investor assets with investment objectives through the development of smart and sophisticated impact investment strategies. At each step in the process—from creating the IPS to setting asset allocation, selecting managers/investments, and creating processes for ongoing investment performance evaluation—there are opportunities to increase the impact of an investor portfolio while ensuring financial objectives are met. While the era of portfolio construction that incorporates risk, return and impact may seem new, the impact products available in every asset class are growing rapidly and build upon a history of investors aligning their capital with their values and impact objectives. A total portfolio approach is far more accessible than it was even 10 years ago and leading investors are providing the proof points that impact investing is not an asset class, but rather an overall approach to maximizing the *total* performance of a portfolio in pursuit of generating sustained, blended value within the world we want to live in and pass along to generations to come.

Notes

This chapter was first published as ImpactAssets Issue Brief # 15 and was revised for this volume.

1 A word about words: While the terms *Unified Investment* and *Total Foundation Asset Management* were introduced in 2002 and *Total Portfolio Activation* in 2012, more recently family offices have begun using the term *Total Portfolio Management* to describe the allocation of all forms of family assets within a single approach to wealth management. This definition includes the allocation of all capital—philanthropic, near-market and market-rate. We prefer and use the term Total Portfolio Management here because, as described in this chapter, it best reflects the reality that all capital has "impact potential" and should be managed to optimize financial performance within a given asset class while maximizing the impact potential of that asset class

2 The steps presented here reference "The Essentials of Portfolio Construction," Consulting Group, Morgan Stanley Smith Barney, April 2010.
3 http://www.socialimpactinvestment.org/about.php, p. 43, Accessed March 26, 2017.
4 The same may not be said of public markets, so the reader is cautioned in that regard.
5 http://www.toniic.com/t100/insights-from-the-frontier-of-impact-investing/, Accessed March 27, 2017. Accessed March 27, 2017, http://www.toniic.com/t100/insights-from-the-frontier-of-impact-investing/.

2

Total Portfolio Management: One Practitioner's Approach

Matthew Weatherly-White

Elsewhere in this book, the reader will discover any number of threads that, when woven together, reveal the tapestry that is Total Portfolio Management (TPM). Better Investing. Better philanthropy. The future of capital markets. Metrics and reporting. How to work with advisors. An inevitable evolution of the way we deploy capital. More responsible stewardship of the environment. Less exploitative markets. And all based on the braided notions that:

1. At some point, it will simply be unacceptable to invest while disregarding the environmental or social consequences of doing so, and
2. Most people, at least subconsciously, want a better world.

This chapter is but one of those threads. And while it has the benefit of a great deal of thought and capital behind it, it should be taken as neither gospel, nor as light-hearted advice, nor as yet another idealistic vision of how the world "should" be. Rather, think of it as a set of reflections on how one might deploy an impact-integrated portfolio along the lines of TPM; guardrails rather than a railroad. For, just as in conventional investing, there are any number of ways to invest well, in impact investing there are any number of ways to create durable, measurable value. In other words, I write not tell you how *you* should pursue impact. I am here to share how *we* pursue impact. And, hopefully, this process of sharing will illuminate your path and provide some amount of encouragement, inspiration or simply permission to get started.

More specifically, this chapter examines one practitioner's application of TPM through the narrower lens of so-called finance first impact investing. Although I have never liked the term *finance first* (we reject the implied impact/finance trade-off), it does capture the essence of how we think about impact investing: solving first for our client's financial requirements, and then pursuing impact to the maximum extent possible within a given asset allocation and a defined thematic orientation. Said differently, we think of investing as deploying capital through various types of investment strategies and instruments to achieve the multiple returns our clients seek—financial performance with integrated consideration of social and environmental impacts. While some of the material in this chapter may occasionally come off as a pitch for my company, I'll ask the reader to understand that this is due to the self-referential nature of this chapter: What I share here is what we do. Other firms—professional fellow impact travelers I hold in high regard—do it differently.

What Exactly Were We Thinking?

Our primary thesis when we began committing firm resources toward building our impact capability in 2007 was simple: we believed that, to invest for impact well, we needed to be able to deploy impact capital with the same rigor, similar risk profile and liquidity characteristics, and wide range of potential financial return objectives as we do on behalf of our conventional clients. In other words, the financial characteristics of an impact port-folio had to reflect similar financial characteristics as those experienced by *all* of our clients ... or we wouldn't do it. We felt at the time—and we believe it now with even more conviction—that if we were to both build credibility in the market and meet our fiduciary obligations, we had to approach impact investing as *investors* rather than activists.

What did this distinction mean? After all, if we accept that impact investing is somehow different, that at its core it is about changing global capital markets as we know them, doesn't that imply some form of activism? And if so, how did we square that with the notion we are investors?

It meant, first, we had to build rational, coherent portfolios. Far too often we have seen portfolios—both impact and conventional—composed of ideas that, when disaggregated, can be individually quite compelling. But those same ideas when viewed within the context of an integrated portfolio may make no sense. Surprising correlations and redundancies. Unexpected illiquidity profiles. Risk characteristics that failed to reflect the client's tolerances for volatility or illiquidity. To be excellent impact investors meant we had to nail the allocation work with the same rigor and authority with which we underpinned our conventional portfolios.

This conclusion, paired with the above observations, inexorably led to the realization there was insufficient capital absorption capacity in the impact markets. Investors, to pursue impact, seemed required to accept irrational portfolios simply because there was not enough investable breadth (or depth) in the impact ecosystem. Put simply: When we began our journey into impact we discovered there were not enough investment products and strategies to build the diversified portfolios we needed. And while this wasn't true in the public markets (more on this later), it was absolutely true in the more arcane asset classes on which we depend to generate steady, attractive risk-adjusted returns through complete business cycles ... and which so many impact-oriented investors define as "impact."

So we had to roll up our sleeves and join others in the gritty, motivation-busting business of field building: evangelizing, networking, structuring, funding, speaking, helping conventional asset managers understand the space and launch products into it and so on. If we didn't join this collective effort, we would have no path to impact portfolios with the same risk, liquidity and financial performance characteristics as our conventional portfolios. And if we couldn't do that, we didn't see how we could offer impact as a viable solution to our clients.

A Valuable (or at Least Informative) Tangent

I reference the above concept of asset classes and then imply many impact investors believe impact can be defined only within the context of certain asset classes (I offer our thoughts on this dynamic below). But ...what exactly *is* an "asset class"? We hear the phrase daily, and its use is just as ambiguous as it is ubiquitous. To level-set this chapter, we'll use the definition offered by Investopedia:

> An asset class is a group of securities [or other investments] that exhibits similar characteristics, behaves similarly in the marketplace and is subject to the same laws and regulations.

Let's accept this definition and use it to highlight an enduring fallacy: that impact investing is somehow an "asset class." It isn't. Period. This notion emerged in the early days of impact investing to create the conditions for an easier commitment. "If people thought they only needed to incorporate impact within their asset allocation," the logic seemed to argue, "then it would be a lot easier to make the commitment." And Wall Street joined in, happily productizing the idea so as to more easily sell it.

But impact investing isn't a discrete asset class. It is a mindset, an investing discipline, applicable across all asset classes. To argue, for example, investing in a municipal bond providing development capital for water treatment infrastructure in Los Angeles is the same thing as making an equity investment in a distributed solar power company in Uganda ... well, just reading that should convince anyone that impact isn't an asset class. Yet, the myth continues to linger. Just recently, I was invited to speak at a family wealth conference in Switzerland that proposed to introduce "the emerging new asset class of impact investing." I declined.

Investopedia then continues by listing three asset classes: stocks, bonds and cash. But just the first page of Google results for a search on asset classes reveals that there are actually four asset classes. Or maybe five. And I've seen a pitch deck from a highly regarded investment advisor that detailed no fewer than a dozen ... all in the public markets!

And the confusion can get even more bewildering in sub asset classes. For example, if you invest in real estate in the public markets via a Real Estate Investment Trust, is that a "real estate investment" or an investment in a share of a publicly traded company? Or if you buy fixed income in a mutual fund, are you actually investing in fixed income, or are you buying a derivative—a share in a pool of capital, the value of which is derived from the underlying value of the bonds? And do such fine distinctions even matter?

We believe the distinctions matter because without them it becomes quite difficult to develop a sense of a portfolio's future behavior ... for all the reasons referenced above. As such, we have settled on six primary asset classes, with any number of sub-asset classes organized beneath them. These asset classes apply to both conventional and impact investments, as they define the *financial* characteristics of the investment (please recall my previous comments on Finance First Impact Investing): liquidity, duration, anticipated financial performance, correlation to other assets and so on. With all of this in mind, The CAPROCK Group's asset class framework is as follows:

- Cash: liquid assets, time deposits, money funds and so on. Held in banks, Community Development Financial Institutions Funds (CDFIs), brokerages and the like. Anticipated returns: 0 percent to 2 percent, depending on the prevailing interest rate environment (in some cases, given global interest rates, returns from some sovereign bonds can be *negative*). Daily liquidity.
- Public Fixed Income: corporate and government debt, traded on a public market (marketable securities). Held by a custodian or (rarely) in certificate form. Anticipated returns: 2 percent to 7 percent, depending on the risk reflected in the instrument and the prevailing interest rate environment. Liquid.
- Public Equity: corporate equity, traded on a public market (marketable securities). Held by a custodian or (rarely) in certificate form. Anticipated returns, over a complete business cycle: 6 percent to 10 percent. Liquid.
- Alternative Investments: typically, either marketable securities or similar instruments, held directly in an unconventional structure like a Limited Partnership (hedge funds are the most common example of this asset class). Anticipated returns: anything from 8 percent to 20 percent, depending on strategy, leverage, securities focus and so on. Semi-liquid.

- Private Investments: illiquid (nonmarketable) debt and/or equity of an operating entity (corporate, nonprofit, sovereign, etc.), typically held directly with the issuing entity or via one of many different fund structures. Anticipated returns: ranging from 8 percent to 25 percent, depending on a wide array of factors. Illiquid.
- Real Assets: illiquid (nonmarketable) investments in tangible property(timber, agricultural, commodities, land, real estate, etc). Anticipated returns: ranging from 5 percent to 30 percent, depending on a wide array of factors. Illiquid.

As you can see, each asset class reflects different liquidity, risk and return characteristics. And each asset tends to perform well (or poorly) in different market conditions. The intended result when blended together is a portfolio that strives to generate attractive risk-adjusted returns through a complete business cycle, while minimizing volatility. Importantly, the point of asset allocation and diversification is never to make a directional or sector bet on the market. And, as such, it is rarely the objective of a diversified portfolio to sharply outperform market benchmarks, particularly over a relatively short time period. For that, asset concentration is required.

So, while the portfolios we build tend to underperform during periods of rapidly rising public equity prices, they also tend to outperform during periods of heightened asset volatility or times of crisis. This performance is entirely by design, and is the objective of many—but not all—market participants. After all, as my first market mentor once told me, "It isn't how much you make that matters, it is how little you give back!"

Asset Classes: A Bit More Detail

It should be noted that entire books have been written on this subject. It is not our hope to deliver a master class on asset allocation, much less a definitive sense of how one might go about performing security analysis and selection. Instead, in the following section we hope to convey the essence of how an investor would take the steps necessary to building a viable impact portfolio.

The fundamental idea behind risk control through diversification is that the future is impossible to predict. Thus, while most investors believe they can make educated guesses based on a rational assessment of prevailing conditions, and can thus impute some sort of "reasonable valuation" thesis to each opportunity, the truth is ... none of us knows. To reference a recent example, who would have built a portfolio based on a Trump presidency, much less on the policies that his administration put into motion in their first 100 days?

More to the point, and more simply, we like diversification. Companies, like investment strategies, face idiosyncratic risks. More diversification should produce more predictable results by commingling these risks. All else being equal, more diversification is better than less diversification. The issue arises in the "all else being equal" bit. And here's where it gets interesting ... the most fascinating aspect of impact investing is that it is – in theory at least - both a risk mitigation strategy (climate change exposure, governance transparency, headline damage avoidance, etc.) and an opportunity screen (industrial disruption, new technology, consumer demand, etc.). If you believe, as we do, that risk control and commitment decisions are the only two levers that are entirely within the control of every investor, the conclusion must be that, when pursued with financial rigor, impact investing may be both a material volatility dampener and, potentially, a performance enhancer.

However, I don't want to create the impression that impact represents a free lunch simply because it is "doing good." Investing is hard. Impact investing, in part because it is a relatively new discipline and in part because it adds dimensions to an already complex process, is harder. Good ideas are rare. There are plenty of ways to lose money, and far fewer ways to earn an attractive return. Given this, why not just concentrate all of one's capital in one's very best idea, forgoing entirely the idea of diversification? On the face of it, this is a sensible enough suggestion. It is hard enough to invest in a few ideas well. Why try to invest in many? Furthermore, assuming an investment were to unfold as expected, it would very likely maximize both financial compounding and impact outcomes over time. Unfortunately, such an approach makes no allowance for fallibility.

The reality is we are dealing with sprawling, complex, dynamic financial and social systems. Outcomes can be surprising. The most rigorous diligence can fail to eliminate "confirmation bias." No matter how much research we do or how much we think we know, there is always some chance that, either for reasons previously unforeseen or just plain bad luck, we lose most (or all!) of our capital in a single investment. If 100 percent of one's wealth is invested in a particular company and that company, for whatever reason, loses all its value, there is no way to recover. The loss would be devastating. If, by contrast, that company represented only 10 percent of one's investment portfolio, a bankruptcy would be a meaningful setback, but is not unrecoverable. Clearly, some amount of diversification is necessary to account for the possibility of a total loss. Yet it is axiomatic that the key to both wealth creation and maximizing impact is through asset concentration, not diversification. This tension is not always easily resolved.

And thus we find ourselves torn between two competing objectives. On the one hand, we want to concentrate as much capital as possible into our best impact ideas to maximize the scope of the solution. On the other hand, we want to ensure sufficient diversification to survive negative financial outcomes. With all of this in mind, I feel obliged to point out that there is no "correct" answer to what constitutes optimal diversification. Academic careers have been made or broken by the turning of the publishing wheel on this subject, and we'll not solve it here.

To help think about how one may begin to resolve this issue, I offer the following:

> While it is impossible for us to know the specific investment environment in which we will find ourselves in the future, we do know the future will fall into two of four basic scenarios, with the depth of that orientation hanging from any number of interlocking factors:
> - rising economic growth,
> - falling economic growth,
> - rising inflation, and
> - falling inflation.

That's it. Despite the millions of words harnessed by the world's financial media to convince us otherwise, *these are the only four driving scenarios that we, as investors can expect to encounter when making an investment.*

To reference my previous section, different asset classes are expected to perform well (or poorly) in each of these four scenarios. The challenge comes not necessarily in identifying current conditions, as they tend to be fairly obvious. Rather, the challenge lies in building a portfolio that will perform well in whatever future an investor imagines will unfold. No matter how short-term an investor's time frame may be, every investment requires a set of assumptions regarding what the future will hold. And the extent to which one is willing to bet on one's ability to predict the future will drive how one allocates capital.

To use Ray Dalio's (founder of Bridgewater, the iconic hedge fund) expression—"The All Weather Portfolio"—an impact advisor might contemplate allocating a quarter of a portfolio's risk budget to each of these four scenarios. In this way, the investor would be protected from their own inevitable ignorance, their possible hubris ... and the potential for an overly cautious allocation. (For a deeper understanding of risk budgeting and its application, I encourage the reader to turn to Google. In this, as in so many things, it is an indispensable resource.)

A Few Thoughts on Pan-Asset Impact Opportunities

It would be absurd to try to list here all of the different strategies that sit under each asset class. However, it would be helpful to at least reference a few to give readers a sense of how the market is evolving, and a feel for the breadth of opportunities now available.

Before proceeding, I should disclose that The CAPROCK Group clients have capital in every single fund referenced below, and in some cases our clients have capital in the management company as well. And please also keep in mind, these are not investment recommendations, but simply examples of products, firms and investment strategies I'm sharing to offer specific examples of how we approach our work. How you approach *your* work will differ based upon your own impact investment goals and objectives. That said, following are the asset class categories we use to create impact portfolios

- **Cash**
  Cash is the most overlooked and underestimated impact asset class. Why? Because some of the most important impact work is

being done in the field of community development, providing start-up, scale and operating capital to small businesses ... yet the vast majority of cash is held in banks and brokerage firms that have zero-interest in unlocking the potential social impact of these deposits. If investors even moved 10 percent of their cash balance to dedicated community banks (for example), the amount of capital focused on providing loans to previously underserved communities would be transformative. Firms such as Beneficial State Bank, New Resources Bank, Southern Bancorp and any number of committed community banks and community-oriented pools of capital are doing extraordinary work. But they are constrained because of capital ratio require-ments, which are in part solved over time by building larger depositor bases. Thus, if an investor wants to pick the lowest hanging fruit on the impact tree ... move your money to a community bank. Do your homework first, of course. But if you leave your cash at a money center bank or your brokerage firm, it is possible your capital is funding companies operating contrary to your values.

- **Public Fixed Income**
  Although a great deal of attention has been paid over the past several decades to the discipline of environmental, social and governance (ESG) factors as applied to public equity portfo-lios, the world of public fixed income has seen less focus. This is surprising on many levels, not the least of which being that, in general, the list of approved (or condemned) equity issuers maps closely to the roster of debt issuers. Even more surprising is the ease with which one might construct a socially respon-sible portfolio of municipal securities, as they typically fund services so essential to economic and opportunity equality. Over the past few years, firms such as SNW Asset Management, Breckenridge Capital and Wasmer Schroeder (all three of which are Certified B Corps[1]) have launched thoughtful, pro-fessional impact-facing fixed-income strategies.

- **Public Equity**
  It is not hyperbole to say the public markets offer the most developed asset class relative to mission/values/impact. The options are nearly endless. Pioneers in responsible investing such as Trillium, Walden and Boston Common introduced

professionalism and credibility to the discipline many years ago. Huge Wall Street firms such as Blackrock, Goldman, JP Morgan, Morgan Stanley, UBS and others have recently launched (or rebranded SRI (socially responsible investing)) impact strategies. A wide range of other asset managers have begun to offer screened versions of their conventional portfolios and newly minted asset managers are branding themselves as responsible/sustainable firms offering products that reflect their values. In addition, technology is now playing a role, with computer-driven customization platforms beginning to appear in the market as well as a bewildering array of Exchange Traded Funds with an SRI/ESG/Impact orientation now available to any investor. In short, public equity investing is likely the easiest way, outside of cash, for an investor to begin her impact journey. (Note: not only is this the most developed asset class in which to pursue impact, it is also the most controversial, with many leaders arguing that investing in the public markets creates no impact whatsoever.)

- **Alternative Investments**
One of the most interesting perspectives to emerge from the impact investing community is that hedge funds are by definition not a legitimate impact option for the simple reason that hedge fund managers hope to profit from the decline of stock prices. To which I reply: soft thinking. After all, if a hedge fund were to do nothing beyond "shorting" coal companies and were to generate impressive financial returns by doing so, how would that differ from another fund that chooses to avoid coal entirely? We believe hedge funds have a role to play in portfolio construction, as during periods of adverse market performance they can dampen portfolio volatility while producing acceptable returns. And if they have the same ESG rigor as a long-only equity fund, they may be in a position to profit from the collapse of a poor ESG-rated company.

Recognizing that "hedge fund" applies to a wide variety of fund strategies, one example of a clearly impact-oriented hedge fund structure is Brevet Capital, a specialty lender and structured finance expert. Most interesting for us is that Brevet's "Impact Sleeve," which is composed of a subset of the all the loans underwritten by the firm, outperforms their conventional portfolio. Note that Brevet is not a conventional long/short equity hedge fund.

- **Private Investments**

  Outside of public equity options, private investing is arguably the most developed impact asset class, particularly in the early growth equity phase.

  A. Seed and angel capital is being deployed steadily, if in a highly fragmented way, with groups such as Investor's Circle, Toniic, CREO, Seattle Venture Partners and a handful of crowdfunding sites (see comments on crowdfunding below) working to unlock early stage impact capital.

  B. There are also several effective early stage venture funds working in the impact space: Village Capital, Unitus Frontier, Golden Seeds and a growing list of others would be on that list.

  C. More typical, growth venture funding is healthy and attracting both capital and deal flow. This category is also continuing to experience positive exits, with firms such as SJF, EIF, Uprising, City Light, Elevar, DBL and many others all contributing leadership to the sector.

  D. At this point, there is surprisingly little late-stage (Private Equity) capital being organized, with Cranemere, TPG's recently announced Rise Fund, and Bain Capital's impact initiatives being the three notable exceptions. We are paying particularly close attention to TPG's acquisition of Elevar Equity and their creation of the Rise Fund which is seeking to raise two billion dollars with the support of the likes of Bono, Richard Branson and other luminaries, as this fund could be the belweather the discipline needs to scale.

- **Real Assets**

  Although Real Assets is not the most richly developed impact asset class, in some ways it offers the most direct and durable link between capital allocation strategy and the creation of extrafinancial value. Mixed-use developers, affordable housing developers, community development lenders and large philanthropic players have all been circling the question of community resiliency for decades. Similarly, sustainable timber harvesting funds such as Lyme Timber and EcoTrust Forest

Management have been reinventing how we utilize a renewable resource like timber in a truly sustainable manner. Lastly, wide-scale conversion of conventional agriculture to sustainable, organic food production at firms such as Iroquois Valley Farms, Farmland LP and Agricultural Capital Management all point to an exciting future for agriculture as a key player in the impact ecosystem.

A Nod to Innovation

In addition to these asset classes that, while perhaps not embraced with unanimity, are at least understood by all capital market participants, there are a handful of impact-specific innovations. The list below is by no means complete, but touches on some of the major developments we've seen over the past few years.

Revenue-based Lending

The premise behind revenue-based lending (RBL) is that start-ups rarely have the cash flow to support debt and entrepreneurs may fail to appreciate that selling equity early in a company's life can be the most expensive capital they ever raise. Investors have tapped into RBL as a way to align deal structure with the reality of early stage business cash flow, the desire to create and hold wealth at the company level (rather than the investment fund level) and to de-risk the investment by triggering a rapid return-of-capital flow to the investor. The downside of RBL (to the investor) is that if you happen to invest in one of the magical, transformative companies that is eventually worth hundreds of millions, you won't capture any of that upside. But, to many impact investors, this is a fair trade-off.

The last point about RBL, which is unfortunately frequently overlooked, is that the structure does not force a transaction. One of the legitimate complaints about conventional venture fund structures for impact investments is that the fund must exit the company to comply with fund life terms or to generate financial returns so the venture firm can successfully raise subsequent funds. This places the entrepreneur in the uncomfortable position of being forced to consider a sale of her company, perhaps to a larger enterprise that is not mission-aligned. RBL sidesteps that concern by beginning to return invested capital quite early in the company's life and by relieving the entrepreneur of the need to sell the company at a high valuation to justify the early sale of equity.

Social Impact Bonds/Pay For Success

So-called Social Impact Bonds (SIB), or as many prefer to refer to them Pay For Success (PfS) Contracts (or more recently, Outcomes-Based Financing), may be the most hyped innovation in the impact world. In a nutshell, they offer:

- the promise of more efficient public funding of social services,
- the potential to unlock billions of market-oriented impact capital, and
- the possibility of an entirely new sub-asset class focused primarily on impact.

They seek to do this by using private capital to front-load costs for proven interventions, relying on the government to redirect future savings to pay the investors a reasonable risk-adjusted rate of return. A rare win-win-win, right? And yet ...

To date, transactions have been expensive, bespoke and time consuming. Proving causation has been fiendishly elusive, despite best intentions and careful modeling. And there remains more than a little confusion in the marketplace as to what exactly these structures are, what problem they are designed to solve and who will be the ultimate beneficiary.

I personally have direct experience with the structure, having launched a PfS initiative in Idaho four years ago. We were able to quickly secure champions in the Statehouse (a mild surprise given the profound rightward tilt in the state's political environment), passing PfS legislation in our first attempt ... only to run into a recalcitrant Department of Education. After overcoming that hurdle, we then encountered resistance from the budgeting office, inconveniently learning there was no line-item appropriation for redirected payments upon which a PfS depends. Successfully negotiating new language in a modified version of the bill, we then bumped into resistance from the teacher's unions, as unrelated concerns of job losses surfaced. Suffice it to say that the learning and structuring curve was depressingly shallow. The irony of this is that, with few exceptions, every person involved actually *wanted* this to happen.

This tortuous experience does not for a moment diminish my careful enthusiasm for the structure, as I believe it can encourage government to embrace risk, can bring commercial capital to bear on otherwise underfunded social enterprises, and can unlock potentially massive amounts of financing for proven, evidence-based social interventions. And of course, there are also organizations now established (Social Finance, Third Sector Capital, The Sorenson Institute and others) on a dedicated basis to manage the process of bringing these types of investments to market. Time will tell, but if it can survive the hype factory that surrounds it, I predict that SIB/PfS financing will within a few years be an important sub-asset class in the impact ecosystem.

Crowdfunding

Though not a prima facie impact instrument, crowdfunding has the potential to transform the way social enterprises raise capital, just as it has changed the face of investing in more than one industry. Real estate crowdfunding sites such as RealtyShares and RealtyMogul have brought increased transparency into a sector that had been notoriously opaque and difficult to access. Equity crowdfunding platforms such as IndieGoGo and KickStarter have brought visibility and capital opportunities to enterprises that would have been all but invisible only a few short years ago. And so-called peer-to-peer lending platforms such as Lending Club and SoFi are disrupting everything from small business loans to student loan refinancing to specialty lending. Even corporations are beginning to crowdfund R&D and prototyping activities. Suffice it to say crowdfunding, made possible by the JOBS Act passed by the Obama administration and the subsequent ruling by the Securities and Exchange Commission (SEC) to remove the crowdfunding equity prohibition, is here to stay.

At the same time, warning signs are flashing. There have been increasingly strident calls for greater disclosure, more transparency, more imputed liability and more evidence regarding how valuations are determined. AIG has begun to sell crowdfunding insurance. And the roster of scams grows at an accelerating rate. All of this leads some investors to shy away and leaves some regulators with the itch to shut it down. To me, these responses, though understandable, are misguided. Crowdfunding is a form of capital raising that is innovative, disruptive and incredibly compelling. It has the ability to transform the way capital is aggregated, as well as the people from whom it is drawn. And it is incredibly difficult to determine if a failed crowdfunded enterprise was a scam ... or just a dud.

Of course crowdfunding will experience growing pains, just as it will surely become the target of Wall Street's army of lobbyists if it begins to carve market share away from the large investment banks. But this is not a reason to torpedo the method. Instead, it is a reason to become informed; to embrace the dictum "caveat emptor." The trick is to be aware enough of the potential for a scam to avoid them, while still being enthusiastic enough by the inspiring stories to remain engaged. And if you are a social entrepreneur trying to crack the capital markets, crowdfunding might be your best solution.

Impact Term Sheets

Of all the solutions the impact community has devised to address the challenges that swirl through the discipline—mission drift, misaligned interests, communicating intention, and so on—none I've seen has the potential that impact-oriented terms sheets offer. Why? Because a term sheet is the only legal document that spells out—in enforceable language—the expectations and intentions entrepreneurs and investors hold when entering a transaction. A well-structured term sheet can:

- link compensation to impact performance, thus ensuring impact fidelity as an investment unfolds;
- lock the mission of an enterprise through a transaction by embedding incentives in the operating agreement (which can be addended to a term sheet);

- articulate the mission of the enterprise seeking funding, so that there are no surprises later in the lifecycle of the business;
- formalize and harmonize the legal landscape around impact investing;
- and more …

I would encourage any impact-oriented entrepreneur, asset manager, advisor or investor to spend time exploring The Impact Terms Project's website.[2] Brainchild of pioneering impact investor Diana Proppert de Callejon and legal mind Bruce Campbell, The Impact Terms Project has been a multi-year, multistakeholder effort to capture the best legal thinking around impact deals. The library of sample terms sheets alone is priceless.

More Color on Risk Control, Diversification and Asset Classes

We have touched on the notion of risk control, particularly relative to asset allocation, and observed that it is a multi-faceted topic, far too nuanced for an overview like this. But it is important to note we do *not* subscribe to fixed risk statistics. Every investment can be either more or less risky, depending on a range of factors, the most critical being valuation. How much one pays for an asset, either debt or equity, when one invests is the primary determination of future returns. As an extreme example, stocks of technology companies were extremely risky in 1999, and much less risky in 2009. Subsequent financial returns reflect this risk variability for one simple reason: the lower the valuation when one is making an investment, the higher potential return on invested capital … a rule that many investors neglect during periods of rising valuation.

This reality leads to our rejection of so-called model portfolios. Since most models usually depend upon static risk calculations, they tend not to reflect shifting market dynamics, and thus may undermine both market-responsive allocation decisions, as well as the discounted cash flow method that undergirds our approach to portfolio construction. Perhaps even more problematically, static risk assessment may distort asset class correlation matrices and capital market return assumptions, leading to hidden risks in the portfolio and a possible mismatch between expected return and what an investor needs. But those conversations are for another book!

We then begin to map investable impact themes and opportunities to each asset class. Below are two graphics that illustrate how we think about the intersection of conventional asset classes (as we define them) and impact. Note that there are other ways to think about this intersection and there are any number of ways to categorize investable opportunities.

The first table is an illustration of the way high-level impact strategies map to different asset classes:

**ASSET CLASSES &
IMPACT CONSIDERATIONS**

CASH	FIXED INCOME	PUBLIC EQUITY
Community Bank CDs Community Bank Time Deposits CDFIs	Impact Overlay Impact Scoring Green Bonds International Aid Bonds	Positive/Negative Screens Impact Mandates Proxy Voting Shareholder Engagement
	Liquid: 0–45 days	*Liquid: 0–45 days*

ALTERNATIVES	REAL ASSETS	PRIVATE INVESTMENTS
Microfinance Long/Short Hedge Funds (Mandate) Structured Finance Small Business Lending Social Impact Bonds	Sustainable Timber/Forestry Land Conservation/Rehabilitation Mitigation Banking Affordable Housing Renewable Energy Infrastructure Project Finance	Venture Capital Private Equity Direct Investments (Seed, Early, Growth) Private Debt Platform Building
Semi-Liquid: 46–365 days	*Illiquid: 1–12 years*	*Illiquid: 1–12 years*

THE CAPROCK GROUP

The second is a more detailed way to reflect some of the opportunities, and the impact and financial characteristic of those opportunities, that map to the Real Assets asset class (an investor might construct a similar table for each asset and sub-asset class, to begin identifying the combination of financial and impact characteristics that are available within their impact focus and to help guide her own portfolio construction process):

Real Assets Overview

Real Estate
- Green (Re) Development
- Single Family
- Multifamily
- Affordable Housing
- Mixed Use/T.O.D

Impact
- Energy Efficiency
- Sustainable Materials
- Health Improvements
- Community Resiliency
- Urban Renewal

Financial
- Leverage
- Style (e.g., Core, Value Add)
- Components of Return
- Tax Efficiency
- Exit Strategy

Land Management
- Timber/Forestry
- Rehabilitation
- Replanting
- Conservation Easements
- Mitigation Banking

Impact
- Ecosystem Restoration
- Forest Regeneration/Conservation
- Sustainable Timber Harvesting
- Watershed Protection
- Biodiversity

Financial
- Harvesting Philosophy
- Income Sources
- Valuation Approach
- Acquisition Strategy
- Exit Strategy

Renewable Energy
- Project Finance
  - Development Phase
  - Construction Phase
  - Operational Phase
- Infrastructure
- Residential Installation

Impact
- Climate Change Mitigation
- CO2/GHG Reduction
- Air Quality Improvement
- Job Creation
- Fossil Fuel Independence

Financial
- Technology Risk
- Monetize Credits
- Project Finance Risks
- Regulation Risk
- Exit Strategy

Agriculture
- Supply Chain
- Acquisition & Conversion
- Crop Management
- Project Finance
- Carbon Credits

Impact
- Sustainable/Organic Practices
- Increased Productive Capacity
- Decreased Land Toxins
- Ecosystem Integration
- Healthier Diets

Financial
- Valuation Approach
- Acquisition Strategy
- Components of Return
- Harvests/Current Yield
- Exit Strategy

THE CAPROCK GROUP

A Practical Suggestion

It may need not be said, but I'll say it anyway: the "All Weather Portfolio" allocation referenced below in no way implies a specific recommendation, for anyone, at any time. It should be read as nothing more than a hypothetical approach to portfolio construction, a way to think about bringing impact to bear across an entire portfolio, specifically for someone who is not an accredited investor. Any investor who deploys capital along these lines is doing so on their own volition, and accepts full responsibility for the results, including 100 percent loss of capital. Got it? In other words: "hot coffee is hot," Consider this appropriately disclaimed.

Continuing the theme of Ray Dalio's All Weather Portfolio, and framing it through the lens of a typical non-accredited investor, the range of investments would apply to the following four economic scenarios:

- Rising Growth Expectations: Stocks, Commodities, Corporate Bonds, Emerging Market Bonds, Treasury Inflation Protected Securities (or other inflation-linked bonds)
- Falling Growth Expectations: Certificates of Deposit, US Government Bonds (specifically treasuries)
- Rising Inflation Expectations: Treasury Inflation Protected Securities (or other inflation-linked bonds), Commodities, Emerging Market Bonds
- Falling Inflation Expectations: Stocks, US Government Bonds (specifically longer-dated securities)

As mentioned above, one would want to try to quantify the risk profile associated with each of these scenarios, assign a weighting to that risk profile and then allocate – for illustrative purposes only - 25 percent of one's total risk budget to each asset class. Understand that this overview does not take into account any of the nuance associated with risk budgeting, as doing so would consume the remainder of this book. The trick, of course, comes with one's assessment of risk. There is no rulebook for doing so. And while machine learning and artificial intelligence have come a long way, computers aren't even close (yet) to being able to assess the risk embedded in a given asset, at a given time, at a given valuation.

Finally, once one has identified with some degree of confidence one's asset allocation, one gets to indulge in the profound satisfaction of beginning to integrate impact into that allocation. Which is where the rubber finally meets the road. . . .

Yet Another Red Herring: Financial Performance

The discussion/debate/argument over financial performance and impact has flowed for years, and it shows no sign of ebbing. As the editor of this book observed in his introduction, this debate seems to rotate more on bias than on fact, a point with which we, as investors, are all too familiar. Rather than point to the ever-expanding body of evidence proving that there are market-rate opportunities in impact (some studies indicate that there may actually be alpha associated with an impact strategy), I'll simply state that our impact portfolios perform in line with both our conventional portfolio and the expectations we set when building them.

I will, however, point to the exercise that sits at the heart of this fact and that relates back to my earlier comments on "finance first" impact investing: working with our clients to build a rigorous, thoughtful, assumption-heavy Lifetime Discounted Cash Flow (LDCF) model.

What is an LDCF? In short, it is a framework designed to capture all known and anticipated future financial events, both assets and liabilities. Some examples might include:

- Assets:
  - Current and anticipated earned income
  - Current invested assets, taxable and tax-deferred
  - Potential inheritance
  - Life insurance proceeds
  - Lottery winnings
- Liabilities
  - Educational costs for children or grandchildren
  - Purchase of a second home
  - Debt associated with real estate or student loans
  - Future car/boat/plane purchase
  - Down-payment on a first home for your children
  - Investing in your children's business
  - And so on . . .

Once as many of these financial events that we can identify have been captured, organized and time-stamped we then apply a discount rate to the liabilities and perform a basic asset/liability present-value calculation. Doing so allows us to answer two absolutely critical questions.

First, given the assumptions in the model, do we have enough *right now* to do everything that we want to accomplish in our life? And second, if not, what rate of return must we achieve from our invested assets to be able to do so (we call this the Target After Tax and Inflation Rate of Return—ATI ROR)? In other words, an LDCF answers the existentially paired questions: "How much is enough ... and do I have it?" The reason this is so important is that answering these questions allows any investor to build portfolios composed of investments that fill specific financial objectives ...thereby permitting a range of target impact outcomes so long as they meet, in aggregate, the required financial characteristics.

I realize this is an oddly circular form of logic, but given impact investors are pursuing two, linked objectives—financial and impact returns—it makes sense. Why? Because, while it is not mandatory that investors sacrifice impact for financial return, doing so is certainly an option. And in some sectors, markets and enterprises, subsidies are required: tax breaks, direct government support, credit enhancements, first loss equity cushions, or even higher asset management fees. Yet if one can understand an investor's capacity to absorb these subsidized costs via concessionary returns, thereby revealing the ability to build a portfolio that supports the development of impact markets ... then why not? After all, impact investors are interested in using market mechanisms to drive capital toward social and environmental challenges. If high transaction costs (for example) can be borne and justified by an investor's ATI ROR, that implies a multifaceted, highly leveragable application of impact.

Which is a long way of saying that once an investor is liberated from the tyranny of an arbitrary market performance benchmark (like the S&P 500), instead anchoring return objectives in clearly defined personal financial needs, the option set for impact is immediately visible.

Rubber? Meet the Road. Integrating Impact

As I've said above, there are many different ways to begin integrating impact into one's investment strategy. After a fair amount of trial and error, we believe the process on which we have settled—identify the financial characteristics of the portfolio and then pursue impact within that framework—works well for us. Why? Because, while it may not be an inspiring way to begin one's journey (it can be far more immediately gratifying to invest in a local artisanal bakery sourcing grains from fields ploughed by rescued oxen), nailing down the financial aspects of a portfolio allows one to think both creatively *and* pragmatically about pursuing impact ... to the extent permitted by the asset classes and sub-asset classes identified by the allocation work. The essence of Total Portfolio Management. Boring, yes. But powerful and potentially liberating.

We have discussed, at length, the process of defining an optimal asset allocation. The next step is drafting an investment policy statement (IPS). The IPS can take any number of forms, can reflect aspirational desires just as much as it can reflect concrete guidelines, can be designed as a communication tool, can be used to inform future generations ... In short, an IPS can be just about anything, so long as it articulates your relationship to impact, and how that relationship influences the selection of investments.

However, at a minimum, the IPS should:

- include language that captures and reflects your values and why that is driving you to pursue impact: the "why";
- present clearly articulated financial goals, liquidity requirements, return expectation, asset allocation ranges and values-based screens: the "how";
- include a description of your timeline—how long you expect it to take for your to either invest cash, pivot an existing portfolio, reallocate an inheritance, move toward philanthropy: the "when";
- provide some insight into the geography on which you would like to focus your attention—local, regional, global: the "where"; and

- perhaps most importantly, detail the various parties involved in this process—family, advisors, board members, beneficiaries: the "who."

We've seen effective IPSs that range from concise three pages all the way to massive tomes. Some have been philosophical. Others entirely pragmatic. Some offer specific investment guidelines. Others give only the vaguest sense of investment direction, leaving the details to be defined, and to evolve, in the future. Some are highly descriptive, with long written passages. Others are a field of bullet points. Some focus entirely internally, on family members and close advisors. Others function as an external communication tool, intended to inform a broad array of stakeholders as to what you intend to accomplish. Some are operational; others inspirational. If you'd like to see a range of great IPSs, visit the Mission Investors Exchange website, where their members share many such documents. I would particularly encourage a close reading of the F. B. Heron Foundation IPS.

The point is that *how* an IPS is composed and what information it includes is less important than the fact that one exists. Once it has been crafted, it becomes a forcing function for action, a set of guidelines to reference as your strategy is implemented, a reminder of why you wanted to pursue impact in the first place, and a communication tool for current and future stakeholders. In short, a well-conceived and dynamic IPS is the armature upon which the impact orientation—through thematic focus and perhaps even a well-articulated Theory of Change—is built.

Elsewhere in this book, a detailed chapter on due diligence and investing methodology is presented. The only element of this process I'd like to add is to highlight the distinction between "values alignment" and "value creation." While this may seem like a distinction in search of a difference (a logical fallacy that regretfully sits at the heart of many poorly conceived impact and other investing strategies), we have found it to be central to effective capital deployment. Why? Because one could make a clearly values-aligned investment that offers precious little in the way of value creation (ESG-screened investing in the public equity markets is a fantastic example), and one could create a great deal of value without that value necessarily being values-aligned (e.g., if one's values incorporates indigenous population education and you were to make an investment in a renewable energy project). Put even more starkly, one could build a theoretical values-aligned portfolio that specifically erodes extrafinancial value by, for example, investing in environmentally destructive companies … presuming that environmental destruction happens to sit at the core of your values!

I have written extensively on this subject on my blog (www. i3impact.com), so will refrain from both treading well-worn ground and consuming unnecessary space in this book. Suffice it to say that when you begin your journey to impact, I encourage you to be intellectually honest and emotionally passionate about where your values lie and how those values may (or may not) shape the specifics of your impact investing strategy.

A Final Word on Investing in the Public Markets

An ocean of ink has been spilled on investing in the public markets, in particular the public equity markets. In particular, the argument on impact availability in the stock markets is a topic of heated debate. As a result, there is very little that I can add to the broad, primarily academic discussion.

I can, however, share our stance:

To coin a phrase, we believe that it isn't "what you own" so much as "what you do with what you own" that matters. In other words, if you sell your shares in Exxon because you believe they misled the world about their role in exacerbating the challenges associated with climate change, the C-suite at Exxon simply doesn't care. There is no functional mechanism to transmit your disapproval through transactions in the secondary market. Yes, if every person who owned Exxon decided to sell their shares, the price would fall enough to get management's attention. But it wouldn't change their essential business. Witness the collapse of Peabody Energy: despite the stock being driven to near zero, they continued to be the largest producer of coal in the United States.

We do believe, however, that here *is* a path to impact in the secondary markets: shareholder activism, engagement and proxy voting. And, fortunately, there are an increasing number of options for impact investors who wish to pursue these options. From activist-inclusive asset management firms to impact-dedicated proxy voting services to shareholder engagement service firms, the avenues to communicate your values to management are robust and accessible. As a result, we believe that an impact investor who is *not* engaging in this way with their public security exposure—either directly or through a third party service provider—needs to take a long, hard look at themselves in the mirror.

The Last Step—Measurement

Sara Olsen, in her chapter on impact measurement, outlines the many issues that simultaneously bedevil and inspire measurement professionals. As advisors, we are not immune to a similar set of challenges and frustrations, nor to the sense of pioneering accomplishment that accrues to those of us who choose to tackle the matter. But, as advisors, we face a specific and surprisingly narrow challenge. It is our responsibility to communicate to our clients, in some fashion, the impact that their capital is having in the world. In other words, we must generate a consolidated impact performance report for each of our clients. And the issues that Sara and her peers face—lack of common standards, a hugely diverse lexicon, informative yet cacophonous reports from our impact investees, a wide array of thematic priorities, and so on—contribute to the difficulty we face. Yet we cannot escape the responsibility. Just as it would be unacceptable to deliver disaggregated financial performance information ("You want to know how your portfolio performed? But why? Isn't it enough that we provide a mountain of performance data related to your portfolio?"), we believe that it will be unacceptable to deliver disaggregated impact performance reports.

The trouble is that there is no off-the-shelf solution for this challenge. So we built it. And, had we known how difficult it would be—seven years of work, an enormous investment in hard and soft costs, and a distressing amount of anxiety, distraction and stress—I don't think we would have done it. But we did, and we believe the solution is powerful. So powerful, in fact, that we were convinced by asset managers, advisors and family offices to spin the platform out into a stand-alone, impact-facing financial technology company: iPAR (www.iparimpact.com).

And while we know that there is a high-value service at the heart of what iPAR does, we don't yet know if there is a business at the heart of what iPAR does. We are nonetheless confident that a company dedicated to bringing transparency and accountability to the impact ecosystem, even if that is only in the form of communicating and reporting (as opposed to measuring or assessing), that company will fill an important gap in the idea-to-execution chain.

Conclusion: It Ain't What You Don't Know That Gets You in Trouble ...

There you have it. Soup to nuts from one leading practitioner. Some basic advice and guidance. A handful of specific examples. The path we use to debunk, demystify, familiarize and structure our approach to impact.

The one thing that we haven't emphasized yet is the temperament necessary to be a good impact investor. Yes, one must know how to invest—the technical aspects of debt versus equity, of private versus public investments. One must be smart enough to understand how to wrap a set of portfolio decisions around a discounted cash flow model. And one must be patient, disciplined and farsighted. But these characteristics are just table stakes for committing capital. To be a good *impact* investor, one must also be capable of independent thought, of pursuing a core belief in the power of the capital markets and in the power of justice and stewardship: a blend of Warren Buffett, MacGyver and Mother Theresa.

But, perhaps most importantly, one must remain humble. For, although the discipline is now well into its third-plus decade, and the evidence that impact is a legitimate, market-facing approach to investing is accumulating rapidly, we are only now moving from proof to scale. And as every businesswoman knows, scaling a business requires a different type of thinking.

Just as nobody really knows how the most important fiscal experiment in history will end—post financial crisis central bank intervention—nobody really knows how the notion of impact investing *at scale* will unfurl. Will Wall Street co-opt the discipline, lowering standards in order to bring institutional capital to bear? Will political events stall the momentum that the discipline has built over the last decade? Will hype lead to unrealistic expectations? And until we do know—*and recall that I believe without reservation that impact is the future of capitalism*—we must continue to ask ourselves hard questions. After all, as Mark Twain may or may not have said: "It isn't what you don't know that will get you in trouble ... it is what you know for certain that just ain't so!"

Notes

1 Certified B Corps have successfully completed a rigorous vetting and evaluation process—the B Survey—designed to reflect best practices in sustainable, responsible business management. The B Survey provides a framework and certification for companies wishing to benefit society as well as their shareholders. More can be found on B Laboratory's website, the certifying entity: www.bcorporation.net.
2 www.impactterms.org.

Case Study 1

STORIES THAT INSPIRE: RON AND MARLYS BOEHM*

Year Started Impact Investing: 2008

Primary Investment Focus: Early stage social and environmental for-profit business

Background: Ron and Marlys Boehm use their business know-how to provide financial and development support to budding social entrepreneurs in developing economies. Typically, the entrepreneurs they work with have a viable product or service, have proven that the concept works and want to take it to the next stage. Ron and Marlys are very aligned with the entrepreneurs, particularly those who are passionately committed to keeping their social mission alive.

Impact Trigger

Ron and Marlys Boehm began their impact investment journey after a business liquidation event. Initially interested in pure philanthropy, the Boehms sought guidance on how they should approach their giving strategy. Their education really began during an organized family trip to Africa where they saw "first hand" nonprofits and for-profit ventures addressing a wide range of issues, including education, economic development and

---

* The book includes case studies of four investor profiles of which the first two are of real people, while the other two are composites.

the environment. Marlys recalls, "We started to realize that we couldn't save the world one check at a time. We also found that we were gravitating toward economic development issues, which makes sense given our business background. That along with the recognition of market realities that happen in a non-profit world led us to go down a different path than pure philanthropy."

Investment Approach

Marlys: We basically jumped into impact investing with both feet. In order to learn a lot, we started off with lots of small investments. We developed an approach along the way where we start small and then add to the company. At this point, we've done over 90 investments in about 40 plus companies.

Along the way we realized that we couldn't agonize for a year making a decision over one investment and we don't want to take critical time away from the entrepreneur. We try to give a "no" in a day and a "yes "within 5 days and fund within two weeks. We also look for reasons to say yes instead of no.

Ron: We have five steps that take us from consideration to investment. The first is based on a feeling. Is this an area we feel positive about? Does it make sense to make an investment at this time? Will investing make a real difference?

The second step is the sustainability of the business model, which usually means the gross margin. The entrepreneur has to be cognizant of what it costs to actually create the goods or services. The cost has to generally be less than 50 percent of whatever the selling price is. There are a lot of early stage entities out there that require a subsidy because the costs of their goods are too close to their selling price.

The third step is scalability. We generally look at The Mulago's Foundation "Design Iteration Format: Designing for Lasting Impact That Goes To Scale"* framework as a guidepost for scalability due diligence. If the company can actually be scalable, who's going to do it and does it potentially reach scale if you can

---

* "Designing for Impact at Scale," Accessed April 14, 2017, http://mulagofoundation.org/ideas/design-iteration-form-dif-and-worksheet.

prove it out? And will it make something that people will potentially repeat? This is scalability.

The fourth step is about listening. Do we feel like they are listening? Not to us but to each other. Do they listen to the market very well? Do they have people on the ground? Are there locals running the company or ex-pats? And the fifth step is "tell me the things that you'd change because of what you've learned that you're doing doesn't work." They may listen but can they learn and change?

These are the five steps that take us from consideration to investment. If we feel good about what we learn after going through these steps, we'll generally make a small investment. That puts us on the same side of the table trying to make our investment pay off. Which it probably will and if the entrepreneur does it right we'll be there to help them at the next stage. And then in the next stage, if they need more and we feel comfortable on how they're spending and managing, we'll probably increase the investment.

Marlys: There are some questions investors don't ask themselves enough. For example, does it matter to you if there's political risk in this country? If the answer is yes, then don't even have a conversation with the entrepreneur. Does it matter to you that you might lose your money? If the answer is yes, you don't want to be in this conversation. You'll probably want to be more in the area of socially responsible investment screening.

The next part that Ron and I are developing now is how to find next stage investors that will take over and add their capital. These investment opportunities are ready to scale. And this is our next adventure in the impact investing space. It's about finding like-minded people that aren't willing to take quite the risk that we did, but are willing to fund somebody that we've been working with for a year or two.

3

Seed Stage Investing: High Impact, But Not for the Faint of Heart

Tim Freundlich, Jed Emerson and Lindsay Smalling

To meet a promising entrepreneur, be convinced their venture will thrive in the market, and subsequently invest at the ground floor; this is the exciting vision of seed stage investing.[1] In this chapter we will explore some of the opportunities and "how to's" of investing in seed stage companies. Although a risky proposition, seed investing has nonetheless attracted investors who want to put their capital where it may be the only chance these ventures have to build and grow a potentially great solution to some impact challenge. An entire ecosystem of venture capital and angel investing has developed to support seed stage technology start-ups and other companies with large-scale potential.

As the market for impact investing has grown, however, it would appear the capital available for seed stage investing has not kept apace.

In the authors' conversations with industry players, it is clear that many believe social entrepreneurs need capacity-building support to make their ventures "investment-ready," and point to accelerators or incubators as a solution. Others advocate for philanthropic dollars to fill the funding gap while an organization tests its product and establishes a customer base. On the capital side, many interpret the seed stage gap as an investor issue; the economics of investing in a round of $500,000 or less in an early stage social venture just doesn't make sense considering the extensive due diligence, term sheet negotiation and ongoing monitoring of investments required by this type of investing. In addition, it can be very difficult to generate the deal flow to match an investor's financial and impact-based expectations as well as their geographic or issue area focus.

Compounding these issues, the whole discussion can be somewhat opaque, with outsiders gaining little visibility into funds, investors, ventures and deals within the seed stage landscape. This creates a level of uncertainty and reluctance to invest in the absence of such transparency and data. Each of these factors contributes to the frustration experienced by both investors and entrepreneurs trying to increase funding flows between impact investors and promising social entrepreneurs. But there are, nonetheless, opportunities in the exciting, risky, "deep end of the pool" that is seed stage impact investing. And for many, "going direct" is what impact investing is all about. Let us walk through some of the characteristics, both the challenges and opportunities, in this category of investment practice.

There are a multitude of sound reasons why many investors do not pursue seed stage investing in the impact space. By taking a closer look at those reasons, this daunting gap can be broken into specific obstacles so the needs and concerns of investors may be more directly addressed.

An Intrinsically Risky Business

Any early stage investment—whether traditional or impact—and especially seed funding, is a fundamentally risky investment. The way this type of risk has traditionally been managed is by making many "tiny bets" and thereby playing the odds that, through wide diversification, one of those bets will result in generating the exponential returns that more than compensate for any lost investment in the other investments of an angel portfolio.

For this approach to make sense, all of the initial investments must have the potential to scale up and produce a return of multiple times the invested seed capital, although only a small percentage will actually do so.

This presents a challenge for seed stage impact investing because the return on the investment is not purely financial. Both the social and environmental impact of social ventures may dramatically outperform previous solutions, but many of these ventures will still have fairly slow and steady financial growth; many more will sputter out, as is true of their conventional counterparts. In fact, the slow and steady growth pattern is a commendable outcome that produces financial return and sustainable impact. These are great impact investments, but someone still has to take the risk at the seed stage, before the business and impact model is fully proven and financial returns generated. There are investors who are willing to take that chance, but it is with full recognition they are taking on high risk that may not result in a correspondingly high financial return.

At this time there are few high impact-oriented ventures that have produced the kinds of multiples of financial return on investment that the venture capital industry has experienced in traditional sectors, especially technology and web-based business models. Importantly, the objective of impact investing is different from traditional investing at its core in that it seeks both financial and social or environmental returns. Impact investors are accepting *both* impact risk and financial risk, and should subsequently evaluate return with a blended approach.

But there are some bright spots! After all, companies such as Honest Tea, Happy Plant and Seventh Generation were once someone's yesteryear seed stage investment. And a growing number of private equity funds offering "broad" as opposed to "deep" impact have come to market in recent years that will offer investors more significant financial return with perhaps lighter impact than direct, seed stage investing may offer. The long-term outcomes and risk-return profile of seed stage impact investing are still somewhat of an experiment at a cultural and market level, with each funded venture providing a new data point. As part of the enthusiasm for social entrepreneurship and impact investing, more and more individuals are being drawn to early stage solutions that have the potential to build a better world. However, they want some benchmarks around risk and return. Over time, the development of better market-wide data on the aggregate return profile of seed investing will allow investors to make more informed decisions regarding the risks they must be willing to take to realize future impact.

Investment Size and the Realities of Allocation

As a risky investment, the allocation to a seed stage investment strategy is typically a small percentage of an investor's portfolio. Within that limited allocation, a common way to decrease the risk is to diversify that segment of an investor's portfolio with multiple small investments, as previously mentioned. An investor with $1 million might reasonably allocate $200,000 to private or alternative investments (and even that would be a quite healthy percentage). Even if all of that is allocated to impact investing, likely no more than a fraction, say 20 percent, would be for seed stage investing. So now such an investor might have $40,000 to place. With reasonable practicalities related to transaction size, this would yield investment in at most one to two ventures, which does not provide sufficient diversification from an overall portfolio perspective. Accordingly, this inability to fully diversify risk may decrease investor appetite for such an allocation.

For an entrepreneur trying to raise a seed round, a significant amount of time goes into cultivating each investor. The relatively small amount they are trying to raise (average range of $250,000–$500,000) falls below the range of consideration for large investors, and raising money from individuals results in piecemeal investments requiring significant time of both entrepreneur and investor. Identifying an investor who can make a sizable contribution of capital out of a diversified impact portfolio is a clear challenge for seed stage ventures.

Expense to Source, Analyze, Monitor Deals

Closely tied to the challenges of investment size, there is often a disproportionate expense associated with making seed stage investments. Regardless of size, these investments must be sourced, undergo thorough due diligence, be negotiated on different, often unique terms and continuously monitored after the initial investment is made. The process is very time consuming and requires special expertise; this level of work could easily require full time attention, either on the part of the investor or her staff. The expense of a single deal is potentially even greater for seed stage investments because the business models are often less developed, requiring additional research and conversations to establish confidence in the investments.

These costs do not scale in relation to the size of the investment, which makes seed stage investments very expensive relative to the amount of capital being put to work. One of the key reasons large investors do not consider investments below $500,000 is that the economics of engaging in due diligence of those deals don't make sense, whereas the same costs are easily accommodated were a multimillion dollar investment under consideration. There is a clear need to streamline seed stage investing; to shrink the hurdles between an investor who believes in the potential of a social venture and their ability to make and monitor such an investment.

Investment Readiness

The cause most often cited for the gap in seed stage impact investing is lack of investment readiness by social ventures. This has prompted the rise of accelerators and incubators tailored to social enterprises, to fortify their business plans, make their financials presentable and polish their pitches. We have only seen the initial swells of a growing wave of social enterprises that in the future will require extensive mentoring and support to develop into viable impact investments. The efficiency with which high-potential ventures and strong leaders can become investment ready is what will set the pace of deal flow.

To be fair, investment readiness also applies to investors. One of the strengths of the venture capital industry is that practitioners are quite ready to invest when an opportunity presents itself and are unabashed in turning away ventures that do not meet their criteria. When an investor makes a personal connection to a social enterprise based on its impact, however, they may extend the conversation with an entrepreneur even if an investment is not on the horizon. This is wasted time that the entrepreneur could spend cultivating other seed stage capital opportunities. Therefore, one of the best things one can do as a seed stage investor is get to "no" quickly, saving both sides wasted time. Furthermore, being clear about whether one is able to jump right in, or needs to follow a lead investor, is also crucial and worth putting on the table.

On the entrepreneur's side, expectation management and an understanding of process are also both significantly important. Investors and their advisors received numerous requests for funding each week. If you're an entrepreneur who is told your proposal is being brought forward for review, you might certainly celebrate—but don't assume you will receive funding! It is not at all unlikely that in the course of the investment committee's discussion what was sincerely viewed as a "good fit" may, for any number of reasons, turn out not to be. This is not the "fault" of those who had been leading due diligence but a natural outcome of a review process. Entrepreneurs seeking capital need to assume there may be interest along with an inability to fund due to any number of factors. Don't forget—the same investor who turned you down this time may be the one who introduces your company to their future seed investor or takes a position in a future round, so be sure not to burn your bridges when told of an unanticipated declination.

These are just some of the reasons why it's hard to do seed investing as well as some perspective on the approach that can help alleviate these challenges. Let's turn our attention to some practical solutions to mitigate the challenges and approach what is still—with its challenges—one of the most exciting propositions in impact investing.

Use a Seed Stage Fund

Finding a seed stage fund can be a way to reach a large, professionally managed portfolio of ventures, allowing investors to place more capital, better and faster. A fund may make upwards of 20 company investments, and may accept as little as $50,000 minimums (though many will be higher than this).

Seed funds anticipate many of their investments will fail, they know the ventures will require extensive mentoring and support and they are willing to accept proxies as evidence of an entrepreneur's capability and potential. Seed funds have found their best investments are often sourced by referrals from prior investees. Many of the strongest prospects don't identify as social entrepreneurs or even realize there are investors specifically seeking social or environmental return. An entrepreneur getting a new business off the ground oftentimes looks to his or her peers for actionable business advice rather than spending time to understand the landscape of investors. For this reason, established entrepreneurs often have the first glimpse into the next great businesses. To identify promising early stage deals, seed funds have built field networks, in addition to their portfolio companies, to gather this street level intelligence. All in all, funds can add a lot of value to investors.

Camp onto an Accelerator Program or an Angel Network

For those investors with a high level of appetite to do direct company investments, but need help in sourcing and diligencing, an accelerator program can be good way to tap into an ecosystem of investment deals, ride along with high engagement support programs and find coinvestors to share in diligence. However, though leveraging program and networks may help reduce some of the pain points, investors are still left with making somewhat sizable investments. There is increasing viability in the area of direct investing, with the JOBS Act increasing access of nonaccredited investors to direct company investments, and development of crowdfunding infrastructure to drive down per deal sizes to as little as $5,000.

The table below is an informational selection of **seed funds** *and* **accelerators** *with impact orientation, and should be viewed as only a jumping off point for deeper exploration of current options (as the landscape is quickly evolving).*

ORGANIZATION	WEBSITE	HQ LOCATION
Agora Partnerships	agorapartnerships.org	Nicaragua/DC
Ashoka	ashoka.org	Washington, DC
Better Ventures	better.vc	Oakland, CA
Civic Accelerator/ Points of Light	pointsoflight.org/civic-incubator/programs/civic- accelerator	Atlanta, GA
Code for America	codeforamerica.org	San Francisco, CA
Echoing Green	echoinggreen.org	New York, NY

(continued)

(cont.)

ORGANIZATION	WEBSITE	HQ LOCATION
Fledge	fledge.co/	Seattle, WA
Global Social Benefit Incubator	scu.edu/socialbenefit/ entrepreneurship/ gsbi/	Santa Clara, CA
GoodCompany Ventures	goodcompanygroup. org/ residency/ program	Philadelphia, PA
Ideaxcelerator/Idea Village	ideavillage.org	New Orleans, LA
Impact Engine	theimpactengine.com	Chicago, IL
Investors Circle/ Patient Capital Collaborative	investorscircle.net	Durham, NC
NESsT	nesst.org	San Francisco, CA
New Ventures	new-ventures.org/	Washington, DC
Rock Health	rockhealth.com/	San Francisco, CA
Unreasonable Institute	unreasonableinstitute. org	Boulder, CO
VentureWell	venturewell.org	Boston, MA
Village Capital	vilcap.com	Atlanta, GA

Use a Donor Advised Fund to Mix and Match

ImpactAssets has seen an increasingly wide range of its clients using their donor advised funds (DAFs) to reach both seed funds and direct company investments in concert with accelerator relationships. Because DAFs aggregate up among multiple accounts, they can drive down minimums even further. And, since individuals receive a tax deduction when they open a DAF (since it is in fact a charitable donation), one might view the tax benefit as an initial "return" of sorts at the point of investment, and then have more support for patience over the long term that these early stage investments demand. See Targeted Impact: Donor Advised Funds and Impact Investing in this volume for more on DAFs.

In Conclusion

Investing in early stage, impact businesses requires specific, often industry or market-level expertise on the part of the investor, as well as portfolio diversification. Therefore, this type of investing has intrinsic challenges for small and large investors alike. Simply put, it is not for the faint of heart. But by leveraging seed funds, accelerator programs and investor networks that can provide support, reduce investment sizes and bring greater diversification to the investor, all the while exploring new modalities available through crowdfunding platforms and DAFs, seed stage investing is at least plausible and increasingly viable for those who find it compelling.

Accelerators are iterating their models to more accurately match entrepreneurs with investors and providing ongoing services to support follow-on financing. In addition, relationships between seed funds and accelerators are being developed that provide a more immediate and ongoing feedback loop between entrepreneurs and investors, in addition to the more efficient vetting resulting from accelerators sharing experiential knowledge of the teams and their ventures.

When all is said and done, there remains a tremendous opportunity for innovation and for intermediaries to alleviate the friction in seed stage impact investing. A small shift in the allocation of capital can make a significant difference, and it is the authors' hope that new products and services will continue to be developed to support increased seed stage impact investing. Directing a steady flow of capital toward promising early stage ventures is critical, for otherwise how will we see the great companies of tomorrow get funded today!

Notes

This chapter was revised and adapted from an ImpactAssets Issue Brief entitled "Seeding the Future: Challenge and Opportunity in Early Stage Impact Investing," originally authored by Jed Emerson, Tim Freundlich and Lindsay Smalling.

1 For the purposes of this chapter, we will consider seed stage to be a venture that is raising an amount of capital less than $500,000 with little to no revenue recognition.

4

Choosing Your Impact
Investment Advisor

Brad Harrison and Stephanie Cohn-Rupp

Aligning your financial assets with your values in a holistic way most often requires intermediaries and advisors, or what is sometimes referred to as the "artisans of impact." This chapter offers a variety of resources, but we must begin with the caveat that we are not endorsing any individual firm, financial product, investment strategy, or even approach. Our comments are not investment recommendations, but rather an effort to offer an overview of the vast landscape of resources available to you. Along with many impact investment advisors, we think about "impact investing" as simply "investing," taking into account the additional risks and opportunities resulting from social and environmental externalities in an increasingly complex financial system—and our hope is that this chapter proves to demystify some of the "impact" rhetoric that may lead to better decision-making.

Our target audience for this chapter includes asset owners ranging from retail investors to high net worth individuals, foundations and institutions ranging from $5 to $50 million. If you are reading this chapter, you may manage your own portfolio or seek the professional advice of a financial advisor, but in either scenario, are interested in going beyond the status quo to explore how to deepen the alignment and positive impact of your investment strategy. We hope to provide practical questions after each section, and offer key considerations, relevant resources, and decision-making criteria. In a sea of many self-proclaimed impact investing products and experts, it is important to know how to find experienced and authentic impact investment advice—not just "advice."

Delphi's Saying

"Know Thyself" (and thy needs) is the precursor to any advisor search. Whether you are an individual, couple, family, foundation leader or appointed trustee, it is paramount to first clarify your needs and values prior to embarking on an advisor search—especially an impact advisor search. Those who desire to activate their impact portfolio in all asset classes will most likely require professional assistance at some point in their journey.

To begin, we would suggest focusing on a few simple questions:

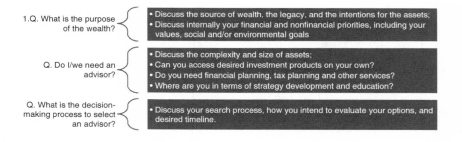

1.Q. What is the purpose of the wealth?
- Discuss the source of wealth, the legacy, and the intentions for the assets;
- Discuss internally your financial and nonfinancial priorities, including your values, social and/or environmental goals

Q. Do I/we need an advisor?
- Discuss the complexity and size of assets;
- Can you access desired investment products on your own?
- Do you need financial planning, tax planning and other services?
- Where are you in terms of strategy development and education?

Q. What is the decision-making process to select an advisor?
- Discuss your search process, how you intend to evaluate your options, and desired timeline.

Retail Investor Options

If you are not working with an advisor, either by choice or circumstance, you can build a mission-aligned impact portfolio, in a variety of meaningful ways, on your own—although we must caveat this assertion as we've seen all too many missteps in this rapidly evolving field. For the true "do-it-yourselfer," the primary challenges tend to lie in strategy development, investment due diligence in all asset classes (one investor may be an expert in venture capital, but may need assistance investing in public markets), impact reporting, and ongoing monitoring of a suite of impact investments. Engaging in meaningful research, including speaking to other investors, reading not only this chapter but other books and reports available online, and even attending impact investing conferences, can all be helpful and are highly recommended.[1]

The lowest hanging fruit when it comes to dialing up the impact of your investments is to consider your banking relationship. As a first step, you may consider moving your savings and checking accounts from a large bank to a community bank whose deposits are used to lend to local entrepreneurs, support minority-owned businesses, or invest in your local community.

Beyond cash, you can begin to assess the individual stocks and bonds held in your brokerage account. A first step is to "know what you own," and a review of your underlying stock and bond exposures is a useful place to start. Depending on how you manage your assets, a transition toward socially responsible investment strategies employing negative or positive environmental, social and governance (ESG) approaches are available to you through various mutual funds. These approaches can screen out harmful sectors (weapons, fossil fuels, etc.) and/or tilt portfolios toward positive corporate behaviors (companies with diverse governance, commitments to environmental disclosures, etc.). These mutual funds or index funds are considered "actively managed" as the managers are actively changing the "ingredients," or underlying stocks and bonds within the fund based on E, S and G factors. Passive approaches, or investing in market indices, can be designed to simply screen for exposures that run contrary to your values and are available through exchange traded funds (ETFs) or index funds.

Retail investors may also access more innovative approaches, such as green bonds (financing environmentally friendly projects aimed at energy efficiency, pollution prevention, sustainable agriculture, fishery and forestry, etc.). The debt options for nonaccredited investors,[2] which include debt products from a variety of sources that provide investment notes, include Community Development Finance Institutions (CDFIs) and Credit Unions. For a list of CDFIs, please refer to Opportunity Finance Network (http://ofn.org/cdfi-locator), which offers a registry of financial institutions with different sectors of focus and geographies. The minimum balance for a loan can be as low as $500 with a single-digit interest rate.

And lastly, there are many other product offerings available to retail investors, including equity crowdfunding and the new, but rapidly emerging "straight-to-consumer" socially responsible "robo-advisors." These investment models and business propositions are still early on in their evolutionary development, but may offer an interesting approach for retail investors over the coming years. The promise here is greater "democratization," lower price points and more streamlined service offerings. If, however, you have decided the complexity of your financial picture requires professional assistance, or seek more innovative approaches to fulfill your goals, we will now turn to reasons for which families, individuals and foundations are seeking professional impact investment advice.

Motivations behind an Advisor Search

For Individuals

Motivations driving high net worth (HNW) individuals to engage impact investment advisors are highly personal, ergo the motto often used by the President of Threshold Group Ed Lazar: "When you meet one family, you've met one family." The press often represents that two demographics, millennials and women, are driving the charge toward impact investing. Although we see this trend playing out, in practice, we have come across a variety of demographics embarking on this journey.

In some cases, the older generation (male or female) may be the ones initiating the process of exploring how best to engage in more than simply traditional investment practices. In some cases, the family has grown to care deeply about a specific social issue, such as supporting local businesses through a CDFI and needs a professional to access these financial products. In other cases, another generation of family members have become philanthropically engaged in an issue such as Women's Rights, or eradication of Modern Day Slavery, and recently learned they could do more through their investments, but their current advisors don't know how to address their requests. And other asset owners are driven by innovation, and have heard of social entrepreneurship, microfinance or mobile money in East Africa, and wonder how they can invest in frontier markets. Asset owners are also increasingly realizing they can have a voice through investment and shareholder engagement—not *only* through divestment—which was better known due to the anti-Apartheid divestment movement.

Another driver is that seasoned impact investors are now being more vocal and engaging social media platforms to communicate their ideas. Traditionally, speaking publicly about money or one's investments and financial returns was taboo or perceived as inappropriate (especially outside of the United States), but the veil of silence around wealth and investing has now been lifted and private citizens of financial means all over the world are willing to share their financial journeys. Experienced asset owners are investing assets in a socially responsible fashion in all asset classes, and trying to encourage others to join them by sharing their stories (successes and failures), portfolios and investment decisions through online publications,[3] public events, social networks and even mainstream media. This has created a tidal wave of demand in the past few years from new entrants. This growth in demand explains the "mainstreaming" of impact investing services from large wealth management outfits and the growth of "impact" advisory firms and asset managers. As a result, asset owners wish to explore how they, too, can take part in the era of the conscientious investor.

For Foundations

Motivations driving foundations to engage an impact investment advisor run the gamut from the moral imperative—that "OMG!" moment when you realize your grants are funded by profits that run contrary to your mission—to the strategic acceleration of your theory of change by unlocking a greater portion of the foundation's assets for social purpose. What has been viewed as a fringe argument by some is gaining considerable traction separate from these other motivations led by the "heart" and the "head." Foundation impact investing may no longer be a matter of reason or responsibility, but a matter of rule. Consider this argument for a second: organizations that have been privileged with federal tax-exempt 501(c)(3) status for the purposes of serving public interest (and the significant tax-advantaged benefits afforded to them) should be required to align their investment portfolios to serve this same public benefit.

As you consider that potentially provocative statement, know a small set of foundations have been among the earliest adopters of impact investing and represent a large (and growing) source of capital to the impact investing ecosystem. This makes sense given many foundations have clearly articulated missions, values and programmatic goals by which to align their investments. Adding to this natural evolution, foundation directors, leaders and staff tend to be experts in assessing the nonfinancial outcomes of their grants, that is: the return on investment (ROI) on their "investments." These internal forces, coupled with strong external policy momentum, are driving foundations to consider the value of impact investing at scale—and seeking the advice of professional impact investors to support their efforts.

Whether you're motivated by principle or prudency—or simply complying with ever-changing regulations surrounding fiduciary duties and prudent financial management—identifying a professional impact investment advisor can be an asset in marrying the often-opaque realm of philanthropy with the more structured realm of investing. At the most basic levels, an impact investment advisor should be well versed in foundation structures, governance, planning, investing, implementation and reporting. But most foundations—especially those reading this chapter—need more than simple formulaic investment advisory, legal and tax services. They often need an advisor who deeply understands (and, we'd argue, cares about) their mission, vision, and values—and can effectively communicate impact integration with the broad set of stakeholders involved in most foundations. The best impact investment advisors are not just great investors, strategists and facilitators, but have a deep grasp on the scientific, policy and social issues that are core to a foundation's philanthropic agenda.

Advisor Landscape

Understanding the skills, experience and styles among investment advisors is fundamental to the search, evaluation and ultimate selection process, no matter where you are in the discovery phase. We have outlined below questions to consider asking as you research and interview a specialized impact investment advisor.

Types of Advisors

A variety of advisors exist, available through individual private consultancies or professional services firms, who may have a socially responsible focus: registered investment advisors (RIAs), stock brokers, chartered financial analysts (CFAs), certified financial planners (CFPs), multifamily office professionals, wealth advisors, investment and strategy consultants, private bankers and trust officers.

A number of highly qualified consultants at Arabella, Bridgespan Group, Hirsh and Associates, Tideline and other firms help foundations develop philanthropic and impact investment strategies and provide structured facilitation, collaboration, coaching and discovery for key stakeholders. For those looking for highly engaged, strategic advisors, thought-leaders such as Jed Emerson (also the editor of this book) have helped families on this personal journey for many years. For individuals, intermediary organizations and collaborations such as ImpactAssets, Investor's Circle, Social Venture Partners and others provide opportunities to interact with practitioners, share deal flow and vet opportunities. Networks like Confluence Philanthropy, Mission Investors Exchange, Toniic and others create thought-leadership pieces, national and regional convenings and share best practices amongst asset-owners. Investment advisors, such as Ivo Knoepfel of OnValues in Zurich, provide investment advice, but do not manage funds directly. That is, these consultants help clients search and select investment managers, but do not directly execute individual fund strategies.

Examples of RIAs that offer advisory services and sell proprietary investment products include Arjuna, Mercer, Nelson, Parella Weinberg, RBC, Sonen Capital and Zevin Asset Management. Examples of RIAs that offer advisory services only but do not sell investment products include Athena, Cambridge Associates, Federal Street, The CAPROCK Group, Threshold Group and Veris Wealth Partners. These advisory firms, whose names have been sourced from Confluence Philanthropy's "Finding Your Way to the Right Impact Investing Advisor" publication, offer investment advisory, implementation and financial reporting services. And last, but certainly not least, large banks and brokerage firms such as Goldman Sachs/Imprint, JP Morgan and Bank of America offer impact investment advisory services, industry research and product development. For a specific list of services offered by these firms, we recommend looking at Confluence Philanthropy's publication, "Finding Your Way to the Right Impact Investing Advisor,"[4] available online.

For asset owners looking for impact portfolio construction in multiple asset classes with deeper impact expertise, we will focus specifically on the RIA market. We encourage you to go online and research advisors through the Securities and Exchange Commission (SEC) Adviser Search portal.[5] There you will find public information pertaining to each RIA's advisory business, management team, governance, fees and compensation, types of clients, methods of analysis, code of ethics and disciplinary information.

Q: Does the advisor have specialized expertise across a broad range of tax-exempt structures?

- Family foundations, private foundations, community foundations
- Public charities, public trusts, endowments
- Social enterprise LLCs, collaborative networks

Registered Investment Advisors versus Registered Investment Advisors with Product Offerings

Most RIAs offer comprehensive wealth management services, including portfolio construction, asset allocation and financial reporting, and some offer proprietary impact investment products (spanning public market solutions, including stocks and bond products and private market solutions, including private equity and venture capital funds). There are pros and cons to each. While some clients may appreciate the "all under one roof" approach, others may feel uncomfortable working with firms that populate portfolios with their own financial products due to potential conflicts of interest (real or perceived). Those with investment products have an economic incentive to place your assets with their own financial products. Other advisors do not offer any proprietary products and, as such, provide arms-length relationships from fund managers (i.e. the investment products), providing a potentially more objective view across products and the ability to terminate relationships at any time. We always recommend asking your prospective advisors which category they fall into and how they handle the potential conflict of interest issues.

Q: How is the RIA compensated?
- Does the advisor only offer investment advisory services or does it also offer products?
- Describe the fee schedule, including both implicit and explicit fees

Size Matters

Impact advisors range from small (<$500 million of assets under management (AUM)) to large firms ($15 billion+ of AUM). Smaller firms may offer a high touch boutique approach to understanding your financial goals and values. These firms typically are able to build highly customized portfolios, and tailor impact reporting, strategy and assessment to you. Larger firms may offer a more institutional-scale approach to aligning investments with your goals and provide access to a platform of institutional investment products through deep investment research functions that may be less bespoke Through the ADV filing with the SEC, RIAs can specify their "assets under management" versus "assets under advisement." Assets under management are those where the SEC has defined as "continuous and regular supervisory or management services of securities portfolios" and assets under advisement as those assets where the firm "provides advice or consultation but for which your firm either does not have discretionary authority or does not arrange or effectuate the transaction," that is, without implementation responsibility. Simply stated, the firm's AUM is a more accurate reflection of an advisor's fiduciary management responsibilities.

One other consideration is the relative size of your asset base compared to the overall AUM of the advisory firm. You may not want to represent a significant portion of the firm's AUM, as you may want to ensure your advisor has significant experience and capacity to manage your assets. Another factor to consider is the financial viability of the firm. A smaller impact investing advisory firm may not have reached sufficient scale to be financially viable whereas a large firm may have a more sustainable revenue model. For a firm managing assets, it is paramount to ask about the overall AUM of the firm, its financial sustainability, investor base and growth plans. For those firms only providing investment advice and not managing assets, the asset base under advisement may not be as relevant, but it is important to ask about the firm's business model and financial viability, as well as its own source of investment for growth.

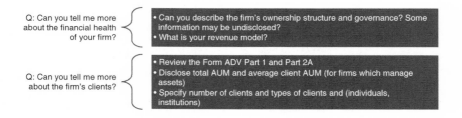

Q: Can you tell me more about the financial health of your firm?
- Can you describe the firm's ownership structure and governance? Some information may be undisclosed?
- What is your revenue model?

Q: Can you tell me more about the firm's clients?
- Review the Form ADV Part 1 and Part 2A
- Disclose total AUM and average client AUM (for firms which manage assets)
- Specify number of clients and types of clients and (individuals, institutions)

Discretionary versus Nondiscretionary Relationships

You can provide your advisor with different levels of authority on your portfolio by establishing a discretionary or nondiscretionary relationship agreement. Discretionary relationships allow your advisor authority to buy and sell securities on your behalf whereas nondiscretionary relationships require that the advisor make investment recommendations that must be approved by the client prior to being purchased. A nondiscretionary relationship will take more investment of your time, as this could also require you to become better educated on values-based strategies, the investment and impact thesis and the role of the investment in your portfolio. Through this, you will work closely with your advisor—but beware—this can become a real time-commitment.

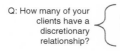

Q: How many of your clients have a discretionary relationship?
- Ask to speak to both discretionary and nondiscretionary clients to understand their reasons for their choice. What is their time commitment?
- Discuss internally your appetite for being involved in investment decisions

Human Capital and Cultural Fit

When speaking to prospective advisors, we recommend asking who exactly would be part of your advisory team. Understand who will be your primary relationship manager, the lead investment professionals and any others who will be servicing your account. This will help you gauge whether their skill-set and interpersonal skills fit with you and your family, or your foundation staff. Some advisors develop close-knit relationships with their clients while others will remain at arm's length. Impact investing advisors are also known for being more socially engaged with their client-base than traditional advisors, which is likely due to their personal connection with the work, interest in social and environmental outcomes and the like. We also recommend asking for a minimum of three client references to better understand how the team would work with you and your family.

Q: What are your firm values? How do you like to communicate with your clients?

- Discuss the firm values and culture
- Spend time in various settings with team members
- Discuss the investors' personal values, and motivations
- Evaluate "communication styles" and trustworthiness

Investment Expertise

Your investment advisor should have significant investment experience, which may be evidenced through professional designations such as Chartered Financial Analyst (CFA), Chartered Alternative Investment Analyst (CAIA) and so on. Understanding their investment experience in managing financial assets, investment philosophy, research processes, decision-making structures and track records are key components in your due diligence.

Q: Does the advisor have investment expertise, provide institutional rigor, and adequate risk management?

- Ability to generate asset growth while meeting operational and grantmaking needs
- Truly aligned investment portfolios with mission, values and grantmaking strategies
- Embed risk mitigation strategies integrated throughout institutional quality due diligence and asset allocation processes
- Developed a goals-based approach to address any inherent tensions between impact and traditional portfolio management
- Strategic planning around long-term sustainability

Impact Investing Expertise

Environment, Social and Governance versus Thematic Focus

Some advisory firms have broad-based experience in socially responsible investing (SRI) or environmental, social and governance (ESG) investing, while other RIAs have developed deep thematic expertise around environmental sustainability, gender lens investing, financial inclusion, education and so on. It's important to ask the advisor which approaches they pursue and how they intend to express specific themes within your portfolio. You may only want to have a general approach to impact investing to support positive social and environmental outcomes—so a more generalist firm may be sufficient. But if you care deeply about providing access to capital for the underbanked, for example, a generalist advisor may not know which private equity fund will be best in class, or which interventions (savings, financial education, credit) are the most catalytic.

Q: Does the advisor represent clients across a broad range of programmatic initiatives?

- Environmental sustainability, climate change and advocacy
- Social justice, diversity and inclusion, indigenous rights
- Healthcare, education, human rights, wellness
- Regional economic development, financial inclusion and rural economic advancement

Impact Washing

Outside of asking about the investment or financial planning credentials (CFA, Certified Financial Planner™ (CFP®), etc.) of your prospective advisor, we would also recommend asking very pointed questions regarding their understanding of underlying issues that you personally care about: climate change, social justice, affordable housing and so on. Over recent years, the sector is seeing a growing number of self-proclaimed "impact advisors" who may not be familiar at all with issues of environmental science, equity, poverty, economic development or fair housing that the asset owner may be seeking to address. The growth of "impact washing" is such that it requires the asset owner to be unafraid to ask about the intentions and knowledge of the prospective advisory firm (e.g., "What motivates you? Why did you choose this career path?"). We recommend asking about their research and what intellectual capital or blogs they have written on a given subject. If the advisor is not knowledgeable about key environmental issues like the Dakota Access Pipeline or social issues like Gender-Parity in the workforce, he/she may not be able to conduct informed due diligence on strategies (public or private funds) in an authentic fashion or informed manner.

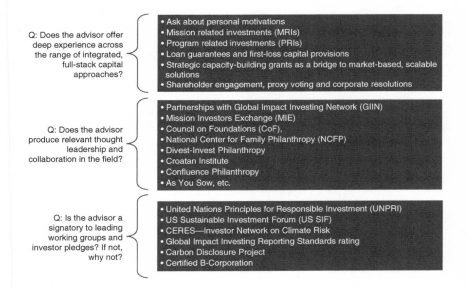

Q: Does the advisor offer deep experience across the range of integrated, full-stack capital approaches?
- Ask about personal motivations
- Mission related investments (MRIs)
- Program related investments (PRIs)
- Loan guarantees and first-loss capital provisions
- Strategic capacity-building grants as a bridge to market-based, scalable solutions
- Shareholder engagement, proxy voting and corporate resolutions

Q: Does the advisor produce relevant thought leadership and collaboration in the field?
- Partnerships with Global Impact Investing Network (GIIN)
- Mission Investors Exchange (MIE)
- Council on Foundations (CoF),
- National Center for Family Philanthropy (NCFP)
- Divest-Invest Philanthropy
- Croatan Institute
- Confluence Philanthropy
- As You Sow, etc.

Q: Is the advisor a signatory to leading working groups and investor pledges? If not, why not?
- United Nations Principles for Responsible Investment (UNPRI)
- US Sustainable Investment Forum (US SIF)
- CERES—Investor Network on Climate Risk
- Global Impact Investing Reporting Standards rating
- Carbon Disclosure Project
- Certified B-Corporation

Total Portfolio Management: Activation for Impact

Most traditional advisors may offer some SRI or ESG funds on their investment platforms or can help build a 5 percent impact carve-out of a total portfolio that is values-aligned. However, a handful of advisors in the United States (at least in 2017) can offer a fully diversified impact portfolio across asset classes. If you wish to embark on the journey of impact investing, moving from a small percentage to perhaps a "total activation" of your portfolio, it's important to ask your prospective advisors about their experience in going beyond "carve-outs." Below you will see an example of an impact portfolio in transition, spanning all asset classes.

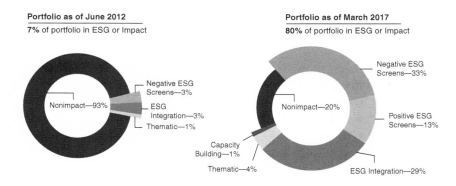

Portfolio as of June 2012
7% of portfolio in ESG or Impact

Nonimpact—93%
Negative ESG Screens—3%
ESG Integration—3%
Thematic—1%

Portfolio as of March 2017
80% of portfolio in ESG or Impact

Negative ESG Screens—33%
Nonimpact—20%
Positive ESG Screens—13%
Capacity Building—1%
Thematic—4%
ESG Integration—29%

For illustrative purposes only

Source: Threshold Group, 2017

Q: Does the advisor have local, national or international leadership on impact investing tools and trends?

- Achieve total portfolio activation, or 100% impact investing across asset classes, if desired
- Implement divestment strategies using all the tools in the toolkit
- Design and implement thematic and place-based investing strategies
- Develop focused carve outs for catalytic, aspirational objectives

Divestment Strategies

One important tool to leverage for asset owners is the option of divesting from securities that relate to sectors or industries you feel do not mesh with your values, as a family, trust or foundation—*while optimizing* for your financial goals. An experienced impact advisor should be able to build a tailored framework for signatories of Divest/Invest to divest from fossil fuels, for example, and then reinvest in clean energy or carbon sinks. Drafting a multi-year divestment and investment plan related to climate change or another topic such as human trafficking/modern day slavery is an important skill-set that may be necessary to further your impact goals. When interviewing prospective advisors, you can ask for examples of such a plan.

Q: Does the advisor have experience developing divestment and reinvestment plans?

- Ask for examples of client portfolios from signatories of Divest/Invest. Advisors can share sample portfolios without disclosing names of clients or fund managers.

Shareholder Engagement

Another catalytic tool to explore with your advisor is his/her experience in shareholder engagement—which can take many shapes. The first step is having the underlying fund managers in your portfolio meet with corporate management to discuss an important issue held by stock-owners, such as excessive executive pay or corporate political campaign donations. Proxy voting is defined as a ballot cast by one person on behalf of a shareholder of a corporation who would rather cast a proxy vote than attend a shareholder meeting. A shareholder resolution is a 500-word maximum proposal that must be included in the company's proxy statement and voted on by shareholders. Actual corporate behavior can change as a result of shareholder engagement—such as McDonald's move from Styrofoam cups to paper cups thanks to the work of the shareholder advocacy organization called As You Sow. An experienced impact RIA should be able to walk you through the many options available to you, and explain which managers and partners they may use.

Q: Does the advisor engage in shareholder activism?

• Does the advisor go beyond manager-led proxy voting?
• Does the advisor help facilitate filing of shareholder resolutions?

Summary of Service Offerings

There is a range of services—some basic and some highly specialized—that must also align with your desired scope of services. At the most basic level, RIAs provide investment advice in the form of asset allocation, portfolio construction, investment recommendations, financial performance reporting and ongoing monitoring. Those are fundamental services that, as a result, have been become fairly commoditized—even robots are doing them. This has led most impact investors to value deeper, more tailored service offerings. We realize that this list is not exhaustive but hope it will help summarize what is a typical scope of services from an impact investing RIA.

1. Relationship Onboarding and Goal Setting

- Creating an inventory of your goals and objectives including capital appreciation, investment stability and liquidity, and impact and mission related investing;
- Understanding your current investment portfolio by reviewing investment holdings, distribution requirements, target returns, risk management, time horizon, tax status, carry forwards, and multi-year commitments;
- Creating a data-driven financial plan to help you meet your investment objectives;
- Utilizing of a diagnostic tools to prioritize non-financial outcomes;
- Developing an integrated Investment Policy Statement (IPS) including impact and non-impact goals.

2. Delivering Comprehensive Investment Management

- Goals-based investment solutions for a variety of portfolio types (private foundations, community foundations, public trusts, endowments, non profits); Fully integrated traditional and impact investing solutions;
- Dynamic portfolio construction including strategic and tactical asset allocation;
- Institutional quality manager research, due diligence and monitoring;
- Investment execution and cash flow management;
- Monthly financial reporting, quarterly performance reporting and annual impact reporting;
- Portfolio stress testing, including sustainability and scenario analysis.

3. Strategic Impact and Mission Related Investing Broad and deep understanding of traditional and impact investments;

- Facilitating impact investing conversations through diagnostic tools and values-based surveys;
- Utilization of the entire investment toolkit including total-portfolio activation, mission related investments (MRIs), program related investments (PRIs), catalytic direct investments, loan guarantees, capacity building grants, etc.
- Access to broad based Environmental, Social, and Governance (ESG) strategies across public equities and fixed income markets;
- Access to thematic and place-based private equity and venture capital;
- Divest-Invest strategies and low-carbon portfolio management;
- Place based investing to align with geographic grantmaking and focus areas;
- Facilitation of shareholder engagement, proxy voting, and corporate resolutions;
- Annual impact reporting, impact evaluation through quantitative and qualitative analysis at portfolio and investment strategy levels.

4. Foundation Board and Committee Governance Expertise (Foundations Only)

- Experience with multi-stakeholder relationships, including intergenerational families, external boards and promoting next-gen leadership;
- Industry best practices around board governance and investment decision making;
- Facilitation of investment committee meetings and updates;
- Development and compilation of Board and Investment Committee dockets;
- Coordination among program staff, accountants, attorneys, advisors and programmatic consultants.

5. Investment Education and Strategic Planning

- Comprehensive educational content for boards, investment committees and staff on a variety of financial and non-financial topics for effective foundation investment management, goal-setting and alignment;
- Planning for changes in perpetuity goals, leadership, mission and governance.

6. Thought-Leadership and Capacity Building

- Support on proactively discussing foundation investment strategy and impact investing through media contacts, website content, etc.
- Partnership on case studies, conference panels, webinars.

Pricing Summary

Although pricing for the services discussed in this chapter are often negotiated and tailored to your unique needs, you should always ask for a prospective advisor's scope of services with their Form ADV Part 2, which includes the fee schedule for their core service offerings. Pricing schedules are confusing to prospective clients, and a general practice is to set pricing floors at specific asset levels. To actually understand the fees you would actually pay on your assets, you will need to calculate a "blended" rate. We looked at some of the most notable impact investing advisors in the market today, and charted out the pricing to give the reader a sense of cost on a blended and annual basis. Please note that this does not include the underlying fees charged by fund managers (i.e., the products) in one's portfolio—this only includes the RIA fees for advising and implementing. For example, a $20 million portfolio, at a 54 basis points rate, means that the client would pay a recurring $108,000. As the AUM grows, the basis point fee decreases, as illustrated below. For full pricing details, you should refer to an advisor's Form ADV Part 2 (the Disclosure Brochure)[6] which, as noted earlier, is publicly available online.

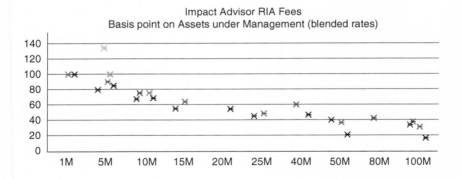

Impact Advisor RIA Fees
Basis point on Assets under Management (blended rates)

Impact RIAs are generally found to be more expensive than similarly sized firms that do not provide impact investing services. This proposition lies in the fact these firms need to be financially sustainable to scale and support their manager research, but they also have the added costs of impact reporting and ongoing training in a growing field where norms on the impact side are not yet set. Though there is a convergence toward using UN Sustainable Development Goals as targets, there is no global authority on impact measurement or auditing. Therefore, we do believe higher pricing is warranted for the time being as the RIAs in the space are investing in a new breed of investment strategies and developing new frameworks.

Q: Does the advisor have different pricing for different levels of impact services?

- Start with defining the scope of work for *recurring* wealth management services.
- Once scope of work is agreed upon, ask for a fee structure
- Some additional services may be offered as a one-off special project— which may require a one-time pricing proposal

Conclusion

Access to impact investing products and services is available to retail investors today, though it is not yet easy or completely "off-the-shelf" since impact investing has not gone fully mainstream. Therefore, hiring an advisor is often necessary—especially at certain levels of wealth. Finding the right advisor can be a time-consuming process, whether you are conducting the search on behalf of yourself or an institution—but it's worth taking this process very seriously. The outcome may not just be the growth or preservation of an endowment or a trust, but also the potential for doing actionable good in the world around you. Since these relationships are long term, built on trust and mutual appreciation, we recommend taking your time and not being afraid to ask questions—you are entitled to know what an advisor would do for you, including what motivations he or she may have for you, their firm and even themselves. When the relationship is a good fit, the services provided should help you for generations to come and help ensure that you leave a positive social and environmental footprint as a lasting legacy.

Notes

1 Although we do not endorse financial products, you can refer to articles that mention retail product examples: they include Fran Seegull's article "How to Make a Difference through Socially Responsible Investing," published by

Conscious Company, April 4, 2015, or "Impact Investing for the Rest of Us," by Marina Leytes and Jérôme Tagger published by Impact Alpha on October 17, 2016.

2 An accredited investor is an individual with net worth of at least $1 million, excluding the value of equity in their primary residence, or net income of at least $200,000 in each of the last two years and a represented expectation of net income in that amount in the current year. For more details on this definition, please refer to www.sec.gov; the term accredited investor is fully defined in Rule 501 of Regulation D.

3 Organizations such as The ImPact and Toniic (www.theimpact.org and www.toniic.com) have documented actual impact investing stories and portfolios to be accessed in the public domain.

4 Confluence Philanthropy published this report in 2016 which we do not specifically endorse, but is indicative of the market at the time http://www.confluencephilanthropy.org/Impact-Investing-Advisor-Guide.

5 The SEC advisor search portal provides access to Form ADV Parts 1 and 2 for registered investment advisors. Form ADV Part 2, the Disclosure Brochure, provides pricing information for each RIA: https://adviserinfo.sec.gov/IAPD/default.aspx

6 https://adviserinfo.sec.gov/IAPD/Part2Brochures.aspx

Case Study 2

STORIES THAT INSPIRE: MORRISON SHAFROTH

Year Started Impact Investing: 2008

Primary Investment Focus: Retail mutual funds, exchange traded funds and individual stocks

Background: Morrison (Mo) Shafroth is an independent investor saving for college for three children and retirement. He has been a lifelong investor—he opened an IRA with savings from a high school summer job and invests primarily in individual securities and mutual funds. About 10–15 percent of his portfolio is in sustainable and impact investing, and he plans to convert a small charitable account into a donor advised fund (DAF) that allows for impact investing.

Impact Trigger

Mo is the owner of a public relations agency in Boulder, Colorado and is busy raising three children with his wife, Barr Hogen. Naturally, investing often has taken the back seat to "day-to-day" life. Mo has worked throughout his adult life, starting with summer jobs in high school and employment in college to pay for incidentals and housing. Growing up, his father and uncle taught him very fundamental lessons about investing: do your research, buy-and-hold investments forever, and save rather than spend.

It was good advice, but the accumulation of assets, rather than the social utility of money was the focus. Money had a singular meaning and a singular purpose, and there was a sense that earning money was a zero sum game.

Money was utilitarian, a tool for personal benefit and it was kept in one bucket. Money for good, such as a UNICEF box at Halloween or passing the plate at church on Sunday, was categorized as charity.

After he moved to Boulder in 2004, Mo was fortunate enough to meet Steve Schueth and George Gay of First Affirmative Financial Network, the founders of the SRI Conference.*

He worked for the conference in 2009 and gained knowledge about sustainable and impact investing. It was eye opening to see how investors at the conference were blending the two notions Mo had about money—as an investment that profited himself and his family and as a benefit to the broader society to create more meaning and impact.

Mo also worked with and helped foster Colorado's early leadership in the development of renewable energy. Amendment 37, the first ever voter-approved Renewable Energy Standard, passed in 2004, ushering in a series of policies that helped the state nurture and grow a vibrant solar and wind industry in the state.

Investment Approach

Once he learned about sustainable and impact investing, it took a few years for Mo to dedicate even a portion of his portfolio to sustainable and impact investing. The United States was mired in the Great Recession and there was limited research and information about sustainable and impact investing. With a family to raise and a business to build, doing the research to understand impact investing and finding the right investment vehicle were put on the back burner.

Today, about 10–15 percent of Mo's investments are in impact. His approach is self-directed. He doesn't work with a financial advisor, so investment research is something that is done in the evening or on weekends. Mo remains a buy-and-hold investor, and he invests almost exclusively in public equities.

* http://www.sriconference.com/.

Mo began his impact portfolio with an active mutual fund manager that invests in the "Next Economy" as a thesis. The fund manager, based in Boulder, held a marketing event at the Impact Hub Boulder, and from there Mo researched the fund online.

This was a good place to start because he wanted his investment to do more than just screen out the bad stocks. The Next Economy fund manager invests in businesses that are building solutions to systemic risks to the global economy from climate change, resource scarcity and economic inequality. With the lessons he learned about saving and investing as a child, Mo also liked the fund's focus on buying stocks based on solid fundamentals.

Mo believes human-caused climate change is a real threat, so investing in innovative solutions gives him an opportunity to earn a return and invest for a better planet for his children. Once he started on the path of sustainable and impact investing, Mo has grown more confident. He has added to his Next Economy mutual fund and is considering other investment options.

Over the past 20 years, he has also set aside about 5 percent of his annual earnings for charity (a legacy of collecting pennies for UNICEF and giving at church), including a small DAF, which he may convert to a fund that allows for impact investing. Mo says he is still in the learning process. The emotional, intellectual and financial reward has been very satisfying and he intends to grow his impact portfolio over time. "I'm on the path and the experience has been positive," says Mo.

5

Targeted Impact: Donor-Advised Funds and Impact Investing

Jointly authored by senior staff of ImpactAssets,
RSF Social Finance and Tides Network

Many of those interested in impact investing come to the practice with thousands to invest—not millions. While those with larger asset sizes often turn to donor advised funds (DAFs) to augment their direct and fund impact investing work, perhaps the best part of DAFs is that they can act as a tool to help "democratize" impact investing since they are available to those of virtually any level of wealth. Even if one just wants to support a set of local charities through making annual gifts—and would also like to move beyond grants to leverage charitable dollars through impact investing— DAFs offer an effective way to expand one's impact. Charitable giving is increasing annually in the United States and internationally and the expanding use of DAFs is a large part of that growth.

In addition to being a good tool to augment one's other impact investing practices, DAFs are also appealing in that they allow the investor without a lot of support or infrastructure to "off-load" on to a community foundation or DAF intermediary (such as the groups profiled below) some of the paperwork, sourcing, reporting and other aspects of impact investing that can be onerous for individuals working on their own. For those who might otherwise create a family foundation, DAFs enable one to plug into an existing administrative infrastructure to support your efforts, while decreasing the need to hire operating personnel to manage your philanthropic investments.

Finally, DAFs offer the impact investor an opportunity to "dip a toe" into impact investing by funding higher risk projects that may still be in seed or early stage development. Depending upon what institution you're working with, your grants can cover research and development or program initiatives while the actual funds you have placed in your DAF may be simultaneously invested in a variety of impact investments, ranging from seed to growth to mainstream market-rate opportunities.

This chapter will help you understand how you may use DAFs to engage in impact investing and build upon your market-rate investments to advance positive change in the world.

The Donor Advised Fund, Defined

The Donor Advised Fund, commonly referred to as a DAF, is a tax-preferred philanthropic vehicle similar to a private foundation. A donor can establish one with an initial tax-deductible contribution, and then recommend the DAF donate funds to other non-profits at a later time. The arrangement allows donors to separate the timing of the tax decision from the giving decision, and to give money out over time while claiming a tax benefit in the year(s) most beneficial to her.

The resemblance to private foundations ends here. DAFs are offered by public charities that draw their support from many donors, whereas private foundations are endowed by one source. Private foundations must pay an excise tax on investment income, while DAFs are exempt from this requirement. Effectively, this means donors' dollars may grow tax free. In addition, the cap on deductible donations to a DAF is higher than to a private foundation. Add to this: no setup fees, no annual accounting and tax filing, no requirement to provide 5 percent in grants annually, and low administration fees. And suddenly, DAFs become a very compelling philanthropic vehicle for many donors!

In 1931, The New York Community Trust established the first DAF to provide living donors with the comparable ability to support their community through their philanthropy. Until the early 1990s

DAFs were offered exclusively by community and public foundations and faith-based organizations. In 1991, Fidelity offered the
first commercially sponsored DAF, and many mutual fund companies and brokerages followed suit. The growth in the field of
DAF providers to include financial institutions offered donors the
ability to closely tie their DAF to their overall financial plan.

In 2010, the total number of donor advised funds operating
in the United States exceeded 152,000, with 72 percent of them
established since 2001. As of 2015 the total number of DAFs operating is 269,180.[1] DAFs now outnumber private foundations by
two-to-one and are the fastest growing charitable vehicle. As a
result, the amount of money under management within DAFs is
significant. In 2015, DAF assets totaled $78.64 billion. This repre-
sents an 11.9 percent growth from a total of $70.27 billion in 2014.
These numbers continue a trajectory of double-digit growth in
assets that began in 2010.[2]

Impact Investing, Philanthropic Capital and the Donor Advised Fund Opportunity

While impact investing may embody many aspects of traditional
investing as explored elsewhere in this book, it also has other characteristics that make it of special interest to those using DAFs as
part of a Total Portfolio Management strategy. First, investing for
impact often requires a longer-term investment horizon—referred
to as "patient capital"—than other mainstream investment strategies. The overall goal of impact investing is the creation of long-
term, sustainable value for investors, stakeholders and the broader
community and planet. The structure of impact investing vehicles
often reflects that consideration for long-term total performance.

Second, impact investing values multiple returns. The level
of return thought to be appropriate for these investments varies
based upon the investor profile and what her long-term goals are
through this investment approach. Generally speaking, investors
expect a level of financial return, unlike in philanthropy where
capital grants are not repaid. But that level of financial return
may or may not be a full market-rate risk-adjusted return (i.e.,
the greater the risk of the investment, the higher the anticipated
financial returns). The measure of social and/or environmental

return may also vary depending upon the type of investment (e.g., microfinance as opposed to, say, water or sustainable timber). In either case, the expectation is that there is a defined level of impact generated through the investment—not simply a general assumption of "good" or broad sense of "social return." Again, this is an exciting and complex area of discussion within impact investing, but this general commitment to financial performance with social/environmental returns is consistent across impact investing.

Finally, the third component of impact investing is the commitment to take risks, to go where traditional market-rate capital either will not or cannot go due to the form of capital it represents. If one thinks of philanthropic capital as being invested in social solutions for market failures and mainstream capital as being invested in market opportunities, impact investing can be considered a bridge across the capital chasm between philanthropic and market-rate capital, leveraging the one against the other. And DAFs may serve as an excellent vehicle in this regard.

Impact investors often seek out ventures to invest in that have the potential to move toward greater market orientation over time but are today viewed as too risky or ill defined for traditional capital. For example, for many years microfinance institutions operated solely with philanthropic support and development aid while they refined their model of making microloans to small-scale entrepreneurs. Over time, they created a track record of both knowledge and lending experience. Those involved in microfinance soon were able to bundle their debt into bond instruments, which they could then offer on the open market. The result: microfinance exploded around the world. This process of moving from philanthropy to market-rate investing would not have been possible without impact investors placing capital in the middle, connecting the parts into a new whole that is today a multibillion dollar investment market bringing significant, appropriate capital to those who most need it.

As discussed above, a DAF is created when a donor allocates a pool of capital for charitable purpose into a defined philanthropic vehicle. A community or public foundation can manage a DAF, but so may a commercial market investment management institution, a university or another entity. This philanthropic capital is money committed to "doing good" and creating positive social or environmental value in the world—as opposed to capital you invest in your child's education, which you hope will demonstrate value in the future! Philanthropic capital may seed new nonprofit programs, support the expansion of existing organizations with proven records, fund public policy advocacy or support high-risk research that promises to cure the diseases plaguing humankind. Since it is money dedicated to promoting the welfare of others and our planet, philanthropic capital values social and environmental returns over financial gains. When one makes a philanthropic investment, one does not expect to receive funds back at some point in the future and instead entrusts the financial stewardship of that gift to the nonprofit organization receiving support.

Strengths and Benefits of Donor Advised Funds

The use of DAFs across the world offers a solid system of charitable giving, but it has its limits. For example, most private charitable funds only make use of their annual payout in pursuit of the mission. (In the United States, it is usually 5 percent of total assets.) The rest of the funds—95 percent!—are most often managed for the generation of financial returns alone. Therefore, the traditional philanthropic model asks donors to reserve 95 percent of their philanthropic investment for doing what those funds were originally doing: earning financial returns. But what if you could use all your philanthropic assets for the charitable purpose you intend? What if you could structure some or all of your funds to support the causes you care about while maintaining your commitment to a philanthropic strategy of charitable giving? That is the impact opportunity offered through DAFs!

DAFs are especially suited to an impact investing strategy for a number of reasons:

- Many DAF providers are small and nimble philanthropic institutions and well positioned to take on innovative strategies for advancing social and environmental agendas.

- Depending on the charitable purpose of the DAF, below-market investments—if selected—are exempt from the traditional regulations regarding prudent investor requirements.
- With a lower administrative cost level than that of most foundations, DAFs make it possible to spend more funds on due diligence and research to help ensure an effective impact strategy.
- If a donor selects a DAF provider with expertise in a certain area, the process is simplified, frictionless and extremely cost effective.
- Depending on the organization, DAFs are highly responsive to donor requests and interests, making it possible to engage in a deeper partnership to address areas of shared interest and concern.

All in all, a DAF makes it possible for donors to pursue philanthropic, impact and traditional investment strategies simultaneously through effective management of these three aspects of capital management. The setup also raises the prospective ability of investors to manage capital for total performance as opposed to simply managing three independent pools of capital.

Furthermore, the structure of a DAF offers donors many benefits:

- The potential pool of DAF assets is significant, totaling $79 billion. If existing DAFs allocated 10 percent of their assets to impact investing, it could represent close to $8 billion in investable assets for the field.
- DAFs have the potential to coordinate outside parties and aggregate capital from many accounts into impact investments.
- DAFs can work to educate their donors, who are in some ways a highly receptive audience for these types of strategies and may potentially create new generations of impact investors.
- The philanthropic capital in DAFs can take greater risks in backing social enterprises or innovative nonprofits than traditional capital could afford. Such capital could also take on a subordinate position in stacked deals, making possible organizational strategies that traditional capital or market-rate capital alone might not be able to accommodate.

- Because DAFs are aggregators of philanthropic capital, they have the potential to allow investors to manage assets across the capital continuum. By providing an easy, positive introduction to impact investing, DAFs increase the likelihood that donors will then build on this successful experience with their nonphilanthropic capital, thus further increasing the overall amount of capital moving into both philanthropy and impact investing. Plus, having funds granted and invested through one vehicle grants principals more fluidity in supporting the growth of a single organization or social venture using various forms of capital (i.e., one could make a seed grant to an enterprise and then provide a later stage investment to scale operations).
- DAFs involved in impact investing could function as an investor "on ramp"—making expanded use of capital already committed to improving the world and potentially recycle that capital for greater leverage, benefit and impact as any sound investor might seek to do.

Total Portfolio Management through Donor Advised Funds

The idea of linking commercial market investing with philanthropic goals may seem new and provocative; however, it is a notion that builds upon many traditional strategies for effectively managing assets.[3] And the Total Portfolio Management approach is explored at length in the first chapter of this book. The core concepts may be summarized as follows:

1. Asset owners should seek to maximize the overall performance of their capital by investing across a capital continuum offering diverse strategies and instruments. This continuum ranges from philanthropic to below-market rate to fully market-rate capital vehicles.
2. Asset owners should have clarity on the unique purpose and goals of their investment—beyond solely financial returns— and these goals should be central to the investment process.[4]
3. The performance of capital should be viewed as consisting of various levels of financial risk and return combined with consideration of social and environmental returns and impact.

4. Consideration of investment opportunities should complement discussions of risk. In fact, investments in emerging markets—both domestic-US and international—are a cornerstone of many sound investment strategies.

5. The possibility of long-term, continuous zero or negative economic growth should be incorporated into an investment strategy by selecting particular sectors and companies where growth can occur rather than relying entirely on a function of rising per capita material consumption.

6. Considerations of risk should include traditional economic analysis as well as consideration of "off balance sheet" risk represented by environmental and social factors such as health, climate change, water and so on—factors that will continue to affect any company's ability to execute its business strategy.

Current Examples of Impact Investing by Donor Advised Funds

A core group of leading DAF providers perform the bulk of impact investing by DAFs today. ImpactAssets, RSF Social Finance and Tides Network have pioneered these practices together with a small but growing movement of community foundations focused on more local opportunities. Impact investing activity among commercial DAF providers has, as yet, not been picking up much steam, though there have been modest, somewhat short-lived experiments at Schwab, Fidelity and Vanguard Charitable.

Specific examples of how this chapter's authors, as leading DAF providers, are working to execute impact investing are discussed below.

ImpactAssets

ImpactAssets offers donors several ways to incorporate impact investing into their portfolios. These options range from ImpactAssets Community Investment Pool to direct investments in individual companies seeking social and environmental as well as financial returns. One can place the offerings into two categories: donor selected and donor sourced.

Donor Selected

While all investments offered to ImpactAssets DAF holders provide positive social and environmental returns in addition to financial returns, there are two that merit additional description. The first is Global Impact Ventures, a platform of private debt and equity impact funds donors may select. These funds offer a range of risk and return across various asset classes and impact issue areas, and are chosen by the top impact investment fund managers. For example, donors may invest in a fund that promotes sustainable agriculture in the developing world, a fund that encourages job growth in green industries in the United States, or a fund that provides capital to public media ventures.

The second is the ImpactAssets Community Investment Pool, a professionally managed portfolio of affordable loans to more than 250 leading nonprofit organizations and social enterprises working in 120 countries that focus on poverty alleviation in key impact sectors (e.g., affordable housing, microcredit, small business funding, and fair trade). By providing affordable capital, the Community Investment Pool offers investment minimums as small as $100 for the option of participating in an impact investment strategy.

3 Ways to Help

Express Opportunities is a partnership between Express Credit Union and Express Advantage in Seattle. Express Credit Union provides affordable financial services to low and moderate income families, helping them build assets and achieve financial security with products specifically designed for them. Express Advantage, their non-partner nonprofit, coordinates financial literacy & education, credit counseling, and language support.

Through her donor advised fund, an Impact Assets donor made grants to Express Advantage. However she wanted to do more. After all, once people understand how to manage their finances and improve their credit, they still need tools to actually do it! Express Credit Union provides affordable car loans and credit building credit cards–the exact tools people need to actualize what they learned from Express Advantage. As a credit union, Express Credit Union is not eligible for a tax-deductible grant. However the donor was able to support the credit union by making an investment directly from her DAF. These investments allow them to increase their capital base, providing more loans to their members. And lastly, the donor also personally helped grow the istitution as a direct consumer by taking a car loan out from Express Credit Union. The interest she pays on that loan is part of the earned revenue that sustains them.

Donor Sourced

ImpactAssets also offers its donors the ability to source their own impact investments. These investments have ranged from a dairy cooperative in New England to a credit union in Seattle to a company utilizing mobile technology to enable convenient and affordable financial services to the "last mile." One particularly compelling example is Village Capital, a nonprofit dedicated to increasing the success of social entrepreneurs worldwide by providing funding and peer support organizations to social innovators. Village Capital established a DAF with ImpactAssets to make 20 direct investments annually in companies that have gone through its social enterprise accelerator program and then selected by their peers for funding.

Finally, it is worth mentioning that for larger accounts, ImpactAssets will create a custom portfolio for a donor, thereby enabling them to target their entire philanthropic investment portfolio toward the realization of customized charitable goals.

RSF Social Finance

RSF Social Finance (RSF) began offering DAFs in 1984 as part of its strategy to provide impactful organizations with a variety of funding options and provide investors with the opportunity to engage in whole portfolio activation. RSF's DAF offerings have evolved as the organization looks to achieve the deepest possible social impact. It does this by backing organizations and funds that are direct, transparent, focused on the long term and relationship-based. RSF has decoupled its investments from Wall Street, and it places a premium on opportunities that strengthen community ties, promote social entrepreneurship and enhance local economies. Areas supported include but are not limited to food and agriculture, environmental stewardship and livelihood improvement. RSF invests new DAFs in its Liquidity Portfolio. (RSF previously offered donor advisors an Impact Portfolio option, but is no longer accepting investments for this offering.)

Liquidity Portfolio

The Liquidity Portfolio is a low-risk portfolio designed to maintain account balances and allow for active grant making. The portfolio is composed primarily of deposits with leading community development and environmental banks, as well as bond offerings that support economic development projects, affordable housing and environmental initiatives. One portfolio company, Southern Bancorp, is the largest rural development bank in the United States and has an approach to community development that combines banking with nonprofit services to reduce poverty and improve education.

Impact Portfolio

The Impact Portfolio aims to grow grant dollars by investing in institutional-quality funds and asset managers that generate competitive risk-adjusted returns. Investments include public and private debt, private equity, and real asset holdings that are consciously dealing with ecological concerns. One holding in the Impact Portfolio that demonstrates RSF's strategy is Elevar Equity. Unlike most private equity funds that invest only in microfinance institutions and then take all returns out of the local communities, Elevar invests in businesses that are adjacent to microfinance lenders, ensuring that more money is recycling within the local economy and that local entrepreneurs are getting more support. RSF is no longer accepting investments into this portfolio.

Tides Network

Tides Network is a philanthropic partner and nonprofit accelerator dedicated to building a world of shared prosperity and social justice, believing that everyone should have a quality education, access to healthcare, a sustainable environment and equal rights. Tides provides its donor partners with philanthropic grantmaking and impact investments opportunities at the intersections of these areas, including granting to nonprofit organizations and investing in social enterprises that address racial and economic justice, LGBTQ and global development issues.

Tides begins the investment management process with the recognition that its responsibility includes not only the traditional goals of maximizing return, minimizing risk and portfolio diversification, but also of benefiting the environment, addressing issues of social and economic justice and promoting healthy communities and societies. Tides' individual and institutional donors invest into various impact-oriented strategies across multiple asset classes. As of March 2017, the following portfolios available to Tides' donor-clients represent over $200 million in impact investments. Clients may invest in:

- a diversified portfolio of equities and fixed income of companies that undergo a comprehensive analysis of company policies and practices to assess their impact on employees, society and the natural environment;
- a fossil fuel free portfolio of equities and fixed income of companies that are not overly dependent on fossil fuels;
- a fixed-income portfolio of overlay strategies in impact areas of gender equity, education and environment; or
- a private equity strategy that focuses on philanthropy for its impact area.

In addition to the above fund offerings, Tides Network also facilitates investment of donor-client funds through Mission-Related Investments in individual for-profit social enterprises that target specific social and environmental impact areas. Tides has made equity investments in innovative green businesses (biochar), fair trade and sustainable business ventures; film and video projects (*Years of Living Dangerously*); and nonprofit real estate and green shared spaces developments (Thoreau Centers in San Francisco and Manhattan). Tides has also made direct loans to nonprofit organizations and microlending institutions, as well as direct land purchases to protect land or to provide nonprofit retreat facilities.

Community Foundations

In addition to the three organizations profiled above, a number of community foundations are also taking on innovative approaches to investing DAF dollars in their local communities.

The Seattle Foundation has invested in three loan funds. One focuses on addressing the needs of small businesses, primarily those operated by immigrant and minority owners, and fostering entrepreneurs with the goal of creating jobs and investment. Another targets commercial or mixed-use projects that support small business development. The third invests in multifamily housing energy retrofits that support job retention and creation and conserve energy and water. These funds are open to Seattle Foundation DAF holders at a $25,000 minimum. The Seattle Foundation is also exploring higher-yield mission-related investment options.

The Greater Cincinnati Community Foundation is also a leader in the field. They began making impact investments in 2008. And with a grant from The Rockefeller Foundation, the foundation documented its efforts via a toolkit that other interested community foundations could use to follow suit. As a result of this work, the Greater Cincinnati Community Foundation has seen a significant uptick in both donors—several new DAFs have opened up—and interest from grantees. It even started a new grantmaking program to help nonprofits increase their capacity to become "investible." The Greater Cincinnati Foundation invests only in Cincinnati, and only in funds—not directly in companies. They endeavor to tie investments to their donors' passions: education, arts, the environment, and health care. It has been challenging for the foundation as many local investment opportunities come from the community investment world and do not address these particular passions. Ultimately, they aim to create another toolkit for community foundations to use for rolling out place-based impact investing.

In spite of these and other inspiring examples, the vast majority of DAFs do not use their assets to further their philanthropic goals. There are many reasons for this. However, it has to do primarily with a lack of donor awareness and demand combined with resistance to change at the management level of some community foundations. Commercial investment management DAF providers such as Schwab and Fidelity have built their reputations by investing conventionally. The clients they attract are drawn to them in part for this reason, so there is neither client pull nor management push for the adoption of impact investing. Community foundations are usually place-based, and the members of their investment committees generally are drawn from the ranks of the local successful business executives who, likewise, have built their reputations on conventional investing. In each case, a lack of familiarity presents obstacles to adoption of impact investing practices.

Another reason for the dearth of impact investing from DAFs is the lack of regulatory incentives. Foundations are required to grant 5 percent of their assets annually and are allowed to count mission-aligned, below-market-rate investments or program related investments as part of their required payout. As DAFs do not have a required annual payout, there is no equivalent to a program related investment for DAFs and, therefore, little regulatory incentive to pursue impact investing strategies.

Future Opportunities for Donor Advised Funds and Impact Investing

In reflecting on where the future of DAFs and impact investing may find us, there are several areas in which we may see expansion:

- Community foundations could facilitate greater amounts of local investing. Expanding the financing of local community development financial institutions (CDFIs) is an easy first step for community foundations. They are FDIC (Federal Deposit Insurance Corporation) insured, operate in geographically bounded communities, and relend the capital to low-to-moderate income populations. While locally specific private equity or debt opportunities are limited, they are growing. For example, La Montanita Fund in New Mexico offers investors the opportunity to invest in a fund that makes loans to local farmers. Community foundations could also invest with fixed-income managers who select bond issues that support local projects such as affordable housing.
- Large, national DAF providers could offer loan guarantees to established social enterprises working at a global scale, such as Accion or FINCA.
- DAF providers could offer donors the opportunity to use their DAF assets to guarantee loans to local nonprofits. For example, Orange County Community Foundation donors can guarantee bank loans to local nonprofits. Since 2006,

this program has leveraged over \$20 million of bank financing with no defaults.[5]

- DAF providers could offer donors the ability to make investment recommendations as well as grant recommendations. Such an offering would require a rethinking of investment policies and fees, but those willing to undertake it would provide a great resource to donors and differentiate themselves from their competitors in what is a dynamic and growing DAF market. For example, a donor at ImpactAssets recommended an investment in her local dairy cooperative, which allowed her to use invested dollars to support her charitable giving in local food and sustainable agriculture.
- All DAF providers could expand their investment options to include impact investments. They wouldn't have to replace all of their investments with impact investments but could augment their options. By rethinking their investment policy statements to address the full complement of returns, DAF providers could mobilize a significant amount of the more than \$28 billion in DAF assets.

Impact investing through DAFs is an exciting, evolving edge of both philanthropy and investing. Individual donors interested in exploring these ideas should either engage the groups mentioned in this chapter or connect with their local community foundation to partner with professionals capable of assisting them in executing an effective impact investment strategy through their DAF. The potential leverage and impact donors can have upon their world literally has no limits!

Notes

1 National Philanthropic Trust 2010, Donor Advised Fund Report, Published 2010, Accessed April 4, 2017 http://www.nptrust.org/images/uploads/DAF-Report-2010.pdf; https://www.nptrust.org/daf-report/market-overview.html.
2 National Philanthropic Trust 2010, Accessed April 4, 2017, https://www.nptrust.org/daf-report/market-overview.html.
3 Most recently, in 2011 RSF Finance released "A New Foundation for Portfolio Management," which joins "Modern Portfolio Theory—with a Twist! The New Efficient Frontier" by Brian Dunn (2006) and "A Capital Idea: Total

Foundation Asset Management and The Unified Investment Strategy" by Jed Emerson (2002) as papers advancing new ideas regarding portfolio management and theory.

4 Please see "A New Foundation for Portfolio Management" by Leslie Christian (2011) for a deeper discussion of this topic.

5 Community Philanthropy Report, Published September 2009, Accessed April 23, 2017, http://www.communityphilanthropy.org/downloads/Equity%20 Advancing%20Equity%20Full%20Report.pdf.

6

Transformational Giving: Philanthropy as an Investment in Change

Kris Putnam-Walkerly

Many investors think of philanthropy as altogether separate from their strategies to build wealth, generate return and make change. While market investments are seen as means to an end, philanthropy is often an afterthought—charitable donations made along the way to "give back" but not necessarily related to an individual's overall goals for business or life and certainly not viewed as part of one's overall capital management and deployment strategy.

But donors who fail to recognize the potential power of their philanthropy to amplify return on investment and contribute to an overall investment strategy are missing a key tool in the investor's tool kit. As described in terms of Total Portfolio Management, rather than an afterthought, philanthropy deserves consideration as another asset class that links to and strengthens other investments within a portfolio.

For example, an investor with a keen interest in the alternative energy industry might provide a philanthropic investment in a green-jobs training program that will ensure a competent workforce for that industry. An investor who believes medical technology is the key to the future might support research institutions that develop those technologies. And an investor who wants to build an empire of organic grocery stores may recognize the importance of supporting nonprofits that help small farmers employ sustainable agriculture practices.

In addition to working hand in hand with market investments, philanthropic investments can provide early venture or seed money from which new innovations and ideas take root and flourish. In fact, many inventions and practices that society now takes for granted—such as public libraries, disease treatments or even white lines along the sides of roadways[1]—were sparked by the charitable investments of others.

The options for effective philanthropy are more varied today than ever. What used to involve simply making financial gifts to qualified nonprofits has now grown to include public-private partnerships, social impact investing, program related investing, crowdfunding and many more avenues for achieving a philanthropic mission. However, giving and grantmaking make up the bulk of philanthropic activity in the world, so it is through the lens of giving and grantmaking that this chapter explores philanthropy.

Taking advantage of these options does not require millions of dollars, nor does it require that an individual create a fully staffed charitable foundation. Individuals, foundations, donor advised funds (DAFs) and corporate giving programs are all considered funders, and they may adopt strategies that align philanthropic investments with a broader portfolio. Doing so, however, requires a funder be strategic and thoughtful about her giving or grantmaking. Regardless of the size of their philanthropic investments, investors must transform their practices and mindsets, shifting away from simple charitable goodwill to a focused, purposeful, well-planned approach. This careful focus and strategy is what shifts giving from purely transactional to transformational. *Transformational giving*[SM] *requires funders to transform their own mechanics and mindsets in order to transform the communities and causes they care about.*

This chapter includes an overview of key avenues individual philanthropic investors or larger, institutional funders may use to make gifts to nonprofit organizations; ways in which funders may transform both the *mechanics* (the processes and practices) and the *mindsets* (attitudes and inclinations) of their giving; and a note of caution about delusional altruism[SM], which can undermine even the most sophisticated philanthropic investor. Using this information, funders of all kinds can become more savvy philanthropic investors and apply their skills and knowledge in ways that lead to transformational giving.

Key Avenues for Giving and Grantmaking

There are many different avenues investors can use to leverage their philanthropic dollars in ways that support their overall desired return and strategy for creating impact in the world, from the local community to global levels. In general, the four most common of these are individual donations, corporate gifts, DAFs and private foundations.

- Individual charitable donations include gifts made by donating cash or other marketable assets directly to a charitable organization. Direct donations allow funders to be immediately responsive to needs and flexible in their giving. Examples of direct donations include regular annual gifts to favorite charities or one-time contributions in response to a natural disaster.
- Gifts through family businesses or corporate entities allow funders to use corporate assets to achieve philanthropic outcomes. These assets could be gifts of cash or products that are donated to a nonprofit organization but could also be shares of corporate stock.
- DAFs are established by donors at community foundations or through larger investment firms. They allow donors to set aside charitable assets to build a corpus for ongoing grantmaking.
- Private foundations can be created by donors with larger amounts of charitable capital. They can be family foundations, in which the donor's family members serve on the board and make grantmaking decisions, or independent foundations led by a board whose members are not related to the founder.

Philanthropic investors often work through more than one of the above avenues. For example, an investor who has a significant number of charitable assets may place the bulk of them into a private foundation and a smaller amount into a community foundation DAF, make corporate gifts from the ongoing profits of a business and make personal direct contributions. Individual donors used to writing smaller checks to specific organizations may opt to become more strategic by establishing a DAF and linking their giving with their the overall impact themes they are most interested in. Each of these avenues comes with its own tax and regulatory features that can also play a role in a funder's overall strategy.

Transformational Mechanics: 11 Core Practices for Effective Philanthropy

No matter whether an investor has thousands of philanthropic dollars to work with or billions, there are some basic core practices of giving and grantmaking that should underpin every giving strategy to ensure the most effective return on charitable investments. The list below contains 11 core practices that every philanthropic investor should consider. While not every practice will be useful to every funder, each can add value to the philanthropic process. Therefore, each merits close consideration as a potential part of the scaffolding for an effective funding strategy.

1. Understanding Mission and Vision

It's hard to make effective charitable investments if an investor is unclear about what he or she is trying to accomplish. A mission and vision, whether espoused by an individual or a foundation, should leave no doubt about that. Mission is the core purpose: It identifies why a funding effort exists and targets the needs it is addressing. Vision is the future an investor desires: It paints a picture of how the neighborhood or the world will be different if the investor succeeds in achieving the mission.

For example, an investor interested in ending homelessness in one city may have a mission to provide the physical spaces and social support services necessary for those in need to find homes and achieve the stability necessary to stay in them. The vision might be a city in which everyone has a place to call home. Or an investor who envisions a community in which everyone is economically self-sufficient may have a mission to support job creation and preparation for all residents.

How does a philanthropic investor develop a mission and vision? It can be driven by the passion, interest or value of the investor, of course, but it also should identify and prioritize the actual needs within the community the investor wishes to serve. For example, an investor may have a passion for women's health, but in the community the biggest needs for women's health may relate to domestic violence or unplanned pregnancies rather than clinical issues.

To identify and prioritize needs, investors can call on a number of resources, including their own past experiences with giving, the services of experts who can conduct an objective scan of needs and community input and engagement.

2. Assessing Capacity to Accomplish the Mission

Achieving a philanthropic investor's mission means more than mustering finances to solve a social problem. It also means applying a range of intellectual assets and skills, which can come from the knowledge and experience of the investor, from paid staff in a family office, from community foundation program staff for donors who hold funds in community foundations, or from outside advisors. In general, investors can consider their capacity needs in three different "buckets": people, knowledge and expertise. Within each area, an investor will likely find existing assets to leverage and gaps that need to be closed in order to better accomplish the mission.

- *People:* Who are the people involved and what roles do they want to play? How engaged does an individual investor want to be and what capacity does he or she bring to the table? Are their board members or staff—and if so what are their roles? Who are the trusted advisors? How can the family office help?
- *Knowledge:* What does the individual investor or the investor's team collectively know about the issues the investor wishes to address? Is additional information readily available or does the investor need help?
- *Expertise:* Does anyone involved have experience in the issues? Do they have experience with individual giving or grantmaking to support those issues?

Answers to these questions will provide a roadmap as to where an investor might want to invest in building organizational capacity and developing a better understanding of where it already exists. He or she may need to spend time building personal knowledge and/or skills, work closely with community foundation staff or outside advisors, increase the board and/or staff in a family office or the investor's foundation, increase administrative capacity so that the board and staff can become more effective, or scale back on the mission.

3. Determining a Funding Focus

What will a philanthropic investor support and what will be set aside? Depending on mission and capacity, the giving focus could include broad program areas such as health or education and fund multiple approaches within them, or it might concentrate on specifics such as increasing global access to safe water and sanitation, or high-quality preschool in a particular neighborhood. For example, an investor who has a keen interest in women-owned businesses and a generous amount of philanthropic capital might invest in a variety of different nongovernmental organizations that provide everything from leadership training to microlending. A investor who shares that interest but has a smaller budget may invest in a single, proven women's entrepreneurship program in the global south.

In general, there are three potential levels of change an investor can affect, based on capacity: changes in people, changes in organizations or changes in fields. For example, if a philanthropic couple is interested in substance abuse treatment, they could fund programs that provide treatment (changes in people). Or they might recognize that the organizations that provide substance abuse treatment are operating on a shoestring budget and need help with staff training, strategic planning or board development, and so determine to provide funding to improve operations (changes in organizations). Or the couple might realize that the stigma of substance abuse prevents people from getting help, so they could decide to fund a national communications campaign to reduce that stigma (changes in the field). Investors of any size can address any of these three levels, using any of the funding avenues listed earlier in this chapter.

What an investor wants to support may also inform *where* they'll place their funding focus—locally, statewide, nationally or globally—and vice versa. For example, if the couple in the example above chooses to create change for individuals, they may decide to start in a single community in their hometown. If they're bound by geography but want to participate in a global effort, then they may need to support participation of local organizations in global networks. The key is to find the most appropriate (or creative) nexus of *what* and *where* to serve the mission within the limits of capacity.

4. Finding Organizations to Fund

Once a philanthropic investor knows the kind of work she wishes to support, how will she find the organizations in which she might invest? It is a natural inclination for individual investors to give to organizations they know, either through personal relationships or by reputation. Individual donors often begin finding organizations to fund by consulting their own networks of friends, fellow philanthropists and professional advisors. But individual investors can also broaden their horizons through personal research. In just a few hours on the Internet, an individual investor could determine which organizations are leading in an issue area, where the experts are who might be willing to speak with the investor to provide further education, and other funders that have invested in the issue. Questions such as "Who's doing the most exciting work on this issue?," "What are the biggest barriers to progress?," "What are the best practices?" or "What kind of returns have other funders seen on their investments with XYZ organization?" can reveal a great deal of information to inform an individual investor's choice of organizations to fund.

Typically, investors who work with community foundations or establish their own private foundations take the road of accepting solicited or unsolicited proposals from nonprofits seeking funding. Solicited proposals are those invited by the investor from organizations they've proactively identified as being effective, aligned with the investor's mission and potentially good partners.

Unsolicited proposals are gathered through an open proposal submission process in which any organization is free to apply for funding, based on advertised criteria.

There are pros and cons to both unsolicited and solicited proposal strategies, and many investors incorporate both in their grantmaking. For example, investors who wish to focus on a specific, evidence-based intervention to address a community need may use a solicited strategy to reach out to a few select organizations that have demonstrated prowess in deploying that intervention. An investor who is interested in early childhood development may be a fan of Nurse-Family Partnership, an evidence-based approach to ensuring a strong start for children up to the age of two. As a result, the investor may wish to offer support only to organizations that have successfully deployed the Nurse-Family Partnership model. On the other hand, a foundation that wants to engage community at the grassroots level to strengthen early childhood development may invite any organization to apply for funding, in hopes of connecting with small but promising community-based organizations as new partners.

5. Creating Grant Strategies

Philanthropic investors have a wide range of strategies to use for giving and grantmaking. The options they choose will be influenced by the size of their giving budget, as well as by mission and capacity, but in general they include the following:

A. *Program support.* Most funders have traditionally offered financial support for a specific program operated by one or more organizations, such as a healthy eating outreach program operated by a community clinic or a grassroots HIV prevention program. Program support is often provided in the form of seed or start-up funds, with the understanding that other funding will eventually sustain ongoing operations.

B. *Core operating support.* Core operating support usually takes the form of unrestricted funding for a nonprofit organization to use as needed to underwrite basic operating expenses, such as rent, salaries, utilities, supplies and so on.

While core operating support does not appear as dynamic as other types of funding, it is a way in which investors often can make the most dramatic difference for a growing non-profit organization.

C. *Organizational capacity building.* Because nonprofits often dedicate their entire budgets to basic operations and programmatic costs, they are rarely able to provide their staff with the tools and training that could improve knowledge and impact. Investors who support capacity-building activities such as staff training, leadership development, executive coaching, skill building or investments in new technology can provide a much-needed boost to an organization's capabilities.

D. *Capital gifts.* A long-time practice of philanthropists, capital gifts support brick-and-mortar investments for nonprofits, such as new buildings or endowments to support ongoing infrastructure needs. Capital gifts often come with naming rights, which are appealing to many investors.

E. *Research grants.* As the name implies, this involves supplying financial support for research. The types of research can vary widely, from a large clinical study at a university to a family-needs survey conducted by a nonprofit in a small city. Investors can also support researching and evaluating the effectiveness of programs or organizations. Such evaluations can help quantify an investor's return on philanthropic investments or show areas where improvements can be made.

F. *Multiyear grants.* While most investors realize that market investing requires a long-term horizon, many tend to see their charitable activity through a very short-term lens. They expect to see results from a single grant or within a one- to two-year time frame, when the time needed to effect lasting social change can be a decade or more.

Philanthropic investors of any size and structure can use any of the strategies listed above. Of course, some may be more suitable than others, depending on an investor's areas of focus and the needs of their potential gift or grant recipients when selecting the types of strategies they use. For example, if an investor wishes to address a relatively rare medical condition or wants to prove that a specific kind of classroom intervention works best for children with dyslexia, he may use research funding as a primary strategy. If an investor knows that domestic violence shelters throughout her state are struggling with daily operations and are unable to collaborate or think strategically, her best bet may be to fund organizational capacity or core support. And if an investor is passionate about feeding the hungry, then support for the programs that deliver services in the community may be the right choice.

6. Developing Grant Guidelines

Investors with community foundation DAFs or private foundations of their own will want to develop funding guidelines. One advantage to community foundations, as well as other organizations that provide DAFs, is that they provide a set of ready-made general grant guidelines, as well as the staff to manage the grant-making process.

Being able to clearly define how, to whom and for what purpose an investor will award grants does more than just provide applicants with a clear set of expectations; it also helps the investor and any staff stay focused and on point with the mission. A good set of grant guidelines puts into writing all of the key decisions made to date: about the mission, the funding focus, program areas, solicited versus unsolicited outreach and chosen grant strategies.

Clarity is absolutely key for funding guidelines. This means that nonprofit organizations can read an investor's guidelines and know immediately whether they are a good fit, which saves them time and frustration. It also means that everyone involved in the funding decisions—from inside staff to outside consultants or advisors—is in agreement about what the investor will or won't support. Length is the enemy of clarity. The more concise and direct an investor's grant guidelines, the clearer they will be for everyone (including the investor).

7. Getting the Word Out

For individual investors, sharing the word about potential giving or grantmaking could be as discreet as hand-picking organizations and mailing checks, or as public as launching a social media campaign to seek bold new ideas. Community foundation donor advised fund-holders often rely on the foundation's program staff to suggest organizations that are doing work that best aligns with the donor's interest.

For foundation funders that have established focus, targets, strategy and guidelines, finding potential grantees can be a challenge, especially when using an unsolicited grant strategy. Foundation trustees may have helpful connections, but most foundations will likely need to cast their nets more broadly.

Basic forms of communication, such as a website, blog posts, or social media are helpful. However, as with other forms of investing, some of the best leads for promising investments come from existing relationships. This is a great time for investors of any size to leverage the connections of grantmaking colleagues, such as other individuals or foundations working in the same geographic area or on the same issue. Many individual investors use their networks of advisors, friends or fellow donors to make connections with likely gift recipients. A investor should take time to explain his or her interests to these philanthropic colleagues and describe the kind(s) of grantees desired. The colleagues can then help point the way to likely candidates for solicited proposals or to networks and communities in which to promote an unsolicited application opportunity.

8. Designing a Process for Proposal Review

Once the requests and proposals start pouring in, who will review them and how? Even individual donors should take the time to develop a manageable process that ensures grant decisions are made thoughtfully and effectively. Again, those who give through community foundation-DAFs will have the resources of the community foundation to guide or assist in this process.

Proposal review processes can be as simple as a thorough read-through and vetting by an individual investor, her program staff or the family office. Or an investor might include a prescreening process with staff or community advisors, site visits to potential grantee locations and/or a group vetting process to discuss the merits of each.

Whether simple or complex, every proposal review process must include basic due diligence. This can mean simply verifying that the applying organization is indeed a 501(c)(3) nonprofit, or it can mean reviewing audit information, confirming staff qualifications or asking for copies of operating agreements between coapplicant partners.

When designing a proposal review process, investors should remember that every step will add to the burden of both reviewer(s) and applicants. Site visits in particular require a deeper level of planning to ensure that both investor and grantseeker make the most of their time together. Before adding a step to the process, every investor should carefully consider its value and purpose against the time and effort involved.

9. Creating a Process for Board Review and Decision Making

Investors who create foundations must consider the information the board will need to make responsible grant recommendations, as well as how the investor or foundation staff will supply that information.

Many foundation staff have horror stories about the extensive time and reams of paper that go into preparing for board meetings. Of course, those thick board dockets don't get read, and all the time spent assembling them could have been better spent on other tasks. Foundation funders or their staff should work with the board to determine how much information they want and need to do their duty, and resolve to give them not one scrap of paper or one extra email more. Allowing board members to decide whether they want to receive their board meeting materials in paper form or electronically further increases their chances of authentic engagement in the decision making.

When a board convenes to make its grants decisions, foundation staff must make sure their discussion is efficient and effective. They should plan in advance the kinds of information they will share with the board during the board meeting—whether a complete set of information or a brief summary. It is best to identify a facilitator for board grant discussions, as is determining ahead of time whether grant decisions will be made by a majority vote or by full board consensus. The approaches to each of these issues can vary, as long as they are based on clear decision criteria that reflect the foundation's grant guidelines.

Individual investors, of course, can streamline this process, but it should still be deliberate and thorough. Just as with market investments, there is no substitute for due diligence. A clearly defined process for selection can help ensure that individual philanthropic investments are more likely to achieve their intended results.

One note of caution: Decision processes can become cumbersome and time consuming, thereby limiting an investor's ability to respond to the capital needs of nonprofits in a timely manner. Investors should always strive to find the right balance between due diligence and making investments when they are most needed or most likely to deliver maximum returns.

10. Awarding Grants and Gifts

Once grant decisions are made, investors will need to notify grantees. Will that be done via email or a phone call, or is a formal letter more in keeping with the investor's style? For individual investors, this is often the last step in the giving process.

Foundation funders and corporate giving programs, however, should follow their grant announcements quickly with a grant agreement letter or contract that both funder and the grantee sign before money is disbursed. This agreement should specify the amount awarded, the purpose, the payment terms, reporting requirements and any other nonnegotiable aspects of the work together as funder and grantee. The grant agreement is a legally binding document that bears careful attorney review before use. Nonprofit and commercial providers of DAFs will have existing grant agreements.

11. Creating Grant Reporting Requirements

Once investors have gone through the process of choosing grantees and investing in their success, they will want to learn what the grantees have accomplished. Simple grant reports can help an investor assess grantee progress; understand the reality of the work; and generate lessons learned that can help the investor, grantees and others in the field hone expectations and improve impact.

Individual investors have relatively little sway in "requiring" progress reports or updates. Smart nonprofits may realize the benefit of keeping the investor in the loop, but will have no legal obligation to do so. Foundation grant agreements, on the other hand, may require some sort of reporting as part of the contract with the grantee.

Writing and reviewing grant reports constitutes an extra burden for both investor and grantee, so keeping them as simple as possible benefits everyone involved. Grant reports should focus only on what is actually useful, leaving sidebars and extraneous details behind. Reports can be as simple as a single page or a series of short answers to specific questions. If an investor's requirements are too long, it may be a sign that the investor is not sure what to ask and should revisit the mission and focus to clarify and streamline.

Grant reports don't have to be written. Investors—particularly individuals—might prefer to conduct a formal post-grant interview, record a video debrief or simply take notes during an informal conversation over coffee. The important thing is to document what counts, in whatever way makes the most sense for both investor and grantee.

Customize the Core Practices for Effectiveness

Obviously, not all of these core practices will apply in the same way to every investor. Individual investors would most certainly find some of the foundation-oriented processes to be cumbersome. Instead, these core practices should be used as a guide to create a process that is meaningful to each investor and meets his or her particular needs.

Learning along the way is to be expected—in fact, it's a sign that an investor is actively working to increase effectiveness. For example, an investor might think site visits are a great idea at first, but then learn that they are too time consuming and the investor (or staff or board members) can't commit to them. Then it's time to change the approach. If the information from grant applicants isn't satisfactory, an investor can and should change funding guidelines. For any of the 11 core practices, the key for any investor, large or small, is to consider how they help achieve philanthropic goals and adapt accordingly.

Transformational Mindsets: 10 Ways Investors Increase Philanthropic Effectiveness

Once an investor has mastered the basics of giving and grantmaking, how can they take their charitable investments to the next level of effectiveness? The following list shares practices that effective philanthropic investors use to go beyond the basics to hone their craft and increase their impact.

Practice #1: Organize Work Around Values

The term *organizational values* can, understandably, lead to eye-rolling. It seems like a phrase on a plaque that is so universal that it means nothing. But when investors are very clear about their values and work to operationalize them, organizational values can have a huge impact.

For example, one foundation conducted a survey of its grantees and was surprised to find they rated their relationship with the foundation much lower than anticipated. The foundation spoke with other foundations whose grantees said their relationships were overwhelmingly positive, and the reason became obvious: All of those other funders had a core value of building strong relationships with grantees. They made this part of everything they did, including how staff allocated their time, application and reporting processes that were not burdensome, and more. When making decisions they asked themselves, "Are we doing this because it would be easier on grantees or easier on us?" If the latter, they wouldn't do it. The foundation in question decided to adopt this same core value.

Another example involves an individual donor who believes strongly in a core value of respecting and accepting everyone, regardless of race, religion, gender or other personal attributes.

This investor makes a practice of specifically seeking advisors and partners who are very different from himself, in order to provide a 360-degree view of his community and his work within it. This core value of respect and acceptance also extends to the gifts the investor makes, because he intentionally looks for nonprofit organizations that demonstrate their shared belief in the core value.

What sets some investors apart is that they live and breathe the values they claim, even imbuing them into their systems and processes so that they are apparent to everyone. Their values have become part of how they do business.

Practice #2: Recognize That Grantmaking Is About Relationships

Investors can have a transactional relationship with their the organizations they support, sending out funding announcements, reviewing solicitations and proposals, emailing them that they've been awarded a grant and sending a check. It's true that by making grants, investors may be making a difference, but a purely transactional process is not very meaningful to either investor or grantee. Relying on transactions alone makes it hard for investors to learn what works and makes it virtually impossible to identify new needs, opportunities or ways to leverage funding for greater impact.

To change that dynamic and get a better understanding of the needs, assets and opportunities in the community, savvy investors work to build stronger and deeper relationships with their grantees. These investors want grantees to feel enough trust to be completely honest about what's working and isn't, so that the investor can help them and they can accomplish more. In the best-case scenario, grantees feel comfortable coming to their investors with a problem—they need to increase their capacity, an executive transition is rocky, a grant is not going as expected but they have a plan to make course corrections. In this situation, a trusted investor has the ability to help grantees by identifying other sources of support or connecting them to people who can help. This in turn continues to build the bonds of trust.

However, investors should always be conscious of the fact that a clear power dynamic exists between those providing funds and those receiving them. Savvy investors seek to mitigate that power differential by listening, learning and recognizing the impact of their requirements and demands and being realistic in their expectations.

Effective investors also build relationships with other funders—both individuals and foundations—to learn more about who is funding what work and what their experiences have been. Funders can help each other perform due diligence with grant-ees, identify new partners who might want to cofund an initiative and share their collective wisdom.

Likewise, other partners, such as researchers or evaluators, experts in a shared interest area or local city or county officials, will also become valuable allies if the investor invests in building relationships with them.

Of course, building relationships requires time and intentional effort. Participating in membership or professional organizations can provide opportunities for this. National and global funding networks, regional associations of grantmakers, local associations of nonprofits or convenings of corporate social responsibility programs are also good places for investors to find others who share their areas of interest. Once an investor has identified people with whom they want to cultivate a relationship, the next step can be as simple as a coffee or lunch invitation to get to know potential partners and allies on a more personal level.

Investors should always act with integrity, regardless of the relationship they're trying to build. The most effective investors listen carefully to the needs of others, demonstrate humility, ask for advice and follow up on commitments. Ultimately, it is these little things that allow effective investors to build trust more quickly and reap the mutual rewards of the relationships they build.

Practice #3: Identify and Leverage Every Asset

Investors of any size have much more to offer than money. Those who take time to catalog their full array of assets and consider how to employ them are better positioned to fulfill their missions. There are many different roles that investors can play, such as catalyst, broker, convenor or ambassador. For example, investors can offer:

A. *Connections.* Investors often know people who might be valuable referrals or resources for their grantees. These could be expert advisors who can provide professional services, talent within the donor's corporation, organizations with similar interests or goals that could be valuable partners, individuals who might make great nonprofit board members or even other investors who might be interested in providing support.

B. *Knowledge and intellectual capital.* Investors often gain valuable knowledge about an issue, the community, local politics or other funders. How and when to share that information merits consideration and discretion, but keeping it a secret may do more to hinder an investor's own agenda than to help it.

C. *Experience.* Chances are individual investors or the staff they employ for giving and grantmaking have specific experience that can translate to guidance for grantees. For example, perhaps an investor has led the scale-up of a business to reach new markets and can apply that skill to a nonprofit. Or an investor who's a self-described "policy wonk" can help inform a grantee's advocacy strategy. Effective investors know to offer their experience with humility when nonprofits are ready for it, never forcing it on grantees.

D. *Reputation.* Whether an investor realizes it or not, their reputation—personal and professional, individual and organizational—can help open doors for grantees. Investors who are well regarded can convey that same respect to grantees by introducing or recommending them to others.

E. *Physical space.* An investor's board room, country club or house can provide valuable meeting space with just the right feel to bring together a grantee's staff retreat, host an event or set the scene for a quiet conversation among diverse community stakeholders to solve shared challenges.

F. *Investments.* The choices philanthropic investors make about their market investments can have a huge impact on grantees. Practices like mission investing and impact investing can boost the capacity and confidence of individual organizations or even entire fields.

G. *Convening power.* The role of convenor is often overlooked by investors, but they have an unmatched ability to bring together disagreeing factions or would-be partners in a safe, neutral and controlled environment. Investors also can provide facilitators or mediators to help move conversations forward and enhance outcomes.

H. *Ability to take risks.* Both individual investors and foundations often are hesitant to try new ideas and learn from them, because they seem to operate under the assumption that failure will somehow discredit them. But as one foundation CEO says, "If this doesn't work, are people going to stop coming to us for money?" Investors have much broader latitude in which to take risks than do government agencies or many businesses. They should use it to greatest advantage.

Practice #4:
Adopt an Abundance Mentality Rather Than a Poverty Mentality

Contrary to what one might assume from the phrase, having an abundance mentality has nothing to do with money. Instead, it has everything to do with an investor's beliefs, organizational culture and approach to its work. At its core, an abundance mentality is based in a belief that almost anything is possible. David conquered Goliath, and a single investor can help conquer just about anything if they are willing to step forward and make an effort and an investment. Both individuals and organizations can embrace an abundance mentality or allow themselves to become trapped in a mentality of poverty. This is true for philanthropic investments as well: The abundance mentality includes the belief that the answers are out there, if only we are willing to invest in searching and experimenting.

Unfortunately, a majority of foundations—and, to a lesser extent, individual investors—have typically operated with a poverty mentality. This is a belief that money should not be spent on internal investment; opportunities are limited by capacity; improvement is always incremental; we should do more with less; and we don't deserve the best, fastest or most efficient path to success. It is based on fear of failure and a misguided belief that maintaining a spartan operation means delivering value for grantees and communities. Investors with a poverty mentality say things like:

- That problem is too big and we are small—we can't make an impact.
- The money we invest in research takes away from our grantees.
- What is the cheapest way we can do this?

Investors often embrace a poverty mentality in the name of stewardship or wise expenditures, like those who refuse to ever include staff salaries in any of their grants. They may fund an evaluation, but not the evaluator's compensation. They may fund an advocacy campaign, but not the advocacy staff. Their fear is based on not wanting to create a dependence on funding for salaries, since their investment will be short term, and they believe that salaries are a basic expense that the nonprofits "should be funding anyway." Instead, investors should ask, "What might the nonprofit discover or develop if we make an investment in their people?"

An abundance mentality, on the other hand, is a belief that internal investment is important, opportunities are a reason to grow capacity, advances can be made in leaps and bounds, success can be replicated and improved, most challenges can be handled (or bounced back from) and the organization deserves investments in order to realize the greatest outcomes. This mentality is based on the belief that the more one puts into life, the more one gets out of it. Investors who embrace an abundance mindset ask:

- Who are the top experts who can advise us?
- What information do we need to take this to the next level?
- What piece of this can we contribute to?
- If our program were to become a national model, what might that look like?

Embracing an abundance mentality doesn't have to be expensive. For example, in creating a new, strategic approach to substance abuse treatment, one investor engaged one of the world's leading experts on the topic for an hour-long phone conversation to tap into his wisdom and guidance. The expert charged nothing, and it was time well spent to attain best-in-class insight. Why not assume every program deserves that investment, rather than assuming one must always find the perceived cheapest or closest available resources? Only by embracing an abundance mentality can an investor attain the freedom to think about ways that a grant of $5,000 (or $50,000 or $500,000) can contribute to dramatically improving how people live, cure a disease, transform preschool education in a community or transform a neighborhood from an area of blight to one of prosperity.

Practice #5: Streamline Philanthropy

Without too much effort, investors can find ways to streamline decision making, application and reporting processes, board meetings, accounting practices, planning and other practices to reduce the burden on nonprofits and the investor himself. It always pays to think about what is the easiest, most simple, most streamlined way of going about everything—especially if an investor has been doing things the same way for years.

For example, one foundation in the California Bay Area realized it had 14 pages of grant guidelines to explain how to submit proposals that only needed to be eight pages—and all that for a $50,000 grant. Another foundation realized it wasn't doing anything with final reports from grantees, so it decided to curb its reporting requirements rather than waste its grantees' time.

To streamline your processes, smart investors ask: What do we really need, and what is the most efficient and useful way to get it? Further, these investors check in on their own processes every few years and ask grantees for feedback as well.

Practice #6: Learn Intentionally

Effective philanthropy requires that an investor create and support a culture of ongoing learning—for himself as an individual and for staff, board or advisors. After all, learning is at the core of all advances.

A culture of learning is one that encourages ongoing inquiry and questioning. It is comfortable with the fact that there is always more to learn and explore, and therefore the work of learning is never-ending. This can be a challenge for investors who are geared toward finding the "one" solution to a challenge, checking it off the list and moving on. But the culture of learning and ongoing inquiry is why cell phones now fit in the palm of the hand, and why more cancers are now curable with less stress for patients.

Learning is less helpful if it's only happening inside the heads of an investor and his or her internal team. Learning should be intentional, documented and shared. Effective investors create systems, processes, plans or timelines that allow for reflection—preferably with board members, staff or trusted advisors. They document that learning and use it to make decisions. For example, an investor who develops new funding guidelines and a process for board proposal review might also commit to a conference call after the first few rounds to find out how the process went and what can be improved. A investor who wants to replicate a new best practice in providing mental health services for returning veterans might convene grantees after the first year to find out what's working, what's not and what can be improved.

Learning cultures can reflect the personalities of their organizations. For example, a leading tech company gives employees one day each week to suspend normal work and focus on inquiry and innovation. A software-development community crowdsources its employee learning, allowing staff to post information they'd like to learn and information they'd like to share. When interests align, those who wish to share join those who wish to learn during a brown-bag lunch. The company also hosts a series of two-hour "deep dive" trainings when staff want to learn more. Many foundations host regular brown-bag lunches for staff to learn about or discuss issues related to their work. Some even maintain a specific reserve fund for "just-in-time" learning. If an initiative or grant-making program appears to be struggling, or a new opportunity arises, these investors can immediately call in an expert, conduct a quick survey, convene key advisors or stakeholders or do any number of things to learn and apply that learning in real time.

Introspection and learning take an investment of time—but it's time well spent. Remember that intentional learning can feel as though an investor is purposefully hunting for failures, so it's important to keep an eye out for things done well in addition to areas for improvement. In either case, the key is to find opportunities that the investor can embrace in real time as his or her work progresses, rather than waiting for a postmortem evaluation, when it's too late to increase impact.

Practice #7: Become Knowledgeable About Target Issues

It's a pretty safe bet that, whatever an investor's focus or issue, someone has already been playing in that sandbox. Before making grants, smart investors scan the landscape of their chosen issue or community to find out who else is focusing on it, what's been successful so far, what hasn't worked, and what the gaps and opportunities for impact are.

Nothing alienates a community or potential partners like an investor who comes into the room with all the answers. Leading with questions and a genuine desire to learn makes for far greater strides and aligns more valuable allies.

Investors also become valuable allies when they bring further knowledge into the mix. For example, an investor might access or underwrite national or regional research that can help inform everyone, or foot the bill for speakers or consultants who can add to everyone's knowledge.

Practice #8: Embrace a Spirit of Collaboration

Investors often expect nonprofits to collaborate, but they less frequently turn that expectation on themselves. Yet there is tremendous opportunity to exponentially expand the impact of research and development investments through funder collaboration. In fact, it is rare for an individual or institutional funder to produce meaningful research or develop an idea all alone. Collaboration allows for greater leverage of ideas, investments and reach to better ensure that research is thorough and conclusive and that new products or approaches work and are relevant to those they're intended to serve.

What does it mean to collaborate? Funder collaborations happen in many different ways, all of which leverage the strengths of each collaborative partner to achieve a common goal. Collaborations can be formal and complex, with written agreements and well-defined roles and structures, or they can be a series of ongoing conversations or even simple handshake agreements. They can be long-term efforts that require a significant commitment of time and funds, or short-term tactical approaches to addressing a common need. They can require a pooling of funds for investment, or simply aligning investments toward a common goal at the discretion of each collaborator.

Collaborations can also take funders beyond the usual allies to build connections with partners who have technical know-how or business knowledge that are not typically part of the philanthropic sphere. For example, one foundation funder who aimed to help California domestic violence shelters better coordinate their ability to serve victims underwrote the services of an app development company. Together, the shelters and app developers created a new smart-phone app that instantly crowdfunds hotel rooms when shelter space is not available.

Collaborations can be messy, but that shouldn't be a deterrent for investors. The key is to plan them well, understand who is leading the collaborative effort and how, communicate openly and often with all involved and recognize that unexpected twists and turns will likely be part of the process.

Practice #9: Remain Open to Prudent Risk

As with market investing, investing in philanthropy means a foundation must be willing to take risks. But not every opportunity is a good one, and not every innovative idea should be pursued. In considering any philanthropic investment, investors should assess each opportunity wisely and take risks that are prudent, calculated and thoroughly explored. Likewise, it's not a good idea to bet the farm on any single idea, product or service. Instead, investors should think of each investment as just one part of a diversified philanthropic portfolio.

There are four criteria that can help foundations assess risk in any philanthropic investment:[2]

1. *Cost.* What investment will this require in terms of grants, staff, outside expertise, new technology, and time?
2. *Benefit.* What are the potential benefits to the investor, community, field? Do the potential benefits outweigh the costs? How long until the effort achieves results?
3. *Strategic fit.* Does this opportunity fit with and advance the investor's mission and strategy? There are many great ideas out there, but no investor should invest in great ideas that take it off course or off mission.
4. *Risk types.* Risk can come in many forms, from potential financial losses to a damaged reputation or strained relationships with partners or community. What kinds of risk are most likely for this particular investment? How severe could they be?

Brainstorming and listing risks with advisors, staff, board and partners can help clarify the realities (and dispel misconceptions) about the risk an investor faces in each philanthropic investment. Once a "risk list" is created, investors should revisit it regularly to consider what's been done—or could be done—to continue to keep risk at a minimum.

Practice #10: Trust and Follow Instincts

Intuition can be a valuable tool for philanthropic investors. If an investor feels doubt about the skills or integrity of the executive director of a nonprofit, or admires the positive culture of a particular group even though it may seem less sophisticated than others, those hunches merit close attention. This is because, at its most basic level, grantmaking is about human relationships. Gut reactions to people and situations can be a valuable tool for determining what feels "right" for achieving an investor's mission.

Avoiding Delusional Altruism: A Note of Caution

Delusional altruism™ is a term coined by the Putnam Consulting Group to describe situations in which philanthropic investors are genuinely trying to make a difference on the issues and communities they care about—while paying absolutely no attention to how they may be getting in their own way by creating operational inefficiency and waste that drains both the investor and grantees of the human and financial capital necessary to accomplish their goals. In terms of market investments, delusional altruism would be the equivalent of any practice or policy that diminishes the ultimate return.

Delusional altruism occurs when a philanthropic investor's beliefs, permissions or practices hamper greater productivity and impact. How many professional development or learning opportunities are deemed too time consuming? How many strategic planning processes take longer than the time to implement the plans themselves? How many hours do investors hide behind administrative tasks instead of interacting with the community?

Philanthropic investors are even more delusional when they create hurdles not just for themselves but for their grantees. One of the most heinous forms of delusional altruism arises when investors simply don't pay attention to the impact that their policies and practices can have on those they most want to help. How many grant application processes end up being more cumbersome than helpful? How often do investors force applicants to deliver far more information than what is needed to make a grant decision? How many people do investors think should do more with less, when indeed they will never hit the mark unless given the chance to do more with *more*?

Manifestations of Delusional Altruism

Delusional altruism is rarely intentional, but it can be pervasive. This is partly because the manifestations of delusional altruism can be difficult to recognize. However, there are eight common examples, many of which are antithetical to the positive practices and mindsets listed previously. Investors who are interested in learning more can take the "Delusional Altruism™ Diagnostic" to rate their performance on each of these manifestations and identify action steps for improvement. It is available at http://putnam-consulting.com.

1. Expecting Others to Do What the Investor Won't

Philanthropic investors are often guilty of looking to grantees to implement big ideas that they refuse to implement themselves.

Examples such as collaboration, innovation and equity come readily to mind. Investors encourage grantees to collaborate on solutions, but are known for sticking to their own agendas. Investors want grantees to pursue so-called innovative solutions but do nothing to innovate within their own walls or practice and often haven't even defined what they mean by the term. And of course, while investors are concerned more and more about equity within the nonprofit organizations and programs they support, few have assessed their own operations and culture with an eye toward equity.

There is a huge difference between talking about or encouraging an idea and actually engaging in the work of developing it. By not thinking about the capacity required to become collaborative, innovative or equitable, investors become delusional about their potential impact.

2. Making Self-Serving Decisions

Throughout the philanthropic field, individual investors and foundations have created a culture of making decisions that are deeply rooted in their own internal perspectives. As a result, they create policies and practices that benefit themselves but not the grantees and the communities they serve.

For example, consider the philanthropic investor who chose to spend most of his time in the office. He expected that potential grantees and partners would come to him, despite the fact that his office was somewhat removed from the communities he served and not easy to get to.

In contrast, another well-meaning foundation conducted a survey of its grantees and grantseekers to assess what they thought of the foundation and their experiences with it. They were surprised to learn that their communication efforts received low marks and immediately set about improving their practices. This foundation dedicated time and resources to listen to its grantees and fix the problems. It was focused on what grantees needed as opposed to what foundation staff thought should be needed or was easiest to provide.

3. Ignoring Customer Service

The words "customer service" are rarely uttered by most philanthropists, foundation staff or foundation trustees. Thinking about customer service isn't part of the culture of most investors, but it has true and lasting implications. In the philanthropic investment context, this doesn't mean treating grantees like paying customers in a business, but rather as people without whom an investor's work would fall flat.

As mentioned above, philanthropy is ultimately about relationships, and poor interactions between investors and grantees can lead to missed connections or opportunities that could have been powerful. Communication is a key to good customer service. The more complex a funding initiative or the more partners it involves, the more communication should play a powerful role. But even in smaller-scale grantmaking, investors should never underestimate the value of a friendly voice at their end of the phone line, one that can provide clear and kind advice or gently explain why a proposal is not likely to be funded. When this is the case, grantseekers are less likely to be surprised or disappointed—even if the ultimate answer to a request is "no."

4. Giving in to Bureaucracy and Sloth

Bureaucracy can creep up on an investor like black mold. It's not something anyone sets out to create ("Hmm, how can I make life more complicated today?"); yet it's everywhere. It often masquerades as productivity, which in turn feeds the delusional-altruism fire.

Layers of bureaucracy can appear with each new set of eyes that develops grant guidelines or reviews a grant proposal, with every additional piece of information received from grant applicants, with every new partner or collaborator that comes on board. In many cases, bureaucracy can grow organically as a philanthropic investor's operation grows from individual giving, to donor advised grantmaking, to having his or her own foundation with a full complement of staff. As this growth occurs, bureaucratic practices can emerge quietly and without question.

Here is an extreme example: one foundation used to send its board members board dockets that were three inches thick. Who had time to read all that information, much less make sense of it? Realizing how bureaucratic and overloaded their process had become, the staff took a systematic approach, looking not just at the board docket but at their entire grantmaking process—from the time an initial letter of intent came in the door to the time a grant check went out. In doing so, they learned that the average grant required hundreds of individual "touches" by foundation staff or board members from start to finish. Hundreds! They have now greatly streamlined their entire grantmaking process, including reducing the board docket to 30 pages.

New grantmakers can sidestep bureaucracy from the get-go, assuming they can avoid a few major pitfalls. One such pitfall is simply adopting practices from other funders without thinking through whether they truly are a best fit for the new venture's mission, goals and culture. Another is not paying attention to how many little decisions can add up to one big mess.

For example, suppose a philanthropic investor who operates a large company wants to create a small start-up foundation with two staff. This investor can hardly expect to maintain the time-intensive practices she relies on in the workplace, such as making personal site visits to every customer (or in this case, grant applicant). Instead, this investor should create a new process more in keeping with the foundation's purpose and capacity. Then, as the foundation grows, she and staff should always be on the lookout for "bureaucratic creep" within internal processes and nip it in the bud.

5. Lacking Urgency and Speed

Foundations and individual investors have virtually no incentive to move quickly. There are few regulations, no shareholders and few vocal grantees to roust funders into fast action. In some cases, a deliberate approach is warranted, but often speed can make a huge difference in terms of impact.

For example, investors frequently delude themselves into thinking that the longer a strategic planning exercise takes, the more relevant the plan will be and the greater impact it will deliver. However, the reverse is more often true. It's almost impossible to plan for anything more than a year or two in advance. When a philanthropic investor spends half or all of that time creating a strategic plan, he's already behind the times. In reality, strategic planning should be an annual process that is completed within in a week. This way investors can get on with the work of helping communities.

One of the most delusional philanthropic investment practices occurs when a funder—usually a foundation—ceases grant-making for a year or even longer in order to "take stock" of its investments, learn more deeply about needs and create a plan for the next decade (or some other far-reaching period). If an investor has engaged in ongoing, intentional learning, then there should be no need to halt all progress in order to reassess footing and vision. A series of staff and board retreats should be sufficient to delve into what an investor has learned and where he or she wants to go. Then it's time to get back to work.

Another example: How long can and should it take for an investor to make a grant? What should be a matter of weeks can evolve into multiple months, as new steps and procedures creep in, adding up to greater complexity and a longer process. Unfortunately, few investors notice or question these developments. But when they do, they can usually reduce their process to a much shorter period of time.

6. Jumping on Bandwagons

We live in a world of trends. Each year, there seems to be another wonderful new thing that every philanthropic investor must adopt. Often these trends are relegated to buzzwords that everyone uses but no one really understands (like "empower," "collective impact," "ideation," "intersectionality"). Sometimes they are actions du jour that make a big splash (like the Ice Bucket Challenge or crowdfunding) but don't deliver impact that's commensurate with the hype.

It's not that any of these practices aren't important, interesting or useful. But as with other investment vehicles, investors delude themselves when they jump on the bandwagon without thinking about how the next big craze aligns with their own strategy. Will the trend advance the investor's work—not just in the moment but in the coming months and years? Is the new trend is in keeping with an investor's culture and practice? The key is to know thyself, and be completely clear about mission and strategy; as a result trends are easier to identify as promising practices or passing fads.

7. Rarely Engaging Diverse Perspectives or Not Engaging Them at All

One of the most common ways philanthropic investors fall prey to delusional altruism is by leaving the people who are affected by the investor's actions out of the decision-making process. Remedying this means more than simply consulting an advisor of color, adding a member of color to an all-white foundation board, attending a community meeting in a specific neighborhood, or signing onto a statement in support of LGBT rights. Increasing connections in these ways is perhaps a start, but making sure voices are continually heard and included is the more critical component for informing an investor's work.

There are many ways to engage diverse perspectives. Philanthropic investors might begin by creating an advisory committee of community members or conducting focus groups and surveys of grantees and community members. For example, an investor who wants to invest in a new pre-K initiative might make a point of talking to parents of preschoolers about what they need and what's stopping them from accessing high-quality pre-K.

But engaging diverse perspectives goes even deeper.

In doing research on equity in philanthropy for the Robert Wood Johnson Foundation, Putnam Consulting Group learned that family, corporate, private and community foundations often delude themselves by genuinely wanting to focus on equity but not turning that equity lens on their own operations. They ask the organizations they fund to prove they have a diverse staff and board, while their own are not. They claim to want to support grassroots organizations, but they make their grant application processes so cumbersome that only a large and sophisticated organization can navigate it. They want to fund economic justice but have never considered whom they hire for their own vendor contracts. While this research only looked at institutional funders, the lesson from this research was clear for foundations and individual philanthropic investors: Engaging diverse perspective starts from within.

8. Creating a Culture of Disrespect

Sometimes the actions of individual investors or the organizational culture of a foundation fuels disrespect. In fact, many of the practices discussed above contribute to that culture of disrespect: not returning phone calls or replying to emails, expecting grantees to assume the burden of traveling to meetings, subjecting nonprofits to overly cumbersome grantmaking processes, moving too slowly or overlooking the values and opinions of those an investor purports to serve and the like.

Most philanthropic investors don't intentionally set out to be disrespectful. It's what happens unintentionally that investors must watch. Cultures of respect grow when investors are willing to communicate openly and honestly with grantees. Through these conversations, both investors and grantees will gain a deeper respect for and understanding of one another, and become better positioned to move forward as allies.

Transformational Giving as a Critical Investment Strategy

Transformational giving can be incredibly powerful. It can result in grantmaking processes that are deeply meaningful and relevant to both the giver and the recipient. It can shape experiences and outcomes for those who supply philanthropic capital just as much as it does for those whose lives are changed because of gifts or grants. And it can effectively leverage other kinds of for-profit investments in ways that bring everyone closer to a desired outcome.

When philanthropic investments are made in a transformational way, they can provide both intrinsic value and amplify returns in the rest of an investor's portfolio. The key is to find the connections between the market outcomes an investor seeks and the social conditions that support those outcomes—then make charitable investments in the organizations that help to create or sustain those social conditions in ways that truly enhance, rather than hinder, the effectiveness of those organizations.

Consider the example of an investor who owns a great deal of timberland. He wants to build the market for his timber, and so he invests in wood processing and paper manufacturing businesses through standard market investment vehicles. But he also wants to ensure that the timber industry continues to be a viable one so that his children and grandchildren can derive benefits from it. This means that the industry must have a skilled and knowledge-able workforce; hence the investor makes philanthropic invest-ments in workforce training programs in his area. It also means that timberlands must be stewarded in a way that preserves the environment for future generations, so he invests in nonprofit organizations that are creating carbon preserves within timber-lands and in a university program that is researching new options for eco-friendly timberland management. The investor makes the connections between these programs and his market investments by clearly understanding his mission, developing an giving strat-egy, and communicating it well.

Further, the investor uses more than just financial gifts to support his philanthropic investments. He leverages his connec-tions in the industry to help find job placements for trainees, business partners for the research university and even scholar-ships for industry workers who want to further their education. He continues to learn alongside the organizations he supports and is a ready and willing collaborator when strategic opportun-ities present themselves. Over time, his investment in traditional markets and philanthropic endeavors become so intertwined that it is hard to say where one ends and the other begins. As an result, his entire investment portfolio is helping to trans-form the future of the timber industry—and the future of his offspring.

When done in this way, transformational philanthropic invest-ments can play a key role in an investor's overall portfolio, as well as in achieving greater vision, increased impact, and deeper mean-ing as part of an investor's total return.

Notes

1 Through the Dorr Foundation, philanthropist and engineer John V. N. Dorr supported the testing and adoption of white lines on the shoulders of roadways in Connecticut and New York in the mid-1950s. The practice has since been adopted nationwide.
2 Michael Robert and Alan Weiss, *The Innovation Formula* (New York: Harper Row, 1988), pp. 63–64.

7

Assessing Your Opportunities: The Challenge and Key Practices of Engaging in Investor Due Diligence

Sandra Osborne

In this chapter we will review in full the process of performing due diligence on a potential investee. We will walk through the various stages of the diligence process and provide key tips and things to keep in mind along the way. We will provide a framework that an investor can adapt and tailor as necessary for a given investment. Some of the key questions that we will address include:

- What is due diligence?
- What are the basic steps involved in a due diligence process?
- How in depth should my diligence be for a given investment type?
- What are the key types of things to look out for during the course of due diligence?

After reading this chapter, you should have the tools you need to develop your own due diligence process and thoroughly investigate an investment opportunity. Ultimately, the goal is to help you make clear and confident investment decision based on the due diligence findings.

What Is Due Diligence?

Due diligence is the comprehensive investigation undertaken on an investment opportunity in order to help the investor assess risk, return and impact as you make your investment decision. Within the impact investing space, this process encompasses both financial and impact analyses. The process begins as early as the first meeting with a fund manager or entrepreneur as any interaction is an opportunity to learn something about the character of the people running the enterprise under evaluation. The process is complete once an investor has thoroughly vetted every relevant aspect of a potential investee and can confidently come to a conclusion about whether or not to make an investment. The purpose of conducting due diligence is to fully understand the business model, identify key strengths and weaknesses and develop a risk-reward analysis, all of which will ultimately inform the final investment decision. Keeping in mind the fact that virtually all investment entails some level of risk, there is no guarantee your investment will perform well with both financial and social returns; but with these key practices in your tool kit, you'll be better prepared to assess the opportunities and understand potential pit falls.

Your due diligence process will vary based on a number of factors including life-stage of a potential investee, type of investment and size of investment. For example, performing a diligence on a start-up enterprise will be very focused on the character of the management team, the quality of the business model and future outlook of the market they are operating within, as very little historical track record will exist. On the other hand, an investor considering an investment in an established enterprise will have much more historical performance available on which to base an investment decision. Furthermore, it is important bear in mind the size and type of investment under consideration when considering the scope of diligence to perform. According to members of Toniic (a leading impact angel network), "due diligence should strike a delicate balance, collecting enough data for rigorous analysis and providing value while not exhausting the entrepreneur in the process. Your due diligence process should focus on information that will get you to a decision and be commensurate to the

Figure 7.1 Stages of Due Diligence and Key Tips to Keep in Mind.

Prescreening	Desktop Due Diligence	On-site Due Diligence	Final Decision
• Initial screen • Investment thesis • Portfolio fit	• Market analysis • Data request and review • Reference interviews	• In person meetings • Non-verbal clues • Tour of office/ factories/branches	• Scorecard • Risk-reward analysis • Clear final decision

Key Tips to Keep in Mind

A. Match the level of diligence with the size and type of the investment
B. Use every interaction with a management team as an evaluation opportunity
C. Prepare thoroughly for in-person meetings to derive the most value
D. Use scorecards to process large amounts of information collected over the course of diligence
E. Make a clear final decision in good confidence after a thorough due diligence

size and type of capital you are planning to deploy."[1] For example, an investor seeking to take a majority equity stake in a start-up enterprise is likely to spend significantly more time investigating a potential investee than would an investor looking to make a relatively small and short-term loan to a known entity.

At the most in-depth level, due diligence typically consists of four stages:

1. Prescreening,
2. Desktop due diligence,
3. On-site due diligence, and
4. The final decision stage.

We will review each in more detail in the ensuing sections but below is a brief snapshot of the key elements of each stage as well as the five key tips to keep in mind throughout the process:

Due Diligence Process

Pipeline Generation

The due diligence process begins with the first contact an investor has with the management team of a potential investment. As mentioned above, every interaction with the management team is in opportunity to ascertain information around the investment's value proposition. As such, deal sourcing is essentially the first step of deal vetting. Sourcing and identifying high-quality investment options is one of the most challenging steps. An investor looking to place capital is likely to be inundated with options; weeding through these options to identify investments of sufficient quality to move forward is the hard part. One option to help facilitate the sourcing is to invest in a structured product or fund. The choice between investing in a fund or investing directly into deals or companies is equally as relevant for impact investors as it is for conventional investors. While we would encourage investors operating independently to focus on a single category or invest in funds or through intermediaries in order not to have to become an expert in each are of potential interest, we present the pros and cons of both below:

If, after weighing the pros and cons of investing in funds or directly into companies, an investor opts for the direct companies, joining an angel group or network could serve as a beneficial aid in deal sourcing. Toniic, recommends finding "value-aligned networks of investors, impact intermediaries, impact banks, advisory firms, incubators, and fund managers who will allow you to coinvest, or select some of their deals."[2] Toniic members further provide the following recommendations:[3]

Figure 7.2   Pros and Cons of Investing in Funds versus Direct Companies.

Funds		Direct Companies	
Pros (+)	*Cons (−)*	*Pros (+)*	*Cons (−)*
• Portfolio diversification	• Removed from direct impact	• Engaged with direct impact	• Undiversified
• Less ongoing monitoring	• Manager fees can be high	• Avoid manager fees	• Ongoing monitoring required
• Lower risk	• No ability to impact direction of companies	• Ability to influence investment	• Higher risk

Figure 7.3 Options for and Benefits of Angel Groups and Networks.

Type	Description
Incubators and Accelerators	Help socially conscious start-ups refine their business models and prepare to pitch to investors.
Business Plan Competitions	Can help early-stage entrepreneurs connect with mentorship, practice pitching to investors and get their plans ready for first infusions of capital.
Networking Groups	Provide learning and community as well as access to resources for impact investors.
Deal Flow and Investor Networks	Can provide a wide variety of services like capacity building on the deal flow side as well as on the investor side, deal vetting, syndication services and more. Frequently only open to accredited investors.
Key Events and Conferences	Can include multisector events and keep you informed of impact investing trends.
Impact Intermediaries	Developing in regions around the world to support entrepreneurs and investors.
Crowdfunding	Provide opportunities both for "retail" investments (for nonaccredited and accredited investors) and "platform" investments (in crowdfunding platform enterprises for accredited investors).

Prescreening

Once an analyst has identified a potential investment, the formal vetting commences. The prescreening stage can be viewed as a relatively high-level review that confirms an investment meets minimum criteria from an investment standpoint and is a good fit from a portfolio standpoint. At this stage, an investor should seek out necessary documentation to form an initial understanding of the potential investment. These documents may include recent audited financials, a business plan (in the case of direct investment), offering documents and preliminary terms. A high level review of each of these will allow the investor to answer the question of whether the investment meets the initial criteria. In addition, prescreening will frequently bring to the surface questions or concerns to be further investigated once full diligence begins. Questions to keep in mind include:

1. What is the investment thesis from a financial and impact perspective?

2. Does this investment provide an acceptable financial risk-return profile?
3. Does the impact value proposition align with the investors values?
4. What are the key risks associated with this transaction and what will an investor need to gain comfort with those risks during the diligence process?

As an example, at ImpactAssets, when we assess potential private debt and equity funds for inclusion on our Global Impact Ventures platform (GIV), we apply the criteria below as our first screen. As you develop your own approach, you might consider developing similar criteria that fits within your own investment philosophy.

Once it has been determined that an investment meets your preestablished criteria, it is also wise to consider how the investment will fit within the overall portfolio, prior to proceeding with full due diligence. Some important questions to ask on the portfolio side include:

- Does this investment fall within targeted asset allocation?
- Does this investment offer diversification benefit to the overall portfolio?
- Does this investment introduce concentration risk to the portfolio?

Figure 7.4 Sample First Screen Criteria.

First Screen Criteria for GIV Platform Candidates

- Private debt or equity, no publically traded investments
- Direct positive social and/or environmental impact; approach to measuring impact
- Strong investment thesis; range of financial returns acceptable
- Track record with previous funds or extensive experience with other funds
- First close by the time the investment panel reviews fund
- Open for at least a year between first and last close

- Does this investment have implications on near-term needs for liquidity (i.e., will the funds be locked up in an investment that can't be exited beyond the time an investor would otherwise need access to the funds?
- Does the time horizon of the investment fit within the needs of the overall portfolio?

With your sourcing process in place and these initial questions addressed, you're now ready to move on to your next step in the process.

Desktop Due Diligence

Once an investment has been prescreened and is determined to be a good potential fit for your portfolio overall, intensive due diligence commences with what is referred to as desktop due diligence. In this stage, an investor will gather and review an exhaustive list of documents and materials on both the potential investee and the market in which it operates. The purpose of this stage is to become as familiar as possible with every aspect of a potential investee. This stage also serves as important preparation for the next phase, on-site due diligence, when you will want to be fully prepared to ask the right questions and understand the venture you are touring. During desktop diligence, a number of questions are bound to arise that the investor should flag for further discussion during subsequent in-person meetings. By the end of the desktop due diligence, an investor should have a solid understanding of both the market landscape of a potential investee as well as a thorough grasp of the ins and outs of the business operations, with any outstanding questions organized in preparation for the next phase of engagement.

Market Analysis

Understanding the space within which a potential investee operates is a key component of desktop due diligence. An investor should seek out market reports, association annual assessments and any industry research available. The purpose of this research is to be able to develop an *independent* strategic view of where the potential investee sits within the broader market and what the total addressable market may be. While the potential investee is likely to provide an investor with their market perspective, it is important to engage in your own research as well. Internally prepared research by a potential investee is likely to present the investee in the best possible light. It is incumbent on the investor to cross-check and verify the company's purported market position and the opportunity they are promoting to you.

Data Request and Review

After the market assessment, the first step of digging into the potential investee itself is to gather and review the necessary legal, financial and organizational documents. This step can take different forms depending on the life-stage or sophistication of a potential investee. An established company or fund will likely have a number of relevant documents available on their website, or be able to provide access to a secure online data room. A virtual data room is an online space dedicated to housing documents and file sharing. If that is not the case, or if the website or data room does not contain everything necessary to complete desktop diligence, it is perfectly acceptable to send an exhaustive diligence request to the potential investee. A responsible investor mindful of the potential investee's time will first identify what information can be sourced independently and then pare down the diligence request to reflect only those items that are still outstanding. It is also important to keep in mind at this stage that the level of diligence undertaken should be proportionate to the size of the investment. A relatively small and shorter-term debt investment may not require the same level of information as a majority equity stake would entail. Below, we present sample documents to request from an investor that assumes a relatively large and high risk investment but should be pared back in the case of smaller, lower risk investments.

The topics that the diligence request will cover include specific documents on recent performance and projections, organizational structure and team, and operations and legal. Specific documents on recent performance and projections are the ones most likely to be found in a potential investee's data room. You should review these documents with a fine-tooth comb looking for any anomalies in the financials or projections or any other red flags, especially any qualified opinions by an auditor. The existence of red flags does not necessarily preclude investing. The purpose of this review is to first identify all red flags in order to prepare follow-up questions with the potential investee in determining whether there are sufficient mitigating factors to offset the red flags and move forward with the investment. The top 10 list of key documents to request that will help facilitate a thorough financial and business analysis in this category are listed below:

1. Articles of incorporation
2. Employee handbook or similar policy documents
3. Audited financial statements for past three years
4. Most recent unaudited financial statements
5. Five-year proforma financial projections
6. Any available third party reports
7. Two most recent annual reports to investors
8. Two most recent quarterly reports to investors
9. Two most recent impact reports
10. Sample of any other reports provided to investors

On the organizational side, an investor should look to gain a deeper understanding of the structure of the organization and key people involved. An investor should seek to learn who reports to whom, how long key team members have been working together and what is the pedigree and experience of the management team and staff. You should also be assessing the fundamental operating and governance systems of the organization. Are appropriate checks and balances embedded in the organizational structure? Does the team seem to chafe at getting you the information you request or in working with each other? In addition, information about the Board of Directors and any advisory positions will help you form an opinion regarding the quality of influential people involved. How often do they meet? How much do they really understand about the venture and its operating practices? Are they individuals with specific industry expertise or more general knowledge? A top 10 list of items to request in this category include:

1. Organizational structure chart with reporting structure chart for management and staff
2. Role, responsibilities and biographies of the board of directors, advisory board, management team and staff
3. Changes in the past 18 months and changes expected in the next 18 months among the board of directors, advisory board, management team and staff
4. Past working relationships among members of board of directors, advisory board, management team and staff
5. Conflict of interest policy and explanation and mitigation of any current potential conflicts of interest
6. Names, titles, tenure, experience, education and responsibilities of management and all staff members
7. Stakeholder diversity: percentage of female and percentage of underrepresented groups (e.g., ethnicities or other minority groups) for (separately) board of directors, management and staff
8. Annual board, management and staff compensation
9. Firm compensation structure, including any performance-based compensation and employee benefits packages
10. List of any significant compensation middle- to senior-level staff receive outside of the firm compensation

On the operations and legal side, an investor should look into the third party associations a potential investee has, including service providers and industry affiliations, and any legal issues they may be facing. Key questions to keep in mind include:

• What key functions have been outsourced?
• Is the investee using "best-in-class" service providers?
• Has there been any legal action taken against the potential investee or is there a risk of any?

The top 10 list of items to request in this category include:

1. List of all firm offices and associated personnel
2. List of any significant parent/subsidiary/joint venture agreements

3. List of any key loans, contracts, conflicts or interrelations
4. List of any current or past legal actions taken against the firm or its funds and outcomes
5. Overview of any third party providers of firm's management information systems, including firm financial management
6. Overview of any other third party service providers, including legal services, tax, auditors and any other service providers
7. List and details of all banking relationships and credit availability
8. List of and documentation for any external regulations complied with or recognitions received
9. List and description of any participation in industry initiatives
10. List of any intrafirm social or environmental policies or initiatives

Recall that every interaction you have with a potential investee is an opportunity to assess something relevant to the due diligence process. In the case of the desktop diligence data request, the pace at which the potential investee is able to provide the requested documents and materials may be informative. Fulfilling an exhaustive data request within 24–48 hours likely indicates a high degree of organization and efficiency. On the contrary, if a potential investee is unable to fulfill a request within one to two weeks, it could be an indication that the organization has poor internal processes in place—which may not bode well for the future! That said, it could also be an indication that the management team is assiduously working to successfully execute on their business plan. Whichever conclusion you reach, it is important to keep in mind this is just one piece of the puzzle that forms the bigger picture you are attempting to sketch out through your due diligence process.

Reference Interviews

The final stage of desktop due diligence is to interview third party references. These are people that are independent from the day to day of the company but have sufficient involvement to be able to provide insights into its future prospects. Key people to consider for a reference interview would be people such as an independent board member, an advisory board member and/or a current investor. As the Bridgespan Group recommends in their blog entitled "Effective Philanthropy, Seven Questions to Ask a Member of a Nonprofit Board in Your Due Diligence," some important questions to ask, which also apply to for-profit investment opportunities, include:[4]

1. Why did you become involved in the organization, and what has your involvement looked like over time?
2. How would you characterize the role of the board of directors/advisory board/investors in the organization?
3. How would you describe the goals of the organization, and how does the organization achieve these goals?
4. How focused on results do you believe the organization is?
5. What attributes does the CEO have that will enable him or her to accomplish the company's goals?

On-site Due Diligence

After desktop due diligence is complete and an investor has gone through all of the necessary documentation, the next step is to pay the potential investee an in-person visit known as on-site due diligence. On-site due diligence is crucial for verifying everything learned thus far. There is no substitute for meeting a management team in person, on their turf, and witnessing firsthand their interactions with one another. In fact, you may well want to have multiple engagements with the management team over several months, depending upon the size and nature of the investment you are considering.

In addition, an investor should want to see for themselves "how the sausage gets made." Whether performing diligence on a company producing a physical product, or a fund or financial institution, a potential investor should take the opportunity to observe the ins and outs of how the business is run and how well processes are followed. During all of the meetings and visits throughout the on-site due diligence, keeping an eye out for staff members putting policies into practice; verifying that behavior aligns with previously reviewed handbooks or manuals is advisable. The bottom-line is that during the on-site visit you want to ensure, to the greatest degree possible, that what they say is what they do!

Similar to the size of the data request for desktop diligence, the amount of time an investor spends performing on-site diligence should vary depending on the size and type of investment under consideration. An afternoon spent discussing repayment capacity and cash flows with the most senior members of the management team could be sufficient for a relatively small or short-term debt investment. On the other hand, an investor contemplating a major equity stake in a company is likely to spend days, possibly over the course of multiple visits, performing on-site diligence. During that time, an investor should make it a point to sit down and meet with each member of the senior management team and each department head on a one-on-one basis. If possible, it is helpful to send a request to the management team in advance of your visit and schedule each meeting. An investor may refer to the organizational chart to determine the list of people who are most important to meet. This list will vary widely depending on the type of company or fund under consideration. As an example, an investor performing diligence on a microfinance institution might ask for the following meetings:

- Chief Executive Officer
- Chief Financial Officer
- Chief Operations Officer
- Head of Risk Department
- Head of Credit Department
- Head of Treasury
- Head of Internal Audit
- Head of Human Resources
- Head of MIS/IT
- Head of Marketing

A well-prepared investor will have a set of questions unique to each of these business heads that relate directly to the function of their departments. Some standard questions that an investor could ask in each interview include:

1. What are some of the key initiatives your department has undertaken in the past 12–18 months?
2. How do you measure success for yourself and your team?
3. What do you view as the three major risks facing your department and the company overall?

While *what* the interviewees say during the interviews is important, *how* they say it can be equally enlightening to a potential investor. Take note of body language during the meeting for clues that an interviewee is holding something back or avoiding an uncomfortable topic. Is the interviewee maintaining good eye contact or constantly averting the investor's gaze? Does the interviewee have their arms crossed in a defensive position? Excessive fidgeting could also indicate nervousness. Also take note of how the team interacts as a group. Do they joke? Is there a comfortable dynamic? It is not at all unreasonable to ask to meet individually as well as with the staff and/or operating managers as a group. A lot of information can be gleaned from these conversations regarding the quality and competency of the interviewee by observing visual clues in addition to the verbal responses.

Another important thing to observe during the interviews is the degree of faith a CEO has in his staff. If the CEO insists on being present for each of the meetings, or send in an observer, this could indicate that the CEO has micromanagement tendencies and may present key man risk, not to mention inefficiencies in running the business. In an ideal scenario, a CEO will grant an investor all of the interviews requested with complete autonomy.

Getting out of the office and "into the field" is also a key component of on-site diligence. An investor should request visits to nearby factories or outposts, as applicable for a given potential investee. This specific request will again vary depending on the type of company or fund under consideration. Going back to the microfinance institution example, an investor would want to go to one or two of the branches for a tour and additional interviews. During the tour, an investor would look to see how the branch is organized, how the tellers interact with customers, how secure the vault is and so on. In terms of meetings, an investor would ideally sit down with:

- branch manager,
- loan officer, and
- teller/cashier

An investor in this scenario should also review loan files at random and request the loan officer walk through the process involved in assessing the credit worthiness of a given client. Through desktop diligence, an investor should have gained a thorough understanding of the lending policy that will come in handy to compare written policies with those actually applied by the loan officer in a specific case. Take note of any discrepancies observed during the review. In this case, the final step of this "in the field" example is to meet with actual clients of the microfinance institutions. During this visit, an investor will have the opportunity to assess the level of client satisfaction and the relationship between the loan officer and this client. Of course, an investor should take everything the client says with a grain of salt as the loan officer is likely to only bring an investor around to meet with star clients. That said, it is possible to catch a lucky break and hear something unexpected. Once on a diligence trip in Laos, I had a client who was presented to me as being a good representative of the types of clients the institution served. When I asked her what purposes she put her loan toward, she essentially confessed to being a loan shark, on lending her loan to friends and neighbors. She was clearly not a star client and we ultimately ended up not making an investment in the microfinance institution.

Final Decision

Once the on-site diligence is complete, an investor should have sufficient materials to make a clear final decision on whether or not to make an investment. Digesting and processing all of the evidence collected and reviewed over the course of the diligence process can be overwhelming. Scorecards can be useful to help evaluate the wide array of factors that play into the final decision. While an investor should determine the specific elements to include in a scorecard depending on the type of investment being considered, the structure should seek to capture the risk and reward profile, both in terms of financial and impact. In order to assess potential private debt and equity fund options for inclusion on the Global Impact Ventures platform, the ImpactAssets Investments team, consisting at the time of Fran Seegull and Joann Chen, developed Quattro, a proprietary scorecard that considers all four key categories: impact risk, impact return, financial risk and financial return. The scorecard contemplates a weighted aggregate of over 80 specific criteria to help map a given fund on the below webs.

The financial return score is calculated through a combination of targeted returns, return benchmarks and historical returns. On the financial risk side, the scorecard contemplates a weighted aggregate of 35 specific criteria across six key categories. Impact return considers the impact generated within the firm such as staff diversity and the impact generated through the firm's investment practices and portfolio. The scorecard aggregates 11 criteria across three categories for a weighted total impact return score. Impact risk is also a weighted score and includes 13 criteria across three categories.

While the ImpactAssets' Quattro scorecard is unique to rating fund managers, many of the elements are relevant to developing a

Figure 7.5 Quattro Risk and Return Webs.

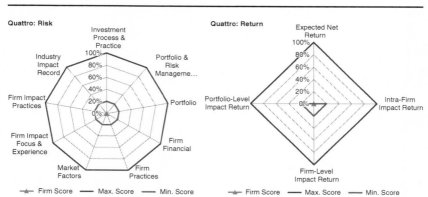

Figure 7.6 Categories to Consider When Developing a Scorecard.

RISK	RETURN
• Firm Financial	• Expected Net Financial Return
• Firm Practices	• Firm-level Impact Return
• Market Factors	• Intra-Firm Impact Return
• Firm Impact Focus & Experience	
• Firm Impact Practices	
• Industry Impact Record	

scorecard for any type of potential investee. To develop your own scorecard, consider using the below general categories within risk and return and identify specific ways of measuring and weighting subcategories within. The subcategories should be specific to the potential investee's business line and market within which it operates. Combining the scored results with the overall impression gleaned during the course of the extensive due diligence process will help inform a clear final investment decision. Readers can refer to the chapter on impact metrics and measurements for additional information on how to approach measuring impact risk and return.

Conclusion

In ultimately making the decision of whether or not to make an investment, there is simply no substitute to a thorough due diligence. Rolling up one's sleeves and digging into the nitty gritty of a company is the only sure way to feel confident and comfortable in the analysis and, ultimately, the investment decision. While consulting other investors is wise and could provide important insights, nothing compares to the knowledge gained from doing the research and hard work yourself. An investor undergoing a first due diligence can use the framework laid out in this chapter as an outline and tailor it to the specifics of the type of investment under consideration. As we wrap up this chapter, we would leave you with the key tips we recommend keeping in mind when

Figure 7.7   Key Tips to Keep in Mind during Due Diligence.

Key Tips to Keep in Mind
- ✓   Match the level of diligence with the size and type of the investment
- ✓   Use every interaction with a management team as an evaluation opportunity
- ✓   Prepare thoroughly for in-person meetings to derive the most value
- ✓   Use scorecards to process large amounts of information collected over the course of diligence
- ✓   Make a clear final decision in good confidence after a thorough due diligence

developing the due diligence process appropriate for a given potential investee:

One final word to the wise:

In general, always remember that the folks you are assessing for a possible investment are usually working hard to keep their venture moving forward while at the same time giving you the time and attention they feel you deserve as a potential investor. Be sure to respect their time and energies as you go through you due diligence process. Remember, as a general rule, it is always good to say "No" fast and "Yes" slowly. You don't want to be the person who leads an entrepreneur on well after you could have informed them that you didn't feel it to be a good fit for you and your portfolio! With the framework laid out in this chapter, tailored to suit the investment at hand, you are well prepared to perform your first due diligence with confidence and, ultimately, make a clear investment decision.

Notes

1 "The 7-Step Framework," Toniic, Accessed April 7, 2017, http://www.toniic.com/the-7-step-framework/.
2 "The 7-Step Framework," Toniic, Accessed April 7, 2017, http://www.toniic.com/the-7-step-framework/.
3 "The 7-Step Framework," Toniic, Accessed April 7, 2017, http://www.toniic.com/the-7-step-framework/.
4 The Bridgespan Group, "Seven Questions to Ask a Member of a Nonprofit Board in Your Nonprofit Due Diligence," June 26, 2012, https://www.bridgespan.org/insights/blog/give-smart/seven-questions-to-ask-a-nonprofit-board-member.

Case Study 3

IMPACT INVESTOR CASE STUDY: "LINDA SHORELY"

Year Started Impact Investing: 2010

Primary Focus: Private equity, debt and venture capital impact funds

Background: Linda is an accredited investor who seeks out professionally managed funds that do seed, early stage venture, later stage venture and private equity investments in mission-driven businesses. The impact funds that Linda invests in generally have minimums starting at $250,000. When Linda invests in impact funds through his donor advised fund (DAF), minimums start at $25,000.

Impact Trigger

Linda's background is in law and during her career she's had the opportunity to work with some of the most disruptive game changers in technology. In 2010, she began to understand that the "real deal" entrepreneurs were those moved by something other than making money. They had a bigger mission. Their satisfaction came from using their creativity and energy toward solving an identified problem as opposed to simply making money. She also started to notice the growing success of companies that are creatively solving for social and environmental challenges, whether in Clean Technology or Fintech (financial technology). It deeply resonated with Linda when she saw that an innovative and sustainable business model could do "financially well while doing good." This intersection of mission and financial return had staying power. It just made sense and Linda began to revise her worldview on the meaning of money. This awareness began to reshape a vision for a future that she wanted for her family and that she wanted to participate in.

Investment Approach

Linda now believes there is no better opportunity than the present to use private capital to solve massive global problems. And she believes impact can actually be the key to finding growth and value in an increasingly crowded marketplace. It's become clear that there is exciting and real potential with companies seeking to solve social and environmental problems. For example, there are more than 2,000 certified B Corps companies globally, redefining success in business because of having a social and environmental mission and not despite it.* Some of the fastest growing and most recognizable companies in the United States are B Corps, such as Warby Parker and Toms Footwear.

Rather than seeking individual investment deals herself, Linda prefers to work with fund managers who have the expertise, focus and passion in finding suitable portfolio bets and appropriately diversifying. There still aren't as many fund managers with a track record of making money in the impact space. There aren't many second- or third-time impact investing funds in the United States. But venture capital pioneers bumped into this same thing 30 years ago. As soon as she hears the old adage that "you can't make money doing this because no one has ever made money doing this," her interest peaks. She focuses instead on her set intentions as an impact investor and to work with funds that are demonstrating the attractiveness of investing for social and environmental impact. At times, she invests in newer or more risky funds using philanthropic capital through her DAF. Doing

* https://www.bcorporation.net/.

so allows her greater flexibility around minimums, risk and return expectations and avoids that annoying K1 reporting.

The risk aspect was a question Linda explored extensively. Are impact fund managers able to consistently deliver both market-rate returns and social or environmental benefit? Are mission-driven businesses different than non–mission-driven businesses? Are they slower growing? Are their margins less attractive? Are they more costly to invest in? Are their exits harder to find? Are their valuations lower? And just like traditional investing, Linda discovered, it all depends on what the investment is. Some investors do prioritize impact returns over financial returns, like those financing social impact bonds to support innovative public sector programs, or those investing with the economic base of the pyramid in emerging markets. And for many impact investors, including Linda, those types of investments play a role in her investment mission. Given the growing number of mission-driven companies that are proving that there doesn't have to be a trade-off, any skepticism should be rethought. There is no doubt that impact investing is an important new force in private capital investing.

Linda believes we've reached a place where most fund managers now recognize strong environmental, social and governance programs can drive real bottom-line value. But she's interested in those that go even further. They see impact as a lens that can help them spot underserved markets where others aren't looking; to work with mission-driven management teams who would otherwise be wary of private equity; and to build economic value by thinking deeply about, and measuring clearly, the social or environmental returns that move in lock-step with earnings growth.

A few examples of funds she has invested in include:

- DBL Investors, which raised over $350 million for its second fund, which invests in high-growth companies that are located in underserved communities or have strong environmental, community or workforce practices.
- Elevar Equity, which raised $78 million for its third fund, focused on commercial investments in early stage companies providing financial services, education, housing and health

care to low-income communities primarily in India and Latin America.

- Better Ventures, which recently closed a $21 million dollar fund focused on start-ups focused on closing opportunity gaps in society in everything from clean tech to health, HR and financial services focused on closing opportunity gaps in society.

8

The Measurement Challenge

Sara Olsen

Ah, impact measurement ...

Perhaps no single topic in this book has this particular quality of being both essential and anathema at the same time. Hold onto your hats, because that combination of opposites means this is a potentially transcendent topic!

At the outset, many investors may doubt one can ever really *know* one's impact, let alone account for it to someone else. I often hear those who are not yet engaged in impact investing say something along these lines: "If it were measurable, wouldn't it already be integrated into conventional investment decision-making?" But as ample and growing evidence presented elsewhere (including in this book) demonstrates,[1] seeking out and including information about the environmental, social and governance (ESG)-related qualities of investments results in a more complete view of not only investments' impact on the world but also of their potential financial performance. In other words, it is increasingly clear that investors' fiduciary duty includes understanding the material ESG qualities of investments.

Although one may intuitively gauge the social or environmental value of one's own investments, intuition is both impossible to transmit to other decision makers up the capital supply chain without supplementary means of communication, and intuition can be wrong. For example, early equity investors in microfinance believed it to have almost miraculous poverty-alleviating benefits– so much so that some I know have felt that asking microfinance operators to stop and measure their social performance would require an unethical diversion of resources away from direct beneficiaries who might otherwise be saved from dire poverty. Yet studies show mixed poverty alleviation results of microfinance across the board, and solid evidence that certain practices in microfinance are what drive more consistently positive impact. These measurement insights combined with volatility in microfinance driven by scandalous negative impact where insufficient attention was paid to social and governance issues are all proof that, despite the surface appearance of obvious and sometimes even miraculous social benefits from impact investments, in order to *have* positive impact, systematically *measuring* impact is important.

What is impact, metrics and reporting in impact investing? How do you do it especially given the fact that privately held companies do not have to disclose their environmental and social performance, and currently there are no publicly available databases of information on the environmental and social impact of alternative investments?[2] Answers are obscured by the current state of practice in impact investing: most of what environmental and social impact data exist are proprietary, often based upon substantially qualitative and custom methods, and frequently not associated systematically with financial performance. Only recently have efforts to standardize definitions and define norms for impact management in impact investing been undertaken[3]; and functional, specialized information technology (IT) systems to support tracking, analysis and reporting of social outcomes relative to investment finally exist on the market today but their adoption is still nascent and these systems tend not to relate social outcomes directly with financial results. Despite all the good work of recent years, today impact information about investments isn't handed to anyone on a silver platter.

In sum, this is not a time in the evolution of the market when you can easily bluff your understanding of what it takes to measure social and environmental impact; therefore, it's important to know the basics. This overview will help you understand what it takes to gauge "impact," how various types of investors are using different approaches and where to go next.

What Is Metrics and Reporting Within Impact Investing?

There are four basic applications for impact assessment within impact investing:[4]

1. When determining your objectives, as you consider what qualities and results of your investments matter to you
2. When deciding whether to make an investment as part of your due diligence process, to check "fit" and potential performance
3. Over the life of the investment relationship in ongoing performance monitoring and reporting, to improve performance
4. At key milestones and/or after exiting the investment, to evaluate results and demonstrate accountability

In other words, impact investing is infused with impact management and vice versa.

Impact Measurement That's Fit for Purpose

At a high level, the kind of impact measurement you will do is based upon the type of investing you will be doing. If you are focused upon public markets and engaging in shareholder advocacy, then the type of measures you're tracking will most likely be based upon already existing, publicly available information, and very likely this will have already been aggregated and even interpreted by a third party; if you're assessing the impact of more targeted, direct investments in the private equity, debt or grants space, then the metrics will likely be a combination of somewhat uniform metrics that consider the investee's social responsibility in general and may already have been produced by others, and more flexible metrics that are both tailored to the particular effects a given investment has on the world, and may be customized to inform your particular objectives and personal goals (and may require you to help pay for if not also do the measurement). For the purposes of this chapter, I will be focusing more on the issue of measurement in the private equity, debt and grants context.[5]

The first application for impact measurement, "when deter-mining your objectives," is highly personal. The next three appli-cations for impact measurement all involve estimating impact. We must approach impact measurement with an eye toward projec-tions and estimates since (unless we have a time machine!) we can never actually *see* both what happened and what would have happened if the investment hadn't occurred.

Impact Measurement for Investors: A Three-legged Stool

There are three fundamental impact issues to understand in investing:

1. The effect your investments have on yourself
2. The particular effects they have on the wider world
3. The degree to which the investments are living up to the social contract

These make up the three-legged impact measurement stool for investors.

Once you've decided you're interested in knowing what envir-onmental or social impact your investing has, the next step is to reflect upon what is most important to you about the impact you seek to have with your capital.

Determining Your Objectives:
What Is the Personal Impact You Seek to Create?

The first leg of the stool is definitely whatever impact you want to have ... on yourself.

Often people answer this by the impact they intend to have on their wallet. Your advisor, if you have one, will be interested in knowing if you aim to preserve your capital, grow it, or even spend it down. Other folks begin by articulating their objectives around impact– what will provide you with the sense of meaning you seek. Generally these personal objectives include one or more of the following:

- Having social or environmental performance that's better than the status quo across the board
- Benefiting a certain place or group
- Reducing a certain kind of change, or promoting another kind of change
- Reducing risk to your portfolio's financial returns

Questions to ask to clarify what your personal objectives are include:

1. What kind of result are you primarily interested in: risk reduction, enhancing financial performance, or achieving a certain type of impact? You may have a combination in mind but it's important to define these clearly and understand which is the priority.
2. Is there a certain population or place you are interested in benefiting, or an environmental issue you want to affect? If so, see the next question; if not, you might be more interested in a review of an organization's across-the-board performance in terms of ESG issues (see "Measuring the Social Contract," below)
3. Have you talked with the beneficiaries you're interested in regarding what they care about, and how it relates to the investment? If not, it is important to do this, and/or talk to others who are well versed in the issue(s).

It is useful to have an idea regarding what your priorities for financial and social/environmental value creation are, or how they will work in concert, and to document this, but it is also important to recognize that you will very likely wish to revise these priorities as you gain greater experience. You might consider the first pass at your personal objectives "version 1.0," and periodically (such as annually) revisit and update them.

And then there's your feelings …

Beyond your intentions regarding your financial returns and intentions for changing the world comes something even more personal: what *other* benefits you are going to get back personally when you make a contribution to changing the world in a certain way; that is, how do you hope to *feel* because of your investments? Do you want to feel:

- reinvigorated by a new challenge?
- powerful?

- relieved of guilt?
- a sense of meaning?
- a sense of community?
- closer to your concept of god?
- confident that your legacy will be one your family is proud of?
- less worried that your kids or future generations at large are "in for it"?

I highlight the personal impact component because (besides having lived in northern California for 18 years ...) all too often these personal motives operate unconsciously but dictate whether investors follow through on the impact part of their strategies. Many folks have gotten their "feels," and their financial returns, and then frankly forgotten to check whether the investment actually did any good out in the world relative to the stated impact objectives. This suggests that what mattered at the end was how the investor *felt*, not what impact was generated for people out there in a particular community much less the larger world. When this happens, these investments are not true impact investments.

But by explicitly distinguishing between (1) your own internal objectives, (2) your own external objectives, and (3) the actual social or environmental results your investments attain, you become able to distinguish these from one another. Your intentions and how the investments make you feel are not the same thing as what actually happens for the people or systems you set out to affect. It is crucial to recognize this, and then to verify what is in fact happening out in the world compared with what you intend and what's happening for you.

Indeed this is a central purpose of impact investing.

Once you have clarity regarding both the personal and financial benefits you seek from your investments, the remaining task is to align both with your actual results so that all three work together. This is the core, thrilling challenge of impact investing!

Pay attention to these questions about your internal and external objectives as you invest, and gradually you may notice how you feel when you support a certain kind of investment or when you get certain information back regarding what is and isn't working.

That will help you reach answers about how you are hoping to benefit.

Now let's turn to the steps to measuring impact.

How to Measure Impact

While it is a bit of a mouthful to say, we need to begin with the understanding that reality consists of the complex, multisensory, physical, emotional, aesthetic, spiritual and economic experience of people, as well as the state of the natural environment. How can we gauge what is changing for each of these as a result of investment?

There are two answers: the theoretically ideal answer and the realistic answer.

Immediately upon setting out to understand the impact of a given investment opportunity you will be confronted with the issue of what resources are reasonable to put into knowing the true impact of an investment. This issue is called "proportionality"—meaning the amount of resources required to assess impact should be in measured proportion to the amount of the investment itself. As you read about the theoretically ideal way to measure impact, you will probably agree that proportionality in impact measurement is a needed principle.

Impact Defined

First let's define the term "impact." There is a general consensus in the impact investing world about what the term "impact" means for impact investment purposes. The G8's Social Investment Task Force's Impact Management Working Group in 2014 defined impact as follows:

> The reflection of social [and environmental] outcomes as measurements, both long-term and short-term, adjusted for the effects achieved by others (alternative attribution), for effects that would have happened anyway (deadweight), for negative consequences (displacement), and for effects declining over time (drop-off).[6]

The diagram below offers a simple way to understand this definition of impact. Note that impact is not only what changes (the outcome) but the difference between the change and what would have happened anyway (in the absence of the entity's activities), or in other words, the additional change caused by the investment (Figure 8.1).

Figure 8.1 Basic Impact Map or Logic Model.

Inputs	Activities	Outputs	Outcomes	Impacts
What resources are used in delivery of the intervention	What is being done with those resources (the intervention)	Products and byproducts of the activities; a summary of the activities in numbers	The changes arising in the lives of beneficiaries and others	The extent to which that change arises from the intervention

Note: GECES Sub-group on Impact Measurement, June 2014. *Proposed Approaches to Social Impact Measurement in European Commission Legislation and in Practice Relating to EuSEFs and the EaSI.*

Source: Author, Social Value International and GECES.

That said, the term "impact" is often used slightly differently by impact investors in practice. In particular the quality of "additionality" is seen by researchers as a defining characteristic of impact but has been treated with some ambivalence by investors, perhaps because it's more difficult both to measure and deliver than outputs or outcomes.[7]

How to Measure Impact in an Ideal World

In the ideal world we wave a magic wand and the answer to what our impact is appears … and then since I'm out of a job I wave it a second time and I become a world-class tango dancer for my next career!

However, the answer to what is ideal from a traditional, methodological perspective goes something like this:

First, before we even finalize our business plan (if we are the investee) or investment thesis (if we are the investor), we develop a picture of how implementation of our still-in-progress investment thesis will cause intended and unintended change. This is done by engaging in preliminary discussions with our stakeholders that help us learn what is changing for them that matters to them, as well as who and what else may be affected. We decide what impact we hope to have, which then informs both the design of the investment and our measures of change through discussions with these stakeholders and with experts in the areas we affect (such as public health, education or environment).

Second, we use these measures to regularly gather information about the state of each distinct stakeholder group and each aspect of the environment that is changing in a significant way, beginning prior to the investment and recurring periodically until we have exited the investment. Ideally we also continue to track what has changed after we exit, for as long as the outcomes we care about take to manifest, so we truly understand whether what we did was effective. We also seek to understand any other outcomes due to the investment, whether positive or negative, that are important to our key stakeholders. This yields valuable information to inform both the ongoing management of the investment and how we will invest going forward. We compare the changes in those outcomes as time goes by to their state when we first invested, and compare them to a very similar group and/or physical setting that didn't experience the investment, to understand the contribution our investment made to the change.

Third, with primary and secondary data in hand, we analyze the information—take into account previous trends, other factors and relevant existing research that might explain the differences we see and help us draw conclusions about the significance of the changes. We do this for all our investments and make meaning of the whole using our skills in comparison and aggregation of different types of investments and their diverse impacts.

Fourth, we create individual reports and roll-ups that summarize and distill insights about our impact for all stakeholders and environmental aspects globally. We regularly present this information in reporting we make available online and offline in versions with levels of detail tailored to our different audiences and their purposes.

Finally, both the investor and the investee make regular use of this information to inform investment, venture management and other decisions.

As you can imagine, this kind of robust data collection, analysis and information management requires diverse skills, and if it is feasible at all it is most likely possible only for entities who do not need to balance the resources spent on impact tracking and reporting with their financial return on investment; that is, governmental entities or foundations whose purpose is to advance the public good. It is therefore no wonder measuring impact, let alone managing impact, is seen as a daunting if not impossible feat by many investors!

Which brings us to the *practical* answer to impact measurement in the context of private investors doing it for their own reasons, not because of a regulatory or funder requirement.

How to Measure Impact in Most Investors' Practical Reality

The practical answer to how to measure impact for investors in the private sector context is to take the previously outlined "ideal" methodology and merge it with what is possible and necessary given five other considerations:

- will
- time
- money
- technology

For the sake of simplicity we will set aside the additional considerations of access and privacy.

While it is tempting to streamline impact measurement efforts to the greatest degree possible, if we do that we risk losing what matters. As the axiom goes, you can't manage what you don't measure, and if we don't measure certain things we not only can't design effective solutions we can't even stay in business. What information about impact is critical to measure?

Simplify but Don't Oversimplify

The metrics that *must* be measured are context-dependent and, in this unregulated arena, ultimately an individual judgment, but some things are relevant for impact investors to measure in general.

What is relevant to measure in impact investing begs the question, "Relevant for whom?" There are three distinct answers to this question that inform the three legs of the impact measurement stool we discussed earlier. One is the impact that is relevant or "important for me": something that either I, the investor, may

Figure 8.2   Two Ways of Thinking About Relevance of Social and Environmental Impacts.

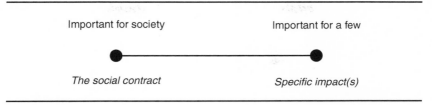

care about quite strongly. Another, which is related to the first in terms of how it is measured, is the impact that is "important for those affected" by the investment, that is, the people other than the investor who are affected by an investment's activities and outputs. The last is the impact that is "important for society generally," that is to say, the social or environmental quality or performance of an investment as seen through the eyes of society at large, or in other words the investment's performance relative to the "social contract" in a given place, day and age (Figure 8.2).

What you do to measure the relevant issues at one of these poles is quite different than what you do to measure the relevant stuff at the other pole.

The Other Two Legs of the Impact Measurement Stool

These two poles have yielded two fundamentally distinct ways of going about measuring impact. The two ways may be thought of as "rules-based" and "principles-based" ways of gauging impact.

Measuring the Social Contract: Rules-based Approaches to Estimating Impact

The third leg of the impact measurement stool is the impact on society at large, or in other words, the investment's "social responsibility." This generally consists of how an investment such as a company treats people and the environment. The best way to gauge this is via a prescribed set of indicators that a sizeable number of society's wisest members have agreed are the right ones over a series of coordinated sessions to gather their input; otherwise the task of gauging it would be unfeasible. Approaches that dictate the metrics and hold them constant across organizations can be considered rules-based approaches. Examples include:[8]

- B Lab B Impact Assessment for B Corp Certification
- B Lab Global Impact Investment Rating System (GIIRS)
- Global Reporting Initiative (GRI) G4 Framework
- Sustainability Accounting Standards Board (SASB) Standards

Impact measurement and reporting approaches that have prescribed metrics most often focus on factors that may be easily compared between different organizations, that is to say, policies, activities and outputs, rather than actual changes experienced by stakeholders or systems (outcomes or impacts). See for example these metrics from one of SASB's 79 reporting standards (Figure 8.3).

Major benefits of prescribed metrics are that no particular skill is required to apply them, and it is relatively easy to compare one organization to another organization using identical metrics. Down sides of this method are that the absolute impact on any given stakeholder or issue area caused by the entity is generally missing from the analysis, and the unique social and environmental differentiators of a given enterprise are buffed out.

The level of effort required to generate an assessment of an organization's impact using one of these standards varies substantially. Generally speaking, B Corp certification is designed for use by privately held, small and medium-sized enterprises, while the methodologies of GRI and SASB are designed for larger publicly traded companies, although these divisions are not rigid (e.g., privately held companies can use the SASB standards, and in late 2014 Natura became the first publicly listed company to become a certified B Corporation).[9] For a very small company it may take about a day or less to fill in the B Corp B Impact Assessment if all your papers are on hand; for a large company to create a highly comprehensive report using the G4 Framework, the time required may be a year or more (at which point the process is similar to painting the Golden Gate Bridge—after one finishes, it is time to begin again!).

Figure 8.3 SASB Commercial Banks Sustainability Accounting Standard, Table 1 (excerpt).

TOPIC	ACCOUNTING METRIC	CATEGORY	UNIT OF MEASURE	CODE
Financial Inclusion & Capacity Building	Percentage of new accounts held by first-time account holders	Quantitative	Percentage (%)	FN0101-01
	Percentage of total domestic loans for underserved and underbanked business segments	Quantitative	Percentage (%) in U.S. dollars ($)	FN0101-02
	Number of participants in financial literacy initiatives for unbanked, underbanked, or underserved customers[7]	Quantitative	Number (#)	FN0101-03
	Loan-to-deposit ratio for: (1) Overall domestic lending (2) Underserved and underbanked business segments	Quantitative	Ratio in U.S. dollars($)	FN0101-04
	Loan default rates for: (1) Overall domestic lending (2) Underserved and underbanked business segments	Quantitative	Rate in U.S. dollars($)	FN0101-05
Customer Privacy & Data Security	Number of data security breaches and percentage involving customers' personally identifiable information[6]	Quantitative	Number (#), percentage (%)	FN0101-06
	Discussion of management approach to identifying and addressing vulnerabilities and threats to data security	Discussion and Analysis	n/a	FN0101-07

Measuring Specific Changes: Principles-based Approaches to Measuring Impact

The second leg of the impact measurement stool is the particular impact out in the world that is created by an investment. While it might be theoretically possible to create a huge list of every conceivable impact on the natural environment, out of which one could ask people to go through and pick the relevant metrics for a given investment, for most investors it is simply not possible to create a prescribed set of indicators to gauge every possible social and/or environmental impact in every context. Something new is always coming along. So a better approach for this situation is to actually engage in research via a process wherein you make a set of judgments along the way that are guided by principles; this methodology is then referred to as a principles-based approach to estimating impact.

Principles-based approaches to measuring and/or reporting impact include:[10]

- International Integrated Reporting Council (IIRC): Integrated Reporting Framework (<IR>)
- Natural Capital Coalition (NCC): Protocol (the "Protocol")
- Social Value International (SVI): Social Value Principles and Social Return on Investment (SROI) Methodology
- Acumen Fund: Lean Data Initiative
- Randomized Control Trials[11]

Principles that tend to be common across different approaches include:

- Clearly articulating the scope and purpose of the analysis
- Identifying and involving stakeholders in the analysis
- Understanding what is changing for stakeholders and/or the environment
- Including the material issues (and not others)
- Transparent reporting

Typically the steps in implementing these approaches involve:

- Determining the purpose of the analysis
- Engaging stakeholders

- Understanding and documenting changes and their import-ance or value
- Considering what else has contributed to the change
- Reporting all of this in a transparent and useful manner

The benefit of principles-based approaches is that they enable organizations to determine what their unique impacts are that help them define their specific value propositions. However, a down side is that they require skill and generally cost more to implement (especially in a comprehensive way) than prescriptive approaches. For example, it would be unlikely to see Unilever consider develop-ing a Social Return on Investment assessment of every part of its glo-bal activities, but it might do so for a specific initiative in a particular region. It's interesting to note that Unilever has considered becom-ing a certified B Corp that would entail completing an impact/per-formance survey that applies to all its global operations.[12]

To understand what is changing for stakeholders it is best to ask them. In principles-based approaches, this can be done in vari-ous ways ranging from observation of the setting people are in and their behavior, to informal conversations with stakeholders, formal interviews, focus groups and surveys. The recent advance of mobile technology means this type of research may be con-ducted at both small and large scale for much lower cost than in the past. Provided one has the phone number or location of one's stakeholders, impact assessment that investigates changes for groups of remote stakeholders can be done for as little as a couple of thousand dollars total.

Streamlined Stakeholder Research

Many organizations have used a streamlined, principles-based approach to assessing changes experienced by stakeholders using SMS- and mobile device-based surveying to obtain both social impact information and more conventional customer feedback. Acumen Fund refers to this as Lean Data, and Root Capital executes a similar approach called Client-Centric Mobile Measurement.[13] Both have used SMS and mobile technology to survey intended beneficiaries of their investments in remote regions of coun-tries in the global south to obtain insights both into whether their intended outcomes such as around poverty alleviation have occurred, and to gain customer feedback that helps them understand better what their beneficiaries value about what is changing, which informs the types of investments they offer.

These practical versions of impact assessment are less strict with regard to establishing specific attribution. As both Acumen Fund and Root Capital state in their report on Lean Data:

> Our principle objective is not to know with certainty that impact can be attributed to a particular action or intervention. Our objective is to collect data with an appropriate degree of rigor that gives voice to our customers, including a more objective window into their experiences of a given product or service, and helps the businesses we invest in use this data to keep an eye on their social metrics and manage toward ever improving levels of social performance.
>
> To avoid confusion in this report, we use the term social performance measurement rather than impact measurement as a more accurate description [than "impact"] of the data we collect and use to assess the social change we believe both we and our respective investees make.[14]

Newer versions of principles-based frameworks such as the NCC Protocol referenced above provide for discretion on the user's part as to the level of effort that is appropriate to gauge what factors are changing. They enable managers to make informed choices regarding what the appropriate impact measurement will consist of in a given situation; and analysts reading the resulting reports to understand what choices were made when the impact was measured and reported, so that both can obtain a fair and true picture of what is truly changing.

Up the Learning Curve

While 10 years ago many doubted it was realistic to expect investors to learn how to measure social impact overall, the level of effort and skill they employ in this task and expect of their investees is rising, as evidenced not only by the willingness of the publisher to publish this book but by the approaches used by impact investors known for their commitment to impact measurement and established practices diagrammed by So and Staskevicius (Figure 8.4).

Figure 8.4 Map of Measurement Methodologies to Measurement Objectives.

	1 Estimating Impact *for due diligence*	2 Planning Impact *through strategy*	3 Monitoring Impact *to improve program*	4 Evaluating Impact *to prove social value*
Expected Return				
• SROI				
Theory of Change				
• Logic Model				
Mission Alignment Methods				
• Social Value Criteria				
• Scorecards				
Quasi-Experimental & Experimental Methods				
• RCT				
• Historical baseline				
• Pre/post test				
• Regression discontinuity design				
• Difference in differences				
Investment Process Alignment:	Due Diligence	Pre-Approval		Post-Investment

Source: So and Staskevicius, "Measuring the 'Impact' in Impact Investing," 2015.

Hybrid Approaches

While rules-based and principles-based approaches differ fundamentally, in practice their combination is becoming more common. Some of the reporting frameworks that began as prescribed lists of indicators such as GRI in more recent iterations are migrating toward versions that permit users to determine what is most important to include,[15] and thus to exercise skilled judgment in their application; this then has evolved into a hybrid approach.

B Corp too has supplemented its fixed assessments and relatively static summaries with its B Impact Analytics platform, which permits users to unpack the details and highlight aspects they deem most important in their own analysis. Impact Reporting and Investing Standards (IRIS), begun as a taxonomy of indicators on the premise that investors could simply pick from among its list and thus have an easier time communicating with each other and in aggregate about impact, is proving to be used most often in combination with custom metrics its users define for themselves. My own firm, SVT Group, both tracks our own customized measures of our impact on customers and relative to our mission, and completes the B Impact Assessment to maintain our B Corp certification. The International Integrated Reporting Framework even provides guidance to publicly traded and other companies on how present their environmental, social and financial performance information in a single annual financial report; after all it's all value that is of interest to investors.

The Will to Measure:
Impact Measurement Behaviors and Beliefs

Although there are efforts being made by investors to understand their impact and overall ESG performance, what a given group of investors consider essential to measure in practice is constantly being defined by the market and actors within it. Today, good practices I see among practitioners and in the literature include the following:

- Be aware of which stakeholders are affected in a way that is important to them, especially including those with the least voice

- Involve stakeholders in efforts to determine what to measure and then in measuring it (think: customer research)
- Gauge whatever is the most important intended impact of the investment
- Measure and reduce material environmental impacts
- Measure what it cost to produce the analysis of impact
- Track how these insights are turned into value by the investor, and what that value is
- Measure the financial performance of the investment relative to expectations
- Assess and monitor "impact risk," that is, the risk that impact will be different than expected
- Align overall measurement practices with the UN Sustainable Development Goals

What is considered appropriate relates not only to what makes sense to actually gauge impact, but also to what is seen as appropriate within a given audience's culture (the "will" issue I mentioned earlier). Some (though not all) newcomers to the space whose peer group have traditionally seen their investments as unrelated to social or environmental impact are being asked if they have social impact investment opportunities by asset owners. These newcomers in turn approach the problem with this question: "What is the least I can do that will qualify to my investor as 'impact'?" This is likely because they believe impact investing is a fad and irrelevant to their core purpose as investors.

Others believe combining attention to impacts on people and the planet with financial performance management is not only socially but commercially constructive. These actors seek to do what they can to demonstrate their impact in a credible fashion within a cost structure they can justify (such as a few basis points that they expect to pay for through enhanced sales). Others may leave their old firms behind and form a new firm specifically devoted to addressing a certain issue, and will formulate more involved approaches to measuring impact.

Some impact investors actively disagree with each others' approaches. For example, there is a group of investors only tracking performance metrics that may simultaneously serve as operational performance indicators. In this case, a lender

Figure 8.5 The Metrics Beliefs Matrix: Investor Impact Measurement Beliefs and Behaviors.

	Measuring does not add value	Measuring adds value
High customization, highly integrated into operations		Pathbreakers Advancers
Low customization, superficially applied to operations	Mainstreamers Laggards	

who intends to reduce poverty may track the number of loans made within a target community, that is, percentage of loans in default. This approach may be viewed as a best practice by some investors, while others point out that tracking only those metrics related to management of the venture leaves open the door that unintended, material *negative* impacts may be occurring (such as over-indebtedness of borrowers that then mires them in poverty—but improves the venture's "impact" performance by increasing the number of clients). I've illustrated the cultural beliefs and behaviors among investors today regarding impact measurement practices in a "Metrics Beliefs Matrix" (Figure 8.5).

Some metrics may be relevant for cohorts of investors, in which case they may all agree to track the same performance indicators. This is the case for the Aspen Network of Development Entrepreneurs (ANDE) who have worked to arrive at a focused number of metrics that are coded using the IRIS system that most of their members already track. Other metrics will be of interest to specific funds, such as the percentage of investees from a certain region, whether the employees of those companies are making living wages, whether more girls are gaining access to quality education and so on. IRIS contains clusters of indicators that have been found to be useful among certain fields of practice and certain well-reputed funds.

This diversity of beliefs will likely remain, although it would be helpful if everyone's social and environmental performance could be understood and aggregated. The UN's Sustainable Development Goals may help: they are a prescribed set of global impact goals with which many investors are looking to align both their individualized and standardized measures and reporting.

The Emerging Profession of Impact Managers and Impact Analysts

While many investors may generate their own impact assessments, there are some who will use impact reporting generated by others to make their decisions. In recent years this has begun to take two distinct roles related to metrics and reporting in impact investing. One is that of the party doing the measurement and reporting, the "Manager." The other is that of the party using this information to make decisions, the "Analyst." Sometimes they overlap in one person or office, but increasingly we're seeing an important distinction between these two roles.

The Impact Manager

The Impact Manager is charged with measuring and managing impact. This role involves producing an estimate of impact, whether by doing it oneself or by commissioning others to do so. As we have been discussing, the process involves defining the scope of the thing to be studied, determining measures, collecting and analyzing data, and reporting information. Measurement fits within the larger role of the Impact Manager, which is to define intended impact, establish measures and performance targets as well as information management systems to track and analyze data, and use data to inform decisions.

A growing number of entities offer training in impact measurement and management for the impact investing context, from businesses to impact investing networks such as the Global Impact Investing Network (GIIN) and TONIIC, to professional associations such as SVI and AEA (American Evaluation Association), and a growing number of academic institutions. (A list of resources and associations supporting impact measurement and metrics will be found at the end of this chapter.)

The Impact Analyst

Often the person deploying capital reads impact reporting produced by others in order to understand the impact itself. Katherine Ruff points out that for every impact report producer, there are likely 100 readers, and reading critically requires an understanding of what issues can cloud or warp the picture of impact. Kate first proposed the idea that, much the way doctors help us laypeople figure out what those medical tests mean or financial analysts help us know which stocks to buy or dump, skilled "impact analysts" who can interpret impact through disparate reporting methods are crucial to enabling investors to make sense of which investments are a good match for their personal objectives. We have elaborated elsewhere on how their skills, along with metrics that are flexible within certain bounds, combine to enable informed capital allocation decisions and grow a well-functioning social capital marketplace.[16]

Qualities of Good Reporting About Impact

Informed by the fields of evaluation and impact measurement, sociology, accounting and economics, SVI (of which Kate and I are members) has distilled a preliminary set of the qualities of good reporting about impact that are summarized in Figure 8.6.

Each of the issues fleshed out in the framework affects whether the impact analyst can understand the true impact underlying what is reported. Social Value US and Canada have also developed this framework into a training seminar in skilled impact analysis, and a professional certificate conferred by SVI, to support the development of this new analyst role.

Figure 8.6 Qualities of Impact Reporting.

Overarching analytical questions: Can we see the impact clearly? Can the impact assessment methods and results be compared to other entities (and their methods and results)?

		Define & measure outputs	Define & measure outcomes	Estimate impact*	Value the impact*
Framing	**Purpose and audience**	What is the purpose of the report? Who is the audience for the report?			
	Boundary and scope	What is the boundary of the entity/program being assessed? Which elements of the value chain are included/excluded? Are indirect effects included or just direct effects?			
	Materiality	Are all material outcomes included?			
Measurement and Analysis	**Validity**	Are measures used good reflections of the underlying reality they are trying to measure?			
	Reliability	Are data used consistent over time and place?			
	Causality	Is the reporting clear on how the organization or program creates impact? Does it try to account for what would have happened without the organization?			
	Valuation	Does the report use appropriate methods for valuing, rather than just measuring or reporting, social impacts?			
Presentation	**Clarity**	Is the report clear and comprehensible to relevant stakeholders? Is information presented in a way that facilitates understanding?			
	Transparency	Is the reporting transparent in how data was collected and analyzed? Can the process be replicated from the information provided?			
	Uncertainty	Does the analysis account for and describe uncertainty in the reporting and analyses?			
	Neutrality	Is the reporting impartial in how it presents the data and findings?			
	Judgment	Are any evaluative judgments justifiable and based on the data and findings?			
	Comparability	Can the results be compared to those of other organizations or programs?			
Cross-cutting	**Engagement**	Were the right stakeholders involved in appropriate aspects of assessing and reporting social impact/value?			
	Proportionality	Were the resources used to assess and report social impact proportional to the size and importance of the impact?			

Source: Social Value US and Social Value Canada, 2017.

Conclusion

It is not new to think that work done with the intent of creating a positive social or environmental outcome ought to be measured systematically to assess if it was successful, but it *is* relatively new to see the private sector deliberately and voluntarily engage in systematic measurement of these extrafinancial outcomes as a way to both enhance profits and create a healthier and more sustainably prosperous world.

You may know—you may even be!—one of the early mission-driven innovators who has become jaded about impact metrics, and views impact measurement as either a power play imposed by impact investors on those already lacking power in the finance equation, or an unfortunate oversimplification that reduces things that are quintessentially valuable to soulless and often wrong numbers on a page that are then used to justify dubious decisions. It is true that getting the metrics wrong is not just a waste of resources; it potentially creates real-world harm.

But a growing number of practitioners and investors are arriving at the conclusion that impact measurement—ubiquitous, high-quality impact measurement—is a crucial navigation aid in the world of impact investing; and that, in fact, it is necessary to enable us to solve the world's problems.

That group is becoming a new profession that will change the face of capital markets worldwide.

Metrics, Reporting Networks and Resources

The following are information and resource networks and information sources that will assist you in your continued process of learning how to understand and best apply performance metrics and reporting in the course of your own impact investing.

Networks and Professional Associations

Quotes below are from the organizations' websites.

- The American Evaluation Association (AEA) "is a professional association of evaluators devoted to the application and exploration of program evaluation, personnel evaluation, technology, and many other forms of evaluation. Evaluation involves assessing the strengths and weaknesses of programs, policies, personnel, products, and organizations to improve their effectiveness. AEA has approximately 7100 members representing all 50 states in the United States as well as over 60 foreign countries." (http://www.eval.org/)

- The Aspen Network of Development Entrepreneurs (ANDE) is "a global network of organizations that propel entrepreneurship in emerging markets. ANDE members provide critical financial, educational, and business support services to *small and growing businesses (SGBs)* based on the conviction that SGBs will create jobs, stimulate long-term economic growth, and produce environmental and social benefits. Ultimately, we believe that SGBs can help lift countries out of poverty." Among other things, ANDE's Metrics & Research Learning Lab organizes webinars for members, and there are regional metrics Learning Labs in Brazil, East Africa, and South Africa that organize in-person meetings. (www.andeglobal.org/)

- B Lab "is a nonprofit organization that serves a global movement of people using business as a force for good™" B Lab is: "1) Building a global community of **Certified B CorporationsTM** who meet the highest standards of verified, overall social and environmental performance, public transparency, and legal accountability; 2) Promoting **Mission Alignment** using innovative corporate structures like the benefit corporation to align the interests of business with those of society and to help high-impact businesses be built to last; 3) Helping tens of thousands of businesses, investors, and institutions **Measure What Matters**, by using the B Impact Assessment and B Analytics to manage their impact—and the impact of the businesses with whom they work—with as much rigor as their profits; 4) Inspiring millions to join the movement through story-telling by B the Change Media." (https://www.bcorporation.net)

- The Chartered Financial Analysts (CFA) Institute has a mission "to lead the investment profession globally by promoting the highest standards of ethics, education, and professional excellence for the ultimate benefit of society." It "seeks to set professional standards for investment management practitioners and

broadly engage other finance professionals through their interest and interactions with the investment management industry.
Improving outcomes for investors advances our social mission
and benefits members through greater demand for educated
and ethical investment management professionals." Recently
the CFA Institute has begun exploring environmental, social
and governance issues. (https://www.cfainstitute.org/)

- The European Evaluation Society (EES) has a mandate "to
stimulate, guide and promote the theory, practice and utilization of evaluation in Europe and beyond. Our vision is a
world where evaluation contributes to human welfare through
social learning. Specifically EES seeks to advance evaluation
knowledge and to encourage adoption of good practices by
fostering evaluation excellence, independence and partnerships. EES activities aim to support improved enabling environments for evaluation, stronger communities of practice,
relevant evaluation research and enhanced evaluation methods." EES has over 550 members from 74 countries. (https://
www.europeanevaluation.org/)

- The Global Impact Investing Network (GIIN) "drives thought
leadership on a variety of key topics and themes within the
impact investing industry. Recent campaigns have served to direct attention to the complexities of a growing industry, as well
as the role of impact investing in achieving the UN Sustainable
Development Goals (SDGs)." The Global Impact Investing
Network (GIIN) also has "an investor-focused membership to
support one portion of this growing ecosystem in service of the
GIIN's mission to increase the scale and effectiveness of impact
investing ... Organizations of all types that make—or plan to
make—impact investments are invited to apply. Organizations
providing—or seeking to provide—services to impact investors, such as law firms, investment advisors, ratings agencies,
and placement agents, are also invited to apply to join the
community." Many early members are institutional investors.
(https://thegiin.org/)

- The Natural Capital Coalition (NCC) "is a unique global multi-
stakeholder collaboration that brings together leading global initiatives and organizations to harmonize approaches to
natural capital." NCC facilitated development of the Natural

Capital Protocol, "a framework designed to help generate trusted, credible, and actionable information for business managers to inform decisions." (http://naturalcapitalcoalition.org/)

- The Social Performance Taskforce (SPTF) "is a non-profit membership organization with more than 3,000 members from all over the world. Our members come from every stakeholder group in inclusive finance. SPTF engages with these stakeholders to develop and promote standards and good practices for social performance management (SPM), in an effort to make financial services safer and more beneficial for clients." (https://sptf.info/)

- Social Value International (SVI) is a membership organization whose "members share a common goal: to change the way society accounts for value. Our pioneering community contains members from over 45 countries, drawn from a huge range of different sectors and disciplines. We work with our members to embed core principles for social value measurement and analysis, to refine and share practice, and to build a powerful movement of like-minded people to influence policy." SVI has roughly 1000 members, 20 country-specific networks that organize trainings and meetings, and hosts an annual global conference. (http://socialvalueint.org/)

- Toniic serves "individuals, family offices, foundations and funds. We increase the velocity of money and services into impact investing to address global challenges. Our members commit to discover, evaluate, nurture and invest in financial products—in all asset classes—that promote a just and sustainable economy. Through the 100%IMPACT members of Toniic, we share portfolios and learn, together, how to best align financial assets with personal values." (http://www.toniic.com/)

Databases of Impact (and Outcome, Output and Activity) Indicators

- IRIS is a free catalog of performance metrics for tracking social and environmental impact of investments. *It* is managed by the Global Impact Investing Network (GIIN). (https://iris.thegiin.org/)

- Global Value Exchange is a free, crowdsourced database of Values, Outcomes, Indicators and Stakeholders. It provides a free platform for information to be shared enabling greater consistency and transparency in measuring social & environmental values. (http://www.globalvalueexchange.org/)

Reports, Books and Articles of Interest

Ruff, K., and Olsen, S. (2015) "The Next Frontier in Impact Measurement Isn't Measurement at All," *Stanford Social Innovation Review.* https://ssir.org/articles/entry/the_next_frontier_in_social_impact_measurement_isnt_measurement_at_all.

Hehenberger, L., Harling, A., and Scholten, P. (2015). *A practical guide to measuring and managing impact.* http://evpa.eu.com/publication/guide-measuring-and-managing-impact-2015/.

Nicholls, J., Lawlor, E., Neitzert, E., and Goodspeed, T. (2012). *A guide to social return on investment.* The definitive guide on how to do social return on investment analysis. http://www.socialvalueuk.org/resources/sroi-guide/

Olsen, S., Kemp, C., and Betancourt, A. (2017) *The pulse of impact management,* SVT Group and the Middlebury Institute at Monterey Center for Social Impact Learning. A "cliff's notes" on impact due diligence, ongoing monitoring and reporting practices among impact investors with a link to 250+ supporting papers and resources. http://miis.edu/academics/researchcenters/social-impact/research.

So, I., & Staskevicius, A. (2015). *Measuring the "impact" in impact investing.* A guide to the combination of measurement approaches seen among impact investing firms known for their commitment to measuring impact. http://www.hbs.edu/socialenterprise/Documents/MeasuringImpact.pdf.

Social Impact Investment Taskforce of the G8. (2014). *Allocating for impact: subject paper of the Asset Allocation Working Group.* A landmark report on impact investing. http://www.social-impactinvestment.org/reports/Asset Allocation WG paper FINAL.pdf.

Social Impact Investment Taskforce of the G8. (2014). *Measuring impact: subject paper of the Impact Measurement Working Group.*

A landmark report on good impact measurement practices within investing. http://www.socialimpactinvestment.org/ reports/Measuring Impact WG paper FINAL.pdf.

Toniic Institute. (2012). *Toniic e-guide to impact measurement.* A practical guide for impact investors and their advisors, with information about use of IRIS and GIIRS. http://www. toniic.com/wp-content/uploads/2011/12/Toniic-E-Guide-to-Impact-Measurement.pdf.

The Impact Management Project (2017): various publications and a glossary that seek to define the emerging conventions governing terms and practices in impact investing and impact measurement within it. http://www.impactmanagementpro-ject.com/.

Twitter Feeds Worth Following

- @meansandrew founder of data analysts for social good, the impact lab. Observer and shaper of trends in data science for impact, impact management and accountability
- @ImpactAlpha news on the industry
- @trisml comments on tech, data & evidence "tools for trans-formation, but we need collective action to make them work." Director of Innovation & Development at NPC in United Kingdom
- @svtgroup news and insights about the impact management industry and wider ecosystem

I would like to acknowledge GRI, SVI, B lab, IRIS and their progeni-tors and champions for helping turning some lights on in a previously pretty dark room, and Kate Ruff, David Pritchard, Michael Harnar, SVT Group, AEA and SVI for the early version of the skilled impact analysts' framework described here.

Notes

1 For example, Mozaffar Khan, George Serafeim and Aaron Yoon, "Corporate Sustainability: First Evidence on Materiality," *The Accounting Review*, Vol. 91, No. 6, (2016), pp. 1697–1724, http://aaajournals.org/doi/abs/10.2308/accr-51383?code=aaan-site; "Sustainable Investing and Bond Returns. Research

Study into the Impact of ESG on Credit Portfolio Performance," (Barclays Bank, October 30, 2016) https://www.investmentbank.barclays.com/our-insights/esg-sustainable-investing-and-bond-returns.html; "Measuring the Impact of Economic Short-Termism," (McKinsey Global Institute, February 15, 2017), http://www.shiftto.org/download/309056/measuringtheeconomicimpactofshortermismmckinsey2017.pdf.

2 B Lab currently has the closest thing to this with a database of about 1,800 (as of Q1 2017) verified company scores, which it makes freely available, but the associated financial performance data is confidential.

3 For example, in 2017 The Impact Management Project facilitated the documenting of a series of current norms and a glossary of commonly misunderstood terms in impact investing, and in 2008 Impact Reporting and Investing Standards (IRIS) was launched to provide standard definitions for ESG indicators frequently seen in impact investing. See impactmanagementproject.com and https://iris.thegiin.org/.

4 For more details on how impact is considered within the three latter of these stages see Sara Olsen, Aislinn Betancourt, and Courtney Kemp **"The Pulse of Impact Management: Current Uses of and Trends in Social and Environmental Impact Measurement in Investing," (SVT Group and the Middlebury Institute Center for Social Impact Learning, 2017)** and Ivy So and Alina Staskevicious, "Measuring the Impact in Impact Investing" (Harvard Business School, 2015).

5 It is possible to do impact measurement and reporting that is integrated across both alternative investments and public equities. The International Integrated Reporting Framework provides guidance as to what this looks like as far as company-facing reporting goes. One clue is that the impact map discussed in this chapter is also at the center of Integrated Reporting. See https://integratedreporting.org/.

6 Social Impact Investment Taskforce of the G8, *Measuring Impact: Subject Paper of the Impact Measurement Working Group. A Landmark Report on Good Impact Measurement Practices Within Investing,* 2014. For more relevant definitions see also the Impact Management Glossary, http://www.impactmanagementproject.com/glossaries/.

7 Although the G8's Social Investment Task Force glosses over additionality in its diagram of impact, referring instead to impact as a long-term, sustained outcome regardless of whether it was caused by the investment activities in question, the elements of additionality are included in the definition of impact in the report's glossary. See *Measuring Impact,* 6, 27.

8 B Lab B Impact Assessment for B Corp Certification, http://bimpactassessment.net/; B Lab Global Impact Investment Rating System (GIIRS), http://b-analytics.net/giirs-funds; Global Reporting Initiative (GRI) G4 Framework, https://www.globalreporting.org/information/g4/Pages/default.aspx; Sustainability Accounting Standards Board (SASB) Standards, https://www.sasb.org/.

9 Fast Company, "A Public Company Has Finally Become a B Corp," December 23, 2014. https://www.fastcompany.com/3040158/a-public-company-has-finally-become-a-b-corp

10 See: International Integrated Reporting Council (IIRC) integratedreporting. org/, Natural Capital Coalition (NCC) naturalcapitalcoalition.org/, Social Value International (SVI) socialvalueint.org, Acumen Fund: Lean Data Initiative http://acumen.org/ideas/lean-data/.

11 The randomized control trial (RCT), often referred to as the gold standard for impact assessment, is a type of experimental design study in which "an intervention is investigated by comparing one group of people who receive the intervention with a control group who do not. The control group receives the usual or no treatment, and their outcome, or the change in measure from the starting point or baseline, is compared with that of the intervention group." Individuals are randomly assigned to either the treatment or control group. In those cases where individuals are not randomly assigned the same structure is called "quasi-experimental design." RCTs are one expression of the scientific research method, also known as experimental method, where there is both a subject and a control group, and you look to see what happens to both in order to assess how the intervention worked.

12 The Guardian. "Will Unilever Become the World's Largest Publicly Traded B Corp?" Published January 23, 2015, Accessed July 12, 2017. https://www.theguardian.com/sustainable-business/2015/jan/23/benefit-corporations-bcorps-business-social-responsibility.

13 For example Good World Solutions and Mobile Metrix are organizations devoted to using mobile and SMS technology to collect information about stakeholder experiences. See goodworldsolutions.org/ and www.mobilemetrix.org/.

14 Acumen Fund and Root Capital, "Innovations in Impact Measurement: Lessons using mobile technology from Acumen's Lean Data Initiative and Root Capital's Client-Centric Mobile Measurement," Published 2015, http://acumen.org/wp-content/uploads/2015/11/Innovations-in-Impact-Measurement-Report.pdf

15 What to include is decided using the principle of "materiality," generally defined in the impact measurement context as change that is considered important by any key stakeholders, not just shareholders.

16 Kate Ruff, "The Role of Intermediaries in Social Accounting: Insights from effective transparency systems" in *Accounting for Social Value*, edited by Laurie Mook. (University of Toronto Press, 2013). And Kate Ruff and Sara Olsen, "The Next Frontier in Impact Measurement Isn't Measurement at All," *Stanford Social Innovation Review*, 2015. https://ssir.org/articles/entry/the_next_frontier_in_social_impact_measurement_isnt_measurement_at_all.

9

Communicating Impact: Frameworks for Messaging

Amy Hartzler

The field of impact investing represents a new frontier of language and understanding about simple and yet very complex issues. This can be inspiring, provocative, hopeful and disorienting, all at once. This chapter is for people investing in impact and those receiving impact investments. If you're investing for impact, it's important to understand key challenges of *communicating* impact. And if you're creating impact, you want to understand how to demonstrate and communicate the good work you've done.

The following pages offer some guiding questions and tested messaging, intended to assist you as you navigate the communications you receive and create. What follows is hardly comprehensive of the inspiring amount of activity in this space, past and present; and there are many new voices, as people seek greater impact and broader reach.

This chapter doesn't offer quick communications fixes to every challenge (especially ones tied to business model, leadership or culture). It does offer the reader:

- Data to better understand a field with limited research;
- Questions to reflect upon, as you consider where to invest, give and why; and
- Tactical insights and themes that have resonated with others on the impact investing journey.

Some grounding reflections, to consider and challenge:

- Impact investing is emergent, and yet part of a long tradition. While it's been called different names over the years—program related investments, mission-related investments, socially responsible investing, and so on—impact investing is largely new in the retail marketplace and to many in the mainstream. This chapter offers ways to hack or adapt existing ideas and language to create shared meaning for the various practices represented by the term "impact investing."

- The first step in communicating about impact investing is knowing the impact you seek; then, identifying ways to achieve it; and then, evaluating and reporting the impact you have.

- Not all aspects of impact investing are positive or will create the future you want. There's no single approach to measure impact and people have a range of priorities and audiences. What does impact investing mean to you? Is it generative, or—perhaps—destructive? What do you want to create, build, scale? Who are your partners? Communicating impact takes many forms.

- People with wealth often have strong counsel to guide financial decisions. Many mainstream retail investors do not; and most do not encounter basic financial literacy curriculum, much less learn about investing. In addition, the financial services industry is not well trusted or liked by many mainstream investors. No disrespect to the thousands of good people in the field; many people on "Main Street" have had, directly or indirectly, negative experiences with the investment and wealth management industries. These experiences represent barriers to communication, and raise issues for those who seek to communicate positive impact.

- Many younger people do not assume the stock market should be part of a wealthbuilding strategy, having seen it crash. They are also keenly aware, they will be left to manage the planet we have created. Any way you approach it, communicating about investing with millennials must speak to impact, responsible wealth management and tangible, positive opportunities for change.

- There are more ways than ever for people to directly invest, lend and save in alignment with their values; from banking locally and crowdfunding, to Goldman Sachs promoting impact investing on its homepage. The volume of noise and lack of shared language is overwhelming and can be confusing to those entering the discussion for the first time.
- In uncertain times stability matters, which many impact investments can plausibly promise. Fidelity's homepage includes a "Tips for Volatility" tool so investors can better self-navigate increasingly bumpy waters. Impact investing through trusted channels can offer a solid track record of repayment with interest. Messaging regarding impact investing can reflect that.
- Access to security and wealth is not equal. People of different races and backgrounds do not have the same access to the same opportunities. What we choose to do with our capital—whether we have a little or a lot—will determine the future for our families, communities and planet, and the degree of equity and justice we share across the globe.
- In the United States, total charitable giving is a penny on the dollar for all of the investable wealth available.[1] Philanthropy can and should function as social risk capital; yet, on its own, it will never address the scale of shared challenges we face, which require substantial investment capital to offset growing need.
- There is no single impact investing template; this work is messy. As you explore, new questions will emerge. Finding trusted guides and translators is key.
- This chapter does not provide focused guidance on communications distribution. Insights about platforms and channels are woven into stories and case studies, where relevant.

It's my intention that the following pages offer useful nuggets to help you navigate your journey through the dynamic landscape involving communications, money and impact. If I've done my part, I've represented the brilliance shared by beautiful, creative and passionate people doing this hard work, by exploring:

1. Context: Our Noisy, Unappealing Landscape
2. Audience: "Psychographic" Characters + Communications Insights by Role

3. Values + Messaging Themes: Case Studies + Qualitative Insights about Impact Investing-Related Language

On with the translation ...

Our Brain + Our Money

Does your brain immediately try to shut down and move along when you're exposed to a financial message? If you work in financial services, do eyes glaze over when you start to explain what you do?

It's not just you. It's the way we have wired ourselves to think.

Scientists have proven it: fMRI scans documented brain activity, showing when we are confronted by an emotional plea to our better angels, and a call for a donation, the happy parts of our brain light up.[2] When we complete a donation the happy parts of our brains light up even brighter as dopamine is released. And when we are confronted by other messages about our money, or the idea of a delayed reward—greater financial "returns" if we don't indulge in immediate spending, or giving—totally different parts of our brain light up.[3] Which is to say, the happy parts power down. It doesn't matter how clever, true or beautifully executed a message about investing might be. Many of us would literally prefer to think of anything else.

Where we mix up communications that trigger all of the happiness we get from giving our money away, alongside the real promise of financial and social returns possible from impact investing, this is where it gets "professionally fascinating and societally important," as a fellow writer noted.

The Context for Receiving and Creating Communications

Our Worlds Are Very Noisy

The average person sees 3,000–20,000 marketing messages a day. One of our most evolved skills, as humans, involves split-second identification of what to delete or ignore. If you're reading this book, you likely receive a disproportionate number of marketing materials about money. From financial firms selling their products, to neighbors, cousins and causes advocating for children, wildlife, water and soil health, this barrage of appeals is a unique burden of privilege. Breaking through and creating a meaningful connection in this context is not easy.

The first and best thing we can do, always, is to ground communications in universal human values. Signal clearly what you are about and then back that up. If there isn't a connection on a personal, emotional level, a dialogue will never start, much less an investing relationship.

Questions to consider:

1. What marketing materials do you give a second glance, or a proper read?
2. What about those communications made you pause and helped make a connection?
3. What voices and channels do you trust and prioritize?

Ordinary Investors Are Waking Up

People have more options than ever to be mindful with money:

- From a general increase in products for the conscious consumer;
- to the rapid growth in partially automated wealth management platforms, such as Betterment, Personal Capital and Wealthfront;
- to the continued mainstreaming of crowdfunding through channels like KickStarter, WeFunder and GoFundMe;
- to resources like the Divestment Guide[4] for moving money out of fossil fuel investments;
- or even more unique products such as CNote[5] (2017 FinTech Innovation award winner at SXSW[6]), a high-yield, low-risk savings product through Community Development Finance

Institutions (CDFIs), offering a projected 2.5 percent return with no fees and flexible liquidity;

and that's not even considering the many funds intentionally generating social and financial returns or the broader economic contribution of CDFIs.

There are so many options. And for many, it's overwhelming.

People are also beginning to realize democracy and capitalism are uneasy mates, and that "voting with your dollars" can, in some ways, mean more than an actual vote as a citizen. For example, $5.42 trillion from 742 institutions and 58,000 individuals has been committed to divest from fossil fuels.[7] Campaigns such as DeFund DAPL,[8] which over just a few months sparked divestment of $4.4 billion from banks funding the Dakota Access Pipeline, helped create awareness that passive savings accounts represent bank investments and may be the object of conscious consumption decisions. Elections, particularly in the United States, continue to reflect the influence of large corporations, financial entities and high net worth individuals who can donate unlimited, undisclosed amounts.

In response to all this and more, many are actively seeking ways to integrate their personal beliefs with how wealth is created and sustained, and how to make our shared systems work for us, not against us. Many individuals are educating themselves to be smarter investors—of course, if you're reading this book, you're one of them. If you're a millennial in particular, skeptical of the market and heavily courted by financial institutions, platforms and brands, you've no doubt taught yourself to evaluate dozens of approachable websites, apps and ads, and made some decisions, more or less independently.

A new generation of financial advisors is emerging—and many more are needed—as existing advisors adapt to harder questions regarding the social and environmental impacts of investing, which don't always have clear or easy answers. We are living between worlds, and shared languages, as old models break down. We can choose positive impact as we invest in, and communicate about, the future we want to build and create.

Ground Rules for Communicating Impact

1. Emotional and Rational Connection Matters

As we satisfy our head's desire for things to "make sense"—from the legitimacy of financial offerings to stability of returns—our hearts seek deeper meaning from our dollars. How do we use words and images to help us see that our money can serve our desire, to be a better version of ourselves, and contribute to the world in a tangible, meaningful way? Before we can move into mechanics—what and how social impact investing works—we must connect with why it matters.

The job of communicators and storytellers is to capture the imagination and strike an emotional chord, through heart-based content, followed by head-based information that satisfies the rational questions that immediately surface. Marketing impact investing is not only about making the business case, conveying positive, quantifiable, tangible results alongside financial returns. And it's not only about heartwarming stories of hard-working entrepreneurs, sleeves rolled up and ready to scale, for example; or even the powerful, concrete ways that many lives have been improved, from more affordable, quality homes to better per-forming schools, or more consistent access to healthcare, and nourishing foods. It's not about selling data and numbers; or stories and people. It's about all of those things, back and forth, over and over.

A predictable series of rational questions emerge, once people are emotionally intrigued by impact investing:

- Where does the money go? Why this instead of that?
- Who decides where the money is invested?
- If money is going to a nonprofit organization (common in impact investing) how do I earn returns? How can I make money on lending to "nonprofits"?
- Who's making money on my money?

Satisfying both curiosity and concern leads to conversion.

2. Show and Tell, Over and Over

When you create or review an impact report, key facts and concepts should speak clearly to the outcomes that have been achieved, not what someone proposes to do—action speak louder than words. This means, of course, you have to measure or otherwise assess your impact. Metrics, monitoring and evaluation are the lifeblood of effective communications—and a whole different book— and also covered in more depth in this volume by Sara Olsen in Chapter Eight. This chapter presumes that, if you are marketing impact investing, you are measuring your positive impact, ideally in a way your audience values.

The AFL-CIO Housing Investment Trust leverages its $5.85 billion in net assets to create quality jobs and affordable housing—81,000 union jobs and 120,000 affordable housing units, specifically. The Trust is an open-end, commingled invest- ment company, commonly called a mutual fund. Its portfolio is internally managed and consists primarily of high credit quality fixed-income securities, and has a history of nearly 50 years of socially responsible investing, putting union capital to work finan- cing housing and creating union jobs nationwide. While the hous- ing industry has struggled to meet the needs of residents across the country, and at a time when quality jobs are in short supply, the results achieved by this unique structure are impressive.

As we emphasize concrete, tangible outcomes of impact invest- ing, and identify and share stories, we have to also remember that for most strategies volume does matter. Think of how many finan- cial services messages have shaped our (largely negative, optimally neutral) reactions, over years. It will take many impressions to un- do that programming and create new pathways of understanding positive impact.

It's also important to remember people will not see every sin- gle communication you produce. You will tire of your messaging long before your audience does. It is vital to show and tell, and engage the heart and the head, over and over.

3. Values-based Communications Transcend

As we mine messages and content around us for meaning, we have a natural, and at times an extreme, affinity for brands that share our personal values. We see engagement with some brands as a way of being more of who we want to be. Clearly signaling what you believe in and the future you want to build will draw more customers and clients to you, and create more loyalty, as you share the results of your work over time. In this way, values-based communications transcend the distance between communicator and audience.

Audience: Human First, Role Second

Most marketers start in the same place: The Audience. Specifically, many will imagine a matrix of boxes for neat talking points, sliced and diced by demographic and role. There are nuances to the way we see, hear and say things, grounded in experience: what and who we have encountered, in life and work; our fluency and comfort in multiple languages, including finance. The following section offers "psychographic" categories for audiences, in addition to messaging insights and tactics by traditional demographics and role. Understanding how the audience is constructed and the types of members may help ground thinking and language in human, universal values that transcend background and bank account size, in addition to considering the functional, transactional needs of specific individuals.

These psychographic profiles help us understand our own role in impact investing; and help those communicating to better understand exactly who they are trying to reach.

Considering Four "Psychographics"

Pragmatic Altruist: an individual wanting to do well and do good

Systems Weaver: someone considering collective assets across sectors, regions

Radical Seeker: an advanced financial activist integrating and aligning total portfolio

The Indifferent: the majority who don't have significant wealth, interest or time

	Risk tolerance	Tangible outcomes	Desired engagement	Financial fluency	Barriers to impact investing
Pragmatic Altruist	Low	Yes	Meh	Medium	Exposure, Many Priorities, Time
Systems Weaver	Low	Yes	Yes please	Low–High	Creative Partners, Time, Regulation
Radical Seeker	High	Maybe	Yes please	Range	Deal flow, Access, Time
The Indifferent	Range	Range	No thanks	Range	Exposure, Easy On-ramps

Questions to consider:

- Which of these categories best describes you as an impact investor?
- How does that affect the way you receive and act on opportunities to activate wealth?
- If you're with an investment group and create communications, which stories are you telling and to what audience(s)?

Let's Meet These Characters ...

The Pragmatic Altruist has always tried to do good things with his money, taking some pride in thoughtful philanthropic activity, in particular. He cares about a number of issues—homelessness and affordable housing, education and animal rights, among others. He gives frequently and often; and so, receives many solicitations. He and his wife prioritize a few major galas and events each year. He is active in his faith community.

Most Pragmatic Altruists first consider impact investing by redirecting philanthropic capital, for example, moving existing donor advised fund (DAF) dollars into fixed-income investment vehicles, targeted to creating positive change in an area of particular interest, such as microfinance or affordable housing. In this sense, impact investing is a "no-brainer": it is a smart place to park and preserve capital, knowing that some good will come from it, along with some returns.

The Pragmatic Altruist does not live in the "weeds" of impact investing, or philanthropy. His good intentions can be tripped up by blind spots. A tendency to analyze, itself the result of privilege, can delay the process of ideas and conversation turning into concrete, mutually beneficial action.

Questions for the Pragmatic Altruist:

1. What do you need to know, to do the most good with your wealth?
2. What kind of counsel do you need?
3. How involved do you want to be in your venture philanthropy and investing?

4. When you look back, what kind of change do you want to have made?

The Systems Weaver considers the big picture. She surveys collective assets—existing pools of capital in an ecosystem—including city budgets, pension funds, bonds, even savings accounts; along with the procurement power of anchor institutions, like hospitals and schools; along with venture philanthropy and investment dollars; along with federal and local incentives.

The Systems Weaver takes it all in, to inform decisive, experimental action. She listens to trusted and new voices. In shifting landscapes, where federal and municipal funding flows become less predictable, she is constantly scanning the horizon for that missing puzzle piece to help things click into place. She operates by instinct at times, always checked, challenged and inspired by data. System Weavers are the people you'll find as the heads of CDFIs (see box below), and at community foundations. They may be working in local, state or federal government; or leading academic or healthcare institutions. They naturally think across systems and sectors, identifying and shaping opportunities for collaboration.

A social entrepreneur is a Systems Weaver by default, since she assumes it is possible to redirect rather than fight market forces to solve chronic social challenges, and seeks to align a constellation of skills with a business model that addresses an underserved market.

Expert weaver Robert Egger, founder of D.C. Central Kitchen and now L.A. Kitchen, has built two nonprofits that are quality job creators for people with barriers to employment. Egger looked at collective assets and activity: every year we throw away 40 percent of what we grow—$150 billion of "waste." His organizations use diverted produce—maybe bruised or very-ripe produce—to create affordable, healthy meals for people with limitations to mobility or income; and good jobs, along the way.

The ways the Systems Weaver engages with social impact investing may include things like designing a "pay for success" program with city government, local philanthropy and the private sector, aligned to create better health or education outcomes for children. A Systems Weaver would be the person at a credit union who sees ways to leverage tax credits and federal small business incentives with a trusted data source, to streamline recruiting for affordable lending dealflow.

The work of a Systems Weaver is complex, dynamic, difficult and sometimes, very fun.

Questions for the Systems Weaver include:

1. Where do you seek the greatest positive impact?
2. Where are possible, if unlikely allies?
3. How do you manage your own energy and prioritize your health, working on long-term, difficult issues?

The CDFI "Communications Problem"

You may well be thinking, what's a CDFI? You're in good company.

CDFIs[9] are community development finance institutions—nonprofit financial institutions long active as responsible stewards of capital, providing credit and investment in communities that are underserved by traditional financial institutions. In addition to a successful track record of leading and participating in large-scale project finance opportunities (including multi-family affordable housing projects, health care centers and schools) over time, CDFIs have grown their capacity as direct small business lenders. By leveraging credit enhancements and federal programs as well as their expertise as "boots on the ground" community lenders, many CDFIs have demonstrated their ability to lend to small businesses that have not been able to secure growth capital.

The fact that this layer of economic infrastructure is largely unknown to its target audiences is, in a real way, "a communications problem" as one Systems Weaver put it. A *Fast Company* writer covering "innovation in community development" had never heard of CDFIs—to be expected for mainstream investors, but a surprise for someone assigned to cover the field. Small and local business owners who need access to capital, and ways to build equity, often have no idea that there is a public/private, nonprofit financial institution, potentially in their own neighborhood, whose mission is aligned with community and business needs. While there are different perspectives about why this is the case, it is more critical, for the sake of positive impact, to address its reality.

There is a robust and growing market of small businesses operating in low- and moderate-income communities, many of which are a great fit for financing and supportive services offered by CDFIs. A recent report from the Association for Economic Opportunity (AEO) noted more than two million small businesses in low-income communities seek credit each year.[10] Unfortunately, CDFIs are only reaching a very small portion of this market (less than 1 percent in 2015), which may contribute in part to many small businesses paying extreme premiums or being unable to secure financing of any kind.[11]

Community Reinvestment Fund, USA (CRF) has been building a core set of tools and strategies that will facilitate increased brand awareness, reach and access for a coordinated national network of mission-driven business lenders. CRF believes that CDFI business lenders must "collaborate to compete," capitalizing on the value added through lower cost financing, flexible underwriting and repayment terms, access to wrap-around small business support services, and complementary/noncompetitive position relative to mainstream financial institutions.

CRF has developed an online marketplace known as Connect2Capital, which helps unbanked and/or underbanked small businesses find responsible sources of capital and advisory services, while reducing customer acquisition costs for mission-driven lenders and service providers. The solution is modeled after the simple, user-friendly prequalification process that has been widely adopted by online lenders. The Connect2Capital Marketplace functions as "connective tissue" to unify the network of responsible lenders by allowing them to establish eligibility parameters for each of their products, which can be matched to incoming financing requests. A small business owner who fills out the prequalification form will immediately be presented with a set of products and services that are available to them based on the eligibility criteria of the network of lending partners.

Oscar Abello, an economist and journalist, noted the rapid increase in individuals and institutions—entire cities, from Seattle and St. Paul to Raleigh—that are actively seeking new banking and investing solutions, and looking for local, values-aligned resources. "In the U.S. there are 5,800 banks. 5,400 of them are technically 'community banks'; it's bewildering." He shared his own method for narrowing down his local bank, in New York. "There are 298 CDFI credit unions that meet several layers of verification in terms of commitment to community." As a financial consumer, and critical analyst, he is more persuaded by a focus on place and local leaders, and knowing that's what his fees are supporting, rather than seeing his bank advertise in magazines or on the side of a bus, for example.

"CDFIs put every dollar into relationship building with my neighbors and local businesses, and that's the best possible use of my money," Abello added, noting "every time you swipe your card—or make any transaction, even online—someone gets a cut, up to 3%. Why not have your funds and your transaction fees all directed to positive, local impact you can see?"

CDFIs have played a critical role in any U.S.-based strategy for community and economic development. That they have remained unknown for so long, by so many, is something that can be addressed in part through effective communications.

Time to meet our **Radical Seeker**.

The Radical Seeker insists and knows money can be a force for good. She also knows the system is rigged. She is (nearly) tireless in researching, educating and trying to always make better decisions, about how she engages in the world, financially. Radical Seekers are not as concerned with the past as building and visioning the future. They are not tinkering with broken models; to paraphrase Buckminster Fuller, Radical Seekers are investing in emergent models, that make the old ones obsolete.

Peter Buffett stepped into a public Radical Seeker role with his provocative *New York Times* op-ed "The Charitable-Industrial Complex," challenging his peers to ask harder questions when they consider their philanthropic and investment priorities:

> *Money should be spent trying out concepts that shatter current structures and systems that have turned much of the world into one vast market. Is progress really Wi-Fi on every street corner? No. It's when no 13-year-old girl on the planet gets sold for sex. But as long as most folks are patting themselves on the back for charitable acts, we've got a perpetual poverty machine.*

President of the Heron Foundation, Clara Miller, also a Radical Seeker, noted in her manifesto, "The World Has Changed and So Must We," that "in much of American philanthropy and social policy, the old narrative and its familiar assumptions linger on, sometimes questioned but rarely departed from."[12] Miller's leadership has inspired other foundations to revisit their strategies, as her own foundation fundamentally altered their strategy "to focus primarily on investing in enterprises that create reliable income streams for people striving to get out of poverty" as well as "organizations that shifted the metrics of the economy as a whole, by measuring the positive and negative social impacts of enterprises of all sizes and kinds, as well as by providing data standards and comparability for like-minded investors and managers." With a change of strategy came a change to Heron as an enterprise: they "removed the division between the investing and the giving operations (traditional in virtually all private foundations), creating a 'team of the whole' to deploy all of Heron's capital in concert for mission."

Jessica Norwood is a Radical Seeker of a different sort: this Alabama-based entrepreneur isn't just trying to make her own business work—she's making sure all black entrepreneurs have access to capital, and can build equity. The Runway Project provides affordable, patient capital in place of the "friends and family" funds that many white entrepreneurs are able to raise from their networks to launch their ventures. "We can't start our businesses by leaning on friends and family, when black families in the U.S. have an average of $11,000 in assets, and the average white family has $141,000." The Runway Project uses a known, "safe" financial vehicle, currently a Certificate of Deposit, to aggregate passive capital—nondirected assets, even modest savings accounts—and then deploys capital through partners, to help create the pipeline of leaders and entrepreneurs of color that so many investors want to resource. An active pilot in Oakland, CA aggregated $500,000 in the first 48 hours.

"We need to question what we mean by 'investing' when the ability of people to participate in the economy is fundamentally challenged," offered another Radical Seeker, Alfa Demmellash. As CEO of Rising Tide Capital in Jersey City, Alfa is building a model for high-quality entrepreneurial development services that can be locally adopted in low-income communities, and used as a catalyst for economic and social empowerment. "Strengthening people where they are, resourcing their ability to access opportunity and create the future, should be the primary concern of investors and community builders. We can no longer expect unfettered economic growth, up and out; we have to go deeper into place."

And, in many ways, it doesn't get more radical than Leslie Christian: from guiding the futures markets on Wall Street in the 1980s, to challenging the very concept of investing as inherently unequal today, Leslie has been a visionary woman leader in a man's world, for decades. Throughout her career, and in her current work as an advisor for Northstar Asset Management, Leslie has carved her own path where one didn't exist. Today that includes advising some of her clients to pursue zero-interest or even negative returns on some investments, as she helps to align capital and values.

Leslie is a Radical Seeker who questions every assumption, starting with the premise that investing is a good thing. "When

I was beginning my career, I saw the financial world as an exciting and worthwhile place to focus as a feminist who wanted to make a mark in business. And I was intellectually fascinated by all of it—especially the bond markets. I hadn't fully internalized the underlying assumptions and implications of our capitalist system. I've come to realize that investing to accumulate wealth inherently perpetuates inequality. The rich get richer; the poor fall behind; the gap widens. If we take 'impact investing' seriously, as a total commitment to values, we have to question the 'laws' of investing; this means sharing financial returns with all who have contributed rather than expecting that investors should receive priority." When asked about trends, Leslie offered that she sees "more women who are questioning the idea of wealth accumulation and seeing it more as hoarding piles of money. They want to see their money circulating, and they are exceedingly generous with time, energy and funds."

Questions for the Radical Seeker:

1. What kind of language inspires greater alignment of capital with values?
2. Would you consider a zero or negative return on a deal you believed in?
3. Would you be willing to directly, personally negotiate loan terms with a borrower of your impact investment capital?

The last character in our psychographic landscape represents the many versions of **The Indifferent.** The Indifferent can be an individual, an intermediary or an institution. The Indifferent includes the average person who holds some assets in a retirement account or pension fund, and has never investigated where her investments are made. She gets a quarterly statement on an account set up years ago, and sees numbers go up, sometimes down, and doesn't pay much attention.

The Indifferent can also include the financial advisor or associate who works for a large services firm, punching the clock and making a living; and who has significant influence, making recommendations and implementing client decisions. The Indifferent may oversee sizable assets, and be happy to guide clients to alternatives that align with their values, if alternatives are easy to explain and execute.

Michael Vitali, a writer with significant experience in traditional financial services, philanthropy and impact investing, reflected on when he was brought in to support a $1 billion capital campaign that had stalled at $700 million. A compelling, personality-driven website with top-notch photography and video content, along with gorgeous print materials, weren't connecting with philanthropists, as time passed.

After reviewing the fundraising process with campaign executives, the first thing Michael did was reorient the communications beyond the philanthropist to include his or her advisors and family influencers. He retro-engineered what amounted to an educational and frictionless process for financial advisors to direct any category of philanthropic assets to the capital campaign, without jeopardizing their control of the client relationship. A series of documents later—offering clearer terms and outlining simple steps in the process, including the technical, financial steps involved—and suddenly the campaign was on its way to adding another $900 million to its goal, topping out at $1.6 billion raised.

Sometimes the best communications solutions are unsexy hacks to streamline a new process, to make it as clear and easy as possible, for people to choose a different option. At the same time, people like Deborah Frieze of Boston Impact Initiative notes, where social impact investing is pitching to the Indifferent, it often "fails to challenge our views about how capital accumulates inequitably in our current financial system." What is the role of communicators, to help expose structural inequality, and offer a path of meaningful inquiry for the Indifferent?

Audience: Theory of Change

If you're creating, measuring and communicating about positive impact, you're operating from some theory of change. Which audience is critical to your strategy? How do you engage and activate them? Communications should flow strategically, and intuitively, from your goals and priorities. Some theories of change in a particular impact portfolio might mean targeting the Indifferent as the biggest opportunity to bring in investors. After all, if they don't really care, in some ways it doesn't matter where investments go. If you want to connect with the Indifferent, you need a compelling answer to the question, what's in it for them? And, it should be very easy and clear, how to take action.

Other theories of change might focus on accelerating the positive impact of a smaller number of highly motivated individuals. Identifying communities of Radical Seekers, and creating meaningful dialogue with them, looks and sounds very different than a mainstream call to Indifferent masses.

And still other theories of change, when designing for impact outcomes, may rely on Systems Weavers, to engage multiple capital streams across sectors. Or an investment initiative might primarily target Pragmatic Altruists, already primed for giving, drawn by the idea of modest earning.

Each of these offers different opportunities, and needs, for communication and connection.

A Millennial Global Perspective

Katharine Tengtio, marketing officer at Calvert Foundation by way of the Cherie Blair Foundation and the London School of Economics, is an efficient, passionate communicator. From her experience in philanthropy, fundraising from high net worth individuals, and now in impact investing, she sees similarities and distinctions, among global markets.

One thing is the same: many impact investors and most philanthropists want scale. Katharine offered, "Most people are less interested in the emotional story about a single person. They want to hear about how big their positive impact can be—how much positive change their money can achieve—the bigger the numbers, the better. There is a focus on outcomes based on quantity over quality."

Money is similarly taboo in most cultures, an inherent barrier to communication: "Brits generally avoid talking about how they invest their money. They are very private people." Beyond that, impact investing and philanthropic activity isn't as intuitive to people who, for example, are shaped by the availability of social systems, like healthcare, education and affordable housing. Government-subsidized services shift perspective on whose responsibility it is to provide support for the underserved. In the United States where there is a greater focus on the separation of state and society, there is an emphasis on the role of the private sector and its responsibility toward charitable giving in general.

The United States seems poised to deliver on the promise to mainstream positive impact investing, if inclined, in part because it "fundamentally aligns with our core values. As much as the U.S. talks about a separation between church and state, the culture is shaped by Christian values, and caring for neighbors. The idea of the American Dream—that everyone has and deserves a chance—is very different than other parts of the world. In the U.S. we champion the idea of opportunity and being able to build yourself from the ground up, which isn't necessarily the same in other cultures, which may focus more on a person's allotted place in the world, and less about social mobility out of it."

In the end, impact investing is similar between the United States and the United Kingdom in that it's still "very niche," as Kat put it. For this idea to really grow, new audiences need to be reached. One way she works to do that is through a particularly challenging aspect of impact investing communications: efficient, meaningful digital content.

For marketers seeking new audiences, limited data show that, "unless you're already thinking about it, 'impact investing' doesn't lend itself to tweeting or Snapchat [158 million daily users Q4 2016], where new and younger audiences can be found. These are complex ideas with endless nuance; if you're lucky you might capture a few seconds of attention. Beyond that, when it comes to doing good, a lot of younger people prefer to take part in an action and have an experience, like volunteering at a soup kitchen, than make a financial transaction." As context shifts, it is important to challenge assumptions about what audiences want, and continue to experiment with messaging and actions.

"What excites me is the growing interest, particularly among my generation. Although it's still not very 'mainstream,' if you look at the trends among business schools worldwide, impact investing is a growing hot topic, and more top MBA programs are focusing on providing more courses, professors, and events on impact investing for their students. This shows a lot of promise for what is to come!"

Audience: Insights by Demographics

Now that we've considered some of the themes that unite audiences across demographics, we'll take a deeper dive into some insights and data about communications targeting specific communities. We will explore Communications Insights in the following areas:

A. Generational
B. Heritage, Identity and Race
C. Place-based and Local Investing
D. Financial Advisor
E. Impact Investor
F. Philanthropist
G. Impact Investment Lender
H. Impact Investment Partner

Let's look at each of these in turn ...

A. Generational

From younger potential investors to those who have been saving and directing funds for decades, there are some unique trends and considerations to reach different age groups. One marketing experiment targeted millennials, through the robust media platform Upworthy, which had emerged as a reliable source for viral video content that would inspire, outrage and activate approximately 800,000 values-aligned do-gooders, each month. The place-based investing initiative, Ours To Own, produced a video[13] in coordination with the Upworthy editorial team and promoted it to their community, in email and social channels.

A thorough series of A/B random tests considered the performance of email subjects and landing page content and design. Any option with terms like economy, money, Wall Street/Main Street failed to generate clicks. Upworthy's editorial team recommended ways to leverage the "curiosity gap" to inspire engagement, to get people to watch the video without knowing what it was about.

One key learning: once people clicked, the Ours To Own video outperformed all other promotional content comparables—with a higher click-through rate to the Ours To Own landing page, higher number of shares, higher time on page. This suggests viewers initially showed less preference for economic content, but once they watched the content, they were more likely to engage than they were with other content. Ours To Own added 2,500 new emails in one week, and nearly 5,000 within six months, through this campaign.

This illustrates a core communication challenge for impact investing, including for those who are interested in doing it: we are predisposed to avoid thinking about it, but once we are involved, we are highly engaged. How do we spark a conversation, in the first place?

Toniic, a community of global social impact investors, produced a report in May 2016[14] focused on millennials and impact investing, which validated insights and data from other experiences, with a more aware and engaged community:

Key findings show that the millennials we surveyed and interviewed are indeed interested in impact investing, with some taking a portfolio approach, and others considering how to align their careers and their philanthropic activities with their values and impact investments.
Challenges shared by millennials surveyed include:
- *Not enough investment knowledge resulting in lowered confidence to act;*
- *Lack of investor education tailored for the needs of millennials;*
- *Resistance from family members; and*
- *Lack of support from financial advisors.*

One Millennial—a venture philanthropist and impact investor—said, "I'm trying to figure it out as I go. It's not easy. I'm trying to bring more joy to it; and, I see that my privilege brings a responsibility, to learn how to translate among those with and without money." Recalling her first days as a "totally hidden" anonymous donor, she later founded a nonprofit committed to "value made visible": specifically, bringing millions of small farmers into markets where buyers are trying to find products. "I think about things like, what does a rainforest ecosystem look like? What is valuable to stakeholders, beyond money, and how do I talk about that from the heart—not checkboxes?"

Younger and older audiences seem to agree: impact investing is worth investigating. Age Strong, a collaboration among AARP Foundation, Calvert Foundation and Capital Impact Partners, is investing $70 million in services for our vulnerable older population—from affordable homes to access to high-quality healthcare and healthy foods, including in rural areas. Testing through the AARP Daily News Alert, which goes to millions of AARP's members, showed the subject headline "Impact Investment Opportunity: A First of its Kind" outperformed subject headlines focused on Age Strong features or outcomes. This suggests that when impact investing is positioned as something people can do, they are more inclined to act on their interest.

More generally, the field of "silvertech"—digital products and services that support the aging process—is struggling to grow[15] at the same pace as our aging communities; and in the United States, the population over 65 will double in the next 25 years.[16] Apps that help people with prescription reminders; devices that can assist in locating loved ones with memory challenges; even Amazon's Alexa, provide accessible technology to automate simple things, like turning on lights before entering a dark area, and adjusting the thermostat, to help people stay comfortable and safe in their homes. There is a massive market opportunity for social entrepreneurs, and investors looking for growing markets and positive impact—and there are serious communications challenges that follow.

"There's a stigma to aging. Period. Most brands don't want to touch it," says Dr. Bill Thomas, an inventor, doctor and impact investor. Dr. Thomas has been visiting communities all over the United States—nearly 100 so far—with a group of other musicians, storytellers and healthcare practitioners, who are seeding new stories about aging. "For millenia, what's changed hearts and minds? Stories."

Dr. Thomas isn't just a storyteller. A geriatrician for more than 30 years, he also invented the rapidly scaling Green House model, designed for 10–12 people whose lives are centered around a big wooden table; a comfortable, open kitchen; shared living space and a hearth; and each person with their own private space. Dr. Thomas continues to innovate new lifestyle solutions for people whose mobility changes over time; and he continues to delight audiences with new ways to think about, and embrace, the complexity and beauty of aging. By focusing on themes of love, community, well-being and connection, Dr. Thomas creates bridges of understanding among younger and older audiences, of why investing in our aging population is viable financially, and important socially and culturally.

While the term "impact investing" and the concept have some cross-generational appeal, as the term continues to gain momentum in mainstream conversations, it is critical to consistently question the actual impact we are having, as we produce and receive communications. Younger audiences want positive, tangible impact for their investment, and do not assume the stock market has to be part of their future planning. Older audiences are generally more conservative, and may need to prioritize financial returns to offset increasing costs of healthcare and longevity. Finding a balance between current and future outcomes, and clearly signaling returns, is critical for both audiences.

Questions to consider in generational impact investing communications:

1. What is the horizon you are thinking about, 3 or 10 years, or 30?
2. What is the one issue you are most concerned about or inspired by?
3. What kind of support do you need to make good decisions about your future?

B. Heritage/Identity/Race

If impact investing communications is a new frontier, one particularly emergent area includes opportunities to align investing with personal identity and heritage. Many impact investors are intrigued by the idea of supporting their country of origin, and communities that are an extension of personal identity, culturally and socially. For impact investing to become more mainstream, it is critical for those designing and providing new financial products, as well as marketing them, to engage a broader population of investors—not only in regard to race and age but in terms of background, wealth and perspective.

Race is an important consideration for impact investors and venture philanthropists looking not only for solid returns—but an opportunity to directly invest in the next generation of leadership and models that will scale measurable, positive impact. JPMorgan Chase CEO Jamie Dimon recognizes that, from a talent standpoint, his company needs to be developing a full pipeline of people of color, dedicating financial and human resources to build the skills and experience needed for success in top leadership roles.[17] Whether you are considering the potential impact of your investment, or designing or marketing a new opportunity, race matters when you communicate about who is being invested in; who is benefiting directly from that investment; and considering who is being marketed to, and what they are being asked to do.

Race in the United States is a complex issue. At a high level, if you are communicating to any one particular community, it is ideal for leadership of your effort or product to look like, represent and deeply understand that community. An organization committed to bold values like equity or inequality, diversity or integrity, can expect people receiving communications to apply more critical filters, especially around money. "What people say, is not always what they do," one marketer noted.

One area of skepticism that communications must address relates to where money goes, and who decides: this is particularly important, and challenging, when white-led North American investors are deploying capital internationally, or within US cities that all have different and deep histories of structural inequity, especially places like Newark, Oakland, Baltimore and Detroit.

Launching new initiatives globally, intermediaries, advisors and brokers will inevitably need to address questions about how they will manage corruption, "business as usual" in many parts of the world. Local leadership, with relationships grounded in many years and deep trust, is vital to any identity- or place-based initiative. (More on that below.)

For white communicators and impact investment product developers, engaging voices of color as true partners early and often is key. If you are white (as I am; and as are 79 percent of financial advisors in the United States,[18] for example) you may well make mistakes; resources exist to develop skills and awareness around white privilege and the benefits conveyed socially and financially because of it. Any white communicator in the impact investing space should consider reading or participating in the growing number of resources dedicated to educating white people on issues of racial justice (Racial Equity Tools,[19] Frameworks Institute,[20] Showing Up for Racial Justice[21] among others). If you are committed to impact that in any way touches on race (which is, all of it) be patient with yourself, invest time in your education, and do not lean heavily and chronically on collaborators of color to be patient with you.

One Example: "Parte de la Solution"

In one initiative, several partners collaborated to engage Latino audiences as "financial activists," encouraging Latinos to recognize and exercise the power of their finances to create a better world. The campaign invites people to be "Parte de la Solution" (PDLS). PDLS partners put money to work for the benefit of Latino communities in the United States and abroad, including Calvert Foundation ("Invest"), Latino Community Credit Union ("Save") and Kiva ("Lend").

PDLS was of interest to media partner Univision, whose CSR commitment includes financial education, and who liked the concept of engaging Latinos financially for social impact. As the fifth largest network in the United States, Univision offers unprecedented access to the US Latino market, and with recent acquisitions of The Root, The Onion and Gawker media properties, access to a multicultural millennial audience.

A paid social media advertisement campaign aimed at millennial Latinos was conducted via Fusion, Univision's millennial-focused multiplatform network, focusing on the "invest" call to action. A community event and kick off to the PDLS campaign was hosted in San Francisco with Univision's social impact unit, Rise Up. While it's not one of Univision's largest markets, San Francisco has a highly engaged Latino audience. With continued marketing, the hope is to see an increase in the number of people signing up to save, invest or lend. The initiative continues to bring on outreach partners whose communities and members might be interested in "financial activism," and will consider other solution partners and potential verticals for growth as the campaign progresses.

Questions to consider in heritage/identity/race–based impact investing:

1. Who are the leaders and partners of this product?
2. What kind of investing relationship do you want to have with investees?
3. What do you need to learn, to feel confident your decisions will lead to the outcomes you seek?

C. Place-based/Local Investing

Impact investors bring a unique hope and skepticism to the idea of place-based investing. Who doesn't want to make their community even better? Because of the promise represented by tangible, local investments, a number of questions quickly arise for the communicator and audience:

- Who is leading and representing the initiative locally?
- Who decides where the money goes?
- Who is making money off my money?
- Can I point my investment directly to Tamara's cafe or Jose's craft brewery? Does that matter?

If you're building or marketing any kind of local effort, there is one secret to success: representation and deep relationships, in that specific place. Slick marketing campaigns and people who helicopter in to strategize, sell and observe cannot replace solid local leadership or expect meaningful, sustained engagement with new audiences of investors. Local guides function as an extension of a sales and marketing team, and they should be true leaders of any authentic place-based effort. Prioritizing and resourcing these leaders will help inform your investor profile, and the traction of your initiative. Countless well-intentioned local initiatives have failed to achieve the effect they seek—and in some cases have had the opposite effect, deepening distrust among audiences. Foundations and anchor institutions rarely engage with their community in a thoughtful, positive, ongoing way. This history shapes how communications are received.

As communicators try to promote a local impact investing initiative, and potential investors want to learn more, operational challenges become marketing breakdowns. For example, many institutional and individual investors are interested in directing substantial capital locally. A lack of "economic plumbing"—a way to deploy significant funds, in a community-responsive way—may make it hard to get money to the businesses and organizations a community wants to support. These all present challenges to effective, satisfying communications.

On the human capital side, outsiders and those with resources often tie up precious time and talent of local leadership—who spend countless hours educating and translating for those with privilege about real, urgent grassroots challenges. If investors are looking for deals, it is often these local leaders and their immediate networks who represent strong investments, themselves.

The number of diverse, place-based initiatives continues to grow—like Benefit Chicago,[22] the Colorado Impact Fund[23] and JumpStart[24] in Cleveland—often through foundation and institutional support. Mainstream individual investors are not as quick to make the leap. Author Amy Cortese noted, "When *Locavesting* was published in 2011, it was still the tail end of the recession; people really understood the value of investing in local, in Main Street. My sense is that has subsided a bit. People tend to have short memories, and when times are good—when the market is high—looking for alternatives is not as urgent."

Questions to consider in place-based impact investing:

1. Who are the local leaders and representatives of the product?
2. Who decides where investments are made? How is the local community involved?
3. What kind of returns are important to you, financially and socially?

D. Financial Advisor

In conversations with a range of advisors, they made it very clear: if you make it easy, there is money that wants to move into positive impact. More and diverse communications resources— infographics, videos, blog posts, media coverage—are needed to unpack financial jargon into accessible, actionable ideas.

For example, a "how it works" infographic has been referenced over and over by advisors grateful for a simple tool to communicate about the mechanics of a place-based investing initiative.

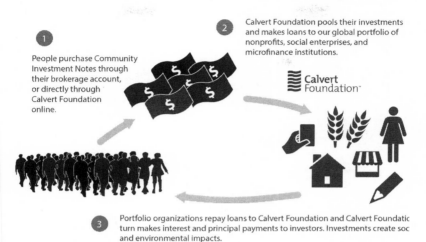

1 People purchase Community Investment Notes through their brokerage account, or directly through Calvert Foundation online.

2 Calvert Foundation pools their investments and makes loans to our global portfolio of nonprofits, social enterprises, and microfinance institutions.

3 Portfolio organizations repay loans to Calvert Foundation and Calvert Foundatic turn makes interest and principal payments to investors. Investments create soc and environmental impacts.

Source: Printed with permission, The Calvert Foundation 2017

That's not to say that there isn't individual and institutional resistance to change—that's human, and understandable. Some even consider new initiatives to be a threat. This must be considered when creating or receiving communications about impact investing. One wealth advisor, a millennial working primarily with older clients, in a private wealth management group for a commercial bank, noted there are different comfort levels in being more and less involved with managing wealth. He is always on the lookout for the "path of least resistance"—where it is easy and transparent that an impact investment clearly aligns with someone's planning goals, and the process is clear, people make the choice to move their money.

Questions to consider for financial advisors:

1. Is your client clear on the impact outcomes that matter most?
2. What are your biggest communications needs—video content, infographics, stories?
3. Where do you turn for guidance and translation? How can you elevate those voices?

E. Impact Investor

People engaged in or drawn to impact investing start with a basic premise: that it's possible to earn financial returns on investments that also create measurable good in the world. The entry point is not about trade-offs or fighting for a limited piece of pie, or seeing the world through a lens of scarcity; it's about making more pie, together. This is difficult to remember, as we've wired ourselves to see other stories, and it's not how many of us experience the world every day. When we communicate through a lens of possibility and abundance, we discover more resources and positive energy for what we are trying to build. Tactically, this means using language like "and" rather than "but"; and thinking about how to collaborate, not compete; and how to create more for more people.

Jenny Kassan helps entrepreneurs grow their business "on their terms," serving as a legal advisor, business consultant and coach for mission-aligned structure and finance. Her work focuses on direct investment in companies—not into pooled or aggregated funds—which "some might say is risky, and it's important to question that assumption." She notes that every opportunity is different. If a business has good counsel, and access to a group of direct investors, there are alternatives to traditional models of investing and raising capital—which require additional messaging, so that people can understand, and ask smart questions, to see whether an investment makes sense for them. Increasingly impact investors desire a direct connection to investees, so while there may be more (or at least different) paperwork, the investment relationship is a deeper partnership, with projected, understood returns.

From a communications and product standpoint, one of Jenny's favorites is Equal Exchange. Their name says it all: the company is dedicated to democratic transactions, grounded in relationship. Their investment option is totally transparent, there is no fee or additional intermediary, and impact investors know their money is going directly to support better livelihoods for more farmers, and more worker-owners within the Equal Exchange co-op. They have also structured the business and investment so there's no pressure to exit to a major multinational corporation; and they target a flat 5 percent dividend, which they have been able to meet nearly every year—which means they have outpaced the S&P 500, over time.

Jenny admits that while she loves making direct investments in companies, these deals are hard to find: whether or not you're making impact investments, it's still very much "who you know." When you do find the right fit, the messaging is easy, because it makes sense.

Where are the breakthroughs, the emerging solutions that address persistent challenges, and produce satisfying financial returns? Who are the people leading teams and products for underserved markets that represent new financial activity, and quality job creation? What are the new structures—from co-ops to employee stock ownership plans (ESOPs)—that impact investors should be considering?

Accelerators, incubators and hubs are growing at an incredible clip, and they can be excellent places for investors looking to resource people, products and services, and potentially earn real returns over time. According to the Brookings Institution, between 2005 and 2015 "172 US-based accelerators invested in more than 5,000 U.S.-based start-ups with a median investment of $100,000. These companies raised a total of $19.5 billion in funding during this period—or $3.7 million per company on average—reflecting both the relatively small investments made in these early-stage companies by accelerators, and the fact that many go on to raise substantial amounts of capital later on."[25]

One thing is clear: investors and philanthropists have under-resourced the talent and infrastructure that would create the deal-flow they seek. Key questions remain of how to reach beyond our networks, to find truly new, emergent voices, and how to begin speaking the same language, to match up where capital wants to flow and cultivate existing talent. Investing in more robust education for entrepreneurs, and economic opportunity for people of color more specifically, is critical to ensuring they can lead, and benefit from, the creative solutions needed to solve shared challenges.

Meanwhile BlackRock[26] has made it clear to investors they will be looking for diverse leadership in companies, as well as proactive steps on climate change, for their portfolio. And "the world's third-largest asset manager [$2.5 trillion State Street Corp.] installed a bronze statue of a defiant girl in front of Wall Street's iconic charging bull statue"[27] to challenge companies they invest in to add more women to their boards.

For impact investors, making sure women and other underrepresented groups are supported in building skills and networks over time is key to inclusive, representative leadership. We must begin to speak new languages to new people, to connect up our worlds.

Questions for impact investors to reflect on, as you evaluate communications:

1. Who is the messenger? What's in it for me, and them?
2. What kind of impact will my investment create?
3. What kinds of outcomes do I want?
4. How often do I want to hear from my advisor, or other financial services relationships?

F. Philanthropist

When communicating with philanthropists, including about impact investing, one successful tactic is appealing to a sense of legacy. Many people who self-identify as philanthropists have a desire to give back to the places and communities that helped shape them. Some want to give to a very specific issue: for example, one philanthropist said he would consider a seven-figure investment if he knew the funds would go to animal rights. When the product was explained, as a general pooled fund, he wasn't interested in combining his capital with other funds for nontargeted community needs.

Communications in philanthropy are often guided by audience: specifically, whether you're speaking with someone who has the autonomy to act, or someone who has to build a case for collaboration—requiring data, stories, introductions, any number of things to get others on board. Similar to financial advisors, many philanthropists don't want to think too much about the details, or get in the weeds of activating their capital for social impact.

Questions to consider for a philanthropist in impact investing:

1. How involved do you want to be in an investment?
2. What issues or outcomes are you most passionate about?
3. What information do you need to feel confident choosing an impact investment?

G. Impact Investment Lender

The Washington Area Community Investment Fund (WACIF) is a CDFI in Washington, D.C. Executive Director Harold Pettigrew finds impact investing is a great doorway for conversations about his work: people have a vaguely positive association with the idea, but don't really know what it is, and he is able to draw a direct parallel between this "new" idea and the historical work of CDFIs. "Impact investing is what CDFIs were founded to do, 30 years ago—invest in under-resourced communities, and earn financial and social returns. So yes, we consider ourselves impact investors."

Pettigrew uses more widely understood concepts, which also convey the realities of his work, to describe a CDFI: "I tell people we are both a nonprofit and a financial institution; that a CDFI is a designation for a type of nonprofit finance organization. Most people have been exposed to nonprofits, so they start to understand we aren't a traditional bank with deep pockets, that we have some common challenges—resources are in high demand, retention of the best talent can be difficult, competing with online commercial banking services is tough. We focus on supporting our community—like through our Ascend Capital Accelerator, for entrepreneurs of color—not running slick marketing campaigns."

"It's the classic marketing dilemma—how to find the people who want to find you," offered Jason Anderson, Sr. Director of Communications & Marketing at Capital Impact Partners. Capital Impact is a national, mission-driven CDFI that has earned an S&P AA rating for its 30-year track record of investing $2 billion into community development.

"As a nonprofit we face two key issues with communications. Because we focus our budget on fulfilling our mission, we don't have resources for campaigns that can compete with large financial institutions or the viral sensation of the day. Second, the problems we are addressing in low-income communities aren't necessarily tangible or immediate to mass audiences. So while they conceptually believe our work is important, they see it as something 'somebody else' must be taking care of."

"This requires our sector to be hyper-focused on those who do care, and then work outward to engage the mainstream slowly. Communicators must work hand-in-hand with sales and fundraising teams to meet their audiences where they are, by understanding their challenges and where they get their information, so we can be there too, with the right message or call to action."

"Once people know us, we do everything possible to reduce barriers to connect: every page of our website invites people to call or email a specific individual. We show their faces. We populate the site with content written by our team to demonstrate expertise. This shows we are about establishing and building strong relationships. We're not only dealing with multimillion dollar transactions, but also helping people fulfill their own mission of helping communities. They want to know the folks on the other end of conversations, and, as we like to say, that we'll be both their lender and their partner."

Questions to consider for lenders in impact investing:

1. Are you reducing barriers to action and encouraging direct, personal connection with leads?
2. What new partners could provide access to potential borrowers?
3. How do you celebrate and promote your borrowers, and engage them in spreading the word?

H. Impact Investment Partner

Successful impact investing often involves deep partnership, across a range of sectors. There are ecosystem leaders doing work at the intersection of philanthropy and investment, government and anchor institutions, grassroots and faith-based communities.

These are true Systems Weavers, and can take many forms, but let's focus on one:

When it comes to language, Boston Impact's Aaron Tanaka is a Jedi. He has grown the Ujima Project into a fully staffed organization with its own Capital Fund, supporting the local economy ecosystem. Tanaka knows where to find deals, and he's helping to create a new community of activated, economically resilient residents.

"Ujima (oo-JEE-mah) is a Swahili word, the celebrated Kwanzaa principle for 'collective work and responsibility.' Ujima inspires us to see our neighbor's problems as our own—and build collective power to solve them together. Boston is one of the most unequal cities in the U.S. Depending on the source, the average net worth of a black family is as little as $7, and for white families, goes up to $250,000.[28] The Ujima Project leadership is rooted in and controlled by the community. Each person has equal say regardless of their share of ownership. We strengthen local economic control and re-center economic power in low-income communities and communities of color." The work of bringing together many stakeholders—from healthcare and academic institutions to impact investors, philanthropists, entrepreneurs and grassroots organizers—is not easy. Tanaka and others have built a strong foundation, where the community cocreated a shared understanding of purpose and language.

Questions for the impact investment partner:

1. Who are we investing in? Who's getting the money? Who's giving, investing, participating?
2. What are we are investing in? What are the goods and services? What are the impacts of the businesses?
3. How are we investing? In structures like worker co-ops and land trusts, which outperform financially and operationally, and build tangible equity and value?

And Now for Some Messaging Nuts and Bolts ...

What content can we provide to effectively engage both hearts and heads? What values do we call on? What are tested themes and lessons?

The following pages include ideas and language you may begin to use to better interpret and create impact investing communications. These examples are just a snapshot of an emergent, rapidly growing field of work.

Values and Resonant Themes, by Audience

In the same way that we are not robots, we are also more than a "psychographic" label. We can't imagine that every Pragmatic Altruist sees the world the same way: some may be deeply motivated by personal faith; others may have grown up in a financially traditional, conservative family; others may be activists in purchasing decisions, but tentative about investing.

While the values mapped below are not representative of every person, for communicators, considering patterns and themes is helpful:

	Belonging Unity Community	Abundance Progress Prosperity	Idealism Innovation Vision	Legacy Stewardship Preservation Sustainable	Equity Resilience Sufficiency Agency	Courage Imagination Love	Diversity Choice Inclusion
Pragmatic Altruist	X	X	X	X	X		
Systems Weaver	X	X	X	X	X		X
Radical Seeker		X	X	X		X	
Indifferent	?	?	?	?	?	?	?

Core values: Belonging, Unity, Community Messaging Themes: In This Together, "Our" + "We"-based Language, Movement, Civic

As we've seen in the rise of successful political campaigns and cause-based organizing, language focused on the collective allows us to imagine beyond any one of us, individually. This bigger paradigm shift from "me-to-we" thinking supports a desired shift in impact investing dollars.

One example is in the name *Ours To Own*, a place-based investment initiative currently active in three US cities. The words signal several ideas quickly:

- Being part of something bigger
- Responsibility and accountability for a community
- Meaningful and relatable to individuals and institutions
- In this initiative, online investments start at $20—making the promise of the name a real opportunity, for a new type of investor
- Suggests a larger community of many (smaller) investments

For the impact investor, actions and communications must engage in a meaningful way. A Pragmatic Altruist, for example, may be drawn to the idea of being part of something without doing anything personally, beyond receiving a quarterly report on social and financial returns. Systems Weavers and Radical Seekers want to participate more actively, presenting opportunities for more focused communications needs.

Shadows: an emphasis on the collective can create a disconnect for some individuals, working hard to leave or make their mark. Often visionary leaders in emergent fields, like impact investing, are initially seen as radicals, revolutionaries, and "rugged individualists" who are not necessarily "joiners."

Core values: Abundance, Progress, Prosperity Messaging Themes: Water + Nature-based metaphors, Pooling, Circulation, Flow, Regenerative

Qualitative observations and feedback brought to the surface a number of specific examples associated with movement and creation, and life and water, specifically. Using natural systems as a metaphor can ground artificial, constructed financial systems in rhythms we can more readily access and understand.

- Many financial advisors and investors talk about making modest impact investments at first as a form of "toe-dipping"—"testing the waters" before "diving in" with larger commitments.
- People consistently respond in a positive way to language like "investments are pooled together" and "your investment is combined with other small and large investments" (when appropriate to the strategy or investment product).
- People like language about money "flowing," in circulation
- Names like Betterment, Beneficial State Bank, Wealthfront and Ascend Capital Accelerator call on a sense of possibility, movement, abundance.
- Impact-related contrasts like "destructive versus generative" and "extractive versus additive" offer natural cycles as context for investments, and help people recognize what is versus what is possible; and remember "this too shall pass," while observing natural trends and market volatility.
- People (in particular women) respond negatively to the idea of "stagnant" or "hoarded" capital, and want their money to move around.

Shadows: "Prosperity" is a complex word in communications about money, commonly understood only as financial prosperity. Some organizations have successfully messaged "Real Prosperity" and "Prosperity for All" to qualify and question the core frame. Taken to its extreme, an antiquated notion of prosperity—where everyone has their own (big) home, (empty) yard, (multiple) cars, endless miscellaneous "stuff"—furthers consumption and investment decisions that lead to destruction of resources. There is also the Prosperity Gospel, which has deep roots in different faith communities; and Americans for Prosperity, a political funding and organizing vehicle for the grassroots conservative movement in the United States "Abundance" has some connections to communities who pray and meditate (vs. create business models, invest, etc.) to manifest financial gain; if used externally, test for audience understanding/fit.

Core Values: Idealism, Innovation, Vision Messaging
Themes: "Beyond," Future, Progress

People who are drawn to impact investing often self-identify as visionaries, interested more in forging new paths than contributing to outdated systems. Striving for more and embracing the new resonates, for many of us, as the way we want to be in the world, even if we fall short, every day.

- One strategic and tactical hack is using the word "beyond" in messaging. While carrying out an audience keyword research for a campaign targeting millennials, a high search rate on "charity" was discovered. "Beyond Charity" was incorporated into ad copy to help with findability, using a word that the audience was searching, while clearly signaling "this is something different." This allows you to call on existing models and frames while clearly saying you are something more, something that is similar but different. This is especially helpful when marketing anything that is new, like impact investing.
- Many advisors and intermediaries will describe impact investing products as being "similar to a bond" or "like a savings account" in that the dollars are, or can be, supporting community development while earning a modest, stable return.
- If you want to talk about Innovation, try to use a more specific word. The word has come to have little meaning. Get clear, and more specific, about what makes you unique.
- Concepts like Freedom and Independence are tricky: free from what? Freedom for who? Who decides who is free, or independent? Impact investors ask hard questions, and expect good answers.

Shadows: Future-focused communications can be so abstract that they fail to connect with people emotionally. Find ways to spark the imagination—perhaps through inquiry-based messages that pose questions to your audiences—while grounding ideas in tangible examples: "Your $20 investment, along with many others, helps create more affordable homes in your neighborhood." Also, if everything is "beyond," what is real? This can quickly become gimmicky if relied on too heavily.

Core values: Legacy, Stewardship, Preservation, Sustainability
Messaging Themes: Community, Honor, Sustainable, Footprint

Many potential impact investors enjoy financial security. Their motives to make an investment—rather than a more straightforward charitable donation (and tax write-off)—can often be activated with a balanced appeal to altruism and ego.

Many people want to give back, especially to people and places that helped generate wealth. As communicators and advisors, how to positively channel that? Connecting on values like Stewardship, Agency and Sufficiency taps a desire to help others without triggering the instinct to, for example, install one's name very large on a building. We can invite people to care for and contribute to shared communities without selling or encouraging ego-based expressions.

We Are Chicago, a capital campaign for The Chicago Community Trust, called on the legendary generosity of the "city of big shoulders." Although not technically impact investing, there are some relevant insights:

- "We"-based language signals this is about something bigger.
- Builds on local "asset," legendary generosity: a report, Giving in Chicago,[29] noted $10 billion in charitable giving in 2013.
- A traditional, high-quality, story-driven execution invited people to identify with other leaders who committed to financially supporting the city in a significant, sustained way.
- The ask is implicit: if We Are Chicago, we are also responsible for Chicago; this campaign makes it possible (through philanthropic activity) to direct capital to the community.

This campaign had the goal of raising $1 billion in six years, to announce at The Chicago Community Trust's 100th anniversary celebration. We Are Chicago netted $1.6 billion for the Trust's endowment, available to be activated in support of the city.

Shadows: "Legacy" appeals focused on the individual are predictably successful with some demographics; trends suggest younger audiences will continue to resonate with more collective, community-based language rather than personal frames. "Sustainability" has become mainstream and has no shared meaning; like impact investing, efforts can range from very specific, narrow definitions to broad and hard to measure. Go deeper to describe sustainability efforts—solar energy capacity, carbon sequestration, soil regeneration—to provide a clearer way for targeted audiences to connect.

Core values: Equity, Resilience, Sufficiency, Agency, Autonomy Messaging themes: Access, Entrepreneurship, Enough, Equip, Quality Job Creation

There are many active narratives around the lack of equal access to equal opportunity.

- Some large foundations have aligned their entire strategy around one core value, and a clear external message, like the Ford Foundation's focus on Inequality (in addition to their leadership, activating $1 billion of their endowment).[30]
- Others in this space may be intermediaries trying to find leaders of color or women entrepreneurs to resource, financially and through networks of support.
- There is a range of intention and sophistication around complex terms like Equity, Agency, Resilience. If you want to use those terms, study them deeply, and shape your external messaging to reflect awareness of shadows, and aspects of your organization or product that are in progress.
- Terms like "Enough" can suggest many things. If one is considering impact investing, they have "enough" that they can afford that choice; their situation is sufficient, content. Enough can also express dissatisfaction—"we've had enough, of this system that doesn't serve us." The word sparks thinking about what is enough, who has enough, and can tap that charitable mindset that makes brains happy.

Shadows: one related word is being replaced for more precise language—"empowerment." People point out, theoretically we all have equal power, we don't grant power; it's just that many are actively disempowered by systems. Similarly, it is best to avoid "enable," as if others are not (cap)able; better to "direct needed resources for others to advance." "Resilience"—the ability to absorb and sustain shock—isn't as inspiring as adopting frames of abundance. The biggest challenge and shadow with any of these values or themes is alignment for impact investors and other discerning observers who look closer. When reality does not align with words, skepticism grows.

Core values: Courage, Imagination, Love Messaging Themes: "No Regrets," What's Possible Together, Imagine, Love

Sallie Calhoun is a Pragmatic, Systemic Radical Seeker, and rancher and impact investor. "All life on earth comes down to the health of soil. We have this idea that it's 'just dirt,' think it's unimportant, but every plant, every animal depends entirely on soil. It's a solution to climate change, and has all these other cobenefits—water, health and nutrition, and so on. It's a no-lose, 'no regrets' solution. It's work that needs doing, and has positive impacts that ripple throughout the systems."

Esther Park, CEO of Cienega Capital, provides more detail: "'No Regrets' is a regenerative asset strategy, activating Sallie's entire portfolio: investing through Cienega Capital; ranching and generating new businesses through soil health and holistic land management, at the 7000+ acre Paicines Ranch; and finally, in her venture philanthropy through the Globetrotter Foundation. All of these together create 'No Regrets.' We use this language to describe simply what we're doing; and also, to encourage other investors and philanthropists to look at their whole portfolio—to think about not just financial capital but in balance with ecological capital, and social capital. And also, we want people to think about soil as part of their strategy. If you care about water, climate, human nutrition, health, hunger—it all comes back to soil."

Communications and Campaign Manager Nikki Silvestri helped land on "No Regrets" to capture what Sallie and Esther are doing for audiences who aren't thinking about soil, to start. A Los Angeles native, she discovered the power of soil late, as a disillusioned, nearly hopeless climate advocate. When she learned about the "simple" science of soil—its natural design, to hold carbon—she knew she could help solve larger systemic problems, in part through communications. "I had no idea what soil carbon sequestration was. And suddenly, I had hope, that there was a way for the ecosystem to balance itself. The day we named this strategy 'No Regrets' I knew we had a powerful meme that could spread."

Hitting on similar values of Courage and Imagination, Love is emergent in communications around impact and money. Mission venture capitalist Joel Solomon, in *The Clean Money Revolution*, invites people to be "billionaires of good deeds, billionaires of love, billionaires of meaning and purpose" who are "driven by love whenever possible, and by tough love when needed." He offers, "The return on that investment will be a great blessing. Dying with the most money is pointless. It's about what we do to help those who will follow us." The use of "love as a verb" and "love where you are"—and a "fierce love" that is "the filter for the hardest decisions about what we build, protect and share"—are woven into place-based investing communications.

Previously mentioned, social entrepreneur Robert Egger drums to a similar beat: "[L.A. Kitchen] is a badass food machine of love. We are a job-training program. We are a food-recycling program. We are a social business—we get contracts to provide healthy, fresh meals for seniors. We create jobs for younger men and women just coming out of foster care, and for older men and women returning to their communities from prison." Eric Garcetti, the mayor of Los Angeles notes, "L.A. Kitchen embodies the values of the city. They help create a greener city, an economically prosperous city, and a healthier city."

The upsides of this type of approach are significant:

- Tapping one's sense of courage, imagination and love creates a deep, expansive connection;
- Increasing the lifetime value of the investor, as these types of dreamers and doers seem more likely to consider long-term commitments for significant progress on difficult issues; and
- Using words like "love" in relation to money is unexpected and can spark interest.

Shadows: Bold thinkers and doers are often dismissed as fringe exceptions and outliers, instead of being acknowledged for the purpose they serve: to redefine the outermost edge of what is possible. People who embrace courageous, messy and big ideas are not easy to fit in a box—and what appeals to them, doesn't always appeal to everyone. Themes around radical innovation and fundamental disruption may confuse and inspire different audiences.

Core Values: Inclusion, Diversity, Choice Messaging Themes: Weaving, Strength in Numbers, Opportunity, Representation

Impact investing provides options to consider more and different returns:

- As in nature, diversity is beautiful, necessary and weaves stronger systems; and more tactically and specifically related to capital, diversity has served (even in "modern" portfolio theory) to ensure returns, in a risk-adjusted way.
- Impact investing goes "beyond" traditional portfolio diversification, to consider a blend of tangible outcomes—like quality job creation, affordable homes, people with new access to healthcare or healthy foods—alongside financial returns.

One example of these values and themes in action is RSF Social Finance's new Integrated Capital Fellowship, teaching "the coordinated use of diverse financing tools (including loans, loan guarantees, investments, and grants), network connections and advisory services to support enterprises that are solving complex social and environmental problems."[31] Over time this program will increase the number of advisors who can support increasingly engaged investors, people "with financial expertise and an activist impulse who want to be at the forefront of fundamentally rethinking the purpose of wealth."

Barbara Alink is in the enviable position of being a market-maker. Her three-wheeled Alinker, called a "walking assist," is providing a greater range of mobility to more people, in a design- and brand-forward way. The insistently happy, bright yellow Alinker is leading a "R-Volution of Inclusion" and claiming a new market of people with a range of mobility, now activated, and experiencing cobenefits of being more physical and less isolated.

Shadows: "Diversity" is often translated to "people of many colors" without real diversity of thought or background. Diversification also has a specific meaning in finance, and for new thinkers and millennials, does not immediately signal a good or bad thing. Words like "inclusion" imply that someone is choosing who is included, a challenged process by default. Consider more straightforward frames like Representation, when that is an accurate (or aspirational) reflection of a situation.

Concluding Thoughts on Communicating Impact

This chapter on communication challenges and opportunities within impact investing was created with the input and reflections of a group of us involved in impact investing and efforts to communicate impact to diverse audiences. It is a privilege to represent the knowledge and experience of so many colleagues and collaborators in this unique work. In reflecting on both the areas we've explored in this chapter and the key points to be considered by those involved in impact investing, I'd ask you to keep the following in mind:

- We live in a noisy world. Many of us have wired ourselves to tune out communications about money.
- The universe of people thinking and talking about impact investing is getting bigger, yet is still small. To grow the field substantially requires talent and resources, to reach new audiences with our message.
- We need to reflect on and communicate not simply the value of impact investing, but the reality that traditional investing—without the intention of creating positive impacts—may be contributing to the problems we share at local, national and global levels.
- It will take many messages, over a long time, "showing and telling" stories of better ways to use capital, to balance the psychological effect of historical financial services marketing.

- The field of impact investing is creating a new language, some-times leaning on or hacking existing language and ideas to communicate.
- Defining the kind of impact we want is the first step in impact investing, from design and measurement to communication.
- Question assumptions. Experiment. There is no template, this is messy work—and can be hugely rewarding!

Pause to enjoy it, and do good better, when you can!

Notes

1 Giving USA, "Americans Donated an Estimated $358.38 Billion to Charity in 2014; Highest Total in Report's 60-year History," June 29, 2015, https://givingusa.org/giving-usa-2015-press-release-giving-usa-americans-donated-an-estimated-358-38-billion-to-charity-in-2014-highest-total-in-reports-60-year-history/ and Andrew Coen, *Financial Planning*, "Investable Assets Hit $33.5 Trillion" https://www.financial-planning.com/news/investable-assets-hit-335-trillion, Total giving every year ($300 bn)/Total investable wealth every year ($30 trillion) = .01.
2 Elizabeth Svoboda, "Hard-Wired for Giving,"' *Wall Street Journal*, August 31, 2013, https://www.wsj.com/articles/SB10001424127887324009304579041231971683854.
3 M. P. Dunleavey, "Do You Have Cheap Genes?," *AARP The Magazine*, February/March 2017, http://www.aarp.org/money/budgeting-saving/info-2017/genetics-and-spending-saving.html.
4 Divestment Guide, "Reducing Climate Risk through Investment Choices," Accessed April 21, 2017, https://divestmentguide.org/,
5 CNote, "Earn 40X* More on Savings with 100% Social Impact," Accessed April 21, 2017, https://www.mycnote.com/.
6 Jordan Roberts, "CNote Wins First SXSW Super Accelerator Pitch Competition," SXSW, March 13, 2017, https://www.sxsw.com/news/2017/cnote-wins-first-sxsw-super-accelerator-pitch/.
7 Fossil Free, "Divest from Fossil Fuels," Accessed April 21, 2017, https://gofossilfree.org/commitments/.
8 Defund DAPL, Stop the Dakota Access Pipeline, accessed April 21, 2017, http://www.defunddapl.org/defund.
9 U.S. Department of Treasury, CDFI Fund infographic, Accessed April 21, 2017, https://www.cdfifund.gov/Documents/CDFI_infographic_v08A.pdf.
10 Association for Economic Opportunity, *The Big Picture: A Larger View of the Small Business Market*, 2014, http://www.aeoworks.org/pdf/the-big-picture.pdf.

11 Opportunity Finance Network, *Inside the Membership: Fiscal Year 2015 Statistical Highlights from the OFN Membership*, October 2016, http://ofn. org/sites/default/files/Inside%20the%20Membership%20FY2015%20 FINAL.pdf.

12 Clara Miller, "The World Has Changed and So Must We," The F. B. Heron Foundation, April 27, 2012, http://www.heron.org/engage/publications/ world-has-changed-and-so-must-we.

13 Calvert Foundation, Video: "Old-school Investing vs. a New Way," https:// www.youtube.com/watch?v=GJZCM2IeUGA.

14 Toniic, *Millenials and Impact Investment*, 2016, http://www.toniic.com/ millennials-and-impact-investment/.

15 Richard Eisenberg, "How to Make Money from the Global Aging Megatrend," *Forbes*, May 9, 2016, https://www.forbes.com/sites/nextavenue/2016/05/ 09/how-to-make-money-from-the-global-aging-megatrend/#54936f5b5a41.

16 Wan He, Daniel Goodkind, and Paul Kowa, "An Aging World: 2015," United States Census, March 2016, https://www.census.gov/content/dam/Census/ library/publications/2016/demo/p95-16-1.pdf.

17 Leah Fessler, "JPMorgan's CEO Admits His Company Has a Black Talent Problem—and the Finance Industry Should Listen,' *Quartz*, April 6, 2017, https://qz.com/951064/jpmorgan-chases-ceo-jamie-dimon-admits-to- diversity-problems-with-black-talent-in-his-2017-letter-to-shareholders/.

18 Elizabeth MacBride, "A Diversity Problem: The Financial Advice Industry Is Among the Least Diverse in the Country and Is Doing Little to Change Its Status," *Investment News*, December 14, 2015, http://www.investmentnews. com/article/20151214/FEATURE/151209979/a-diversity-problem.

19 Racial Equity Tools, Accessed April 21, 2017, https://www.racialequitytools. org/act/communicating

20 Frameworks Institute: Race, Accessed April 21, 2017, http://www.framework- sinstitute.org/race1.html.

21 Showing Up for Racial Justice (SURJ), Accessed April 21, 2017, http://www. showingupforracialjustice.org/.

22 Benefit Chicago, Accessed April 21, 2017, http://www.benefitchi.org/.

23 Colorado Impact Fund, Accessed April 21, 2017, https://coloradoimpact- fund.com/.

24 JumpStart, Accessed April 21, 2017, https://www.jumpstartinc.org/.

25 https://www.brookings.edu/research/accelerating-growth-startup- accelerator-programs-in-the-united-states/.

26 http://www.reuters.com/article/us-blackrock-climate-exclusive- idUSKBN16K0CR.

27 Rachael Levy, "A $2.5 Trillion Asset Manager Just Put a Statue of a Defiant Girl in Front of the Wall Street Bull," *Business Insider*, March 7, 2017, http://www.businessinsider.com/stage-street-global-advisors-girl-statue-in- front-of-wall-street-bull-2017-3.

28 Federal Reserve Bank of Boston, *The Color of Wealth in Boston*, March 25, 2015. https://www.bostonfed.org/publications/one-time-pubs/color-of-wealth. aspx.

29 Chicago Community Trust, "Giving in Chicago," Accessed April 21, 2017, http://givinginchicago.com/.
30 Darren Walker, "Unleashing the Power of Endowments: The Next Great Challenge for Philanthropy," Ford Foundation, April 5, 2017, http://www.fordfoundation.org/ideas/equals-change-blog/posts/unleashing-the-power-of-endowments-the-next-great-challenge-for-philanthropy.
31 http://rsfsocialfinance.org/integrated-capital-fellowship/.

10

A Journey to Impact: Initial Steps toward Impact Investing

Jennifer Kenning

Reflections from an Impact Investing Advisor

I was in the prime of my wealth management career. About to turn 30, I managed investments for 20-plus multigenerational high-net-worth families. I'd spent several years climbing the corporate ladder, and finding "success." And then the epiphany struck—success wasn't about titles and more money; there had to be something deeper. I started to see a clear separation between people of wealth and people of scarcity—the poor and struggling individuals with whom I came in contact from volunteering. I realized I could bridge the gap, and that I had the empathy, passion and skill-set to help.

It took me until age 33 to fulfill one particular goal, to travel in Africa. It marked an entry into impact investing, a process by which people define their values—what they care about, the change they want to see—and link them to both their financial goals.

I entered this business because I truly believe there is enough money to change the world, it simply needs to be allocated effectively. With the rise of impact investing, we have the power to utilize our money to not only garner a financial return, but change a life in the process. I challenge each of you reading to close your eyes and imagine the one issue that means the most to you. Whether it be with time, money or personal resources, I invite you to invest in that issue in whatever way you can at this moment to welcome you into the world of impact investing.

Investment Strategy Approach

How is an effective impact strategy built? It involves the following four elements:

1. Uncover Values and Goals

Impact investing is similar to traditional investing, just a step or two deeper. Traditional investing fundamentals are carried through to an impact investing strategy. The process is designed to identify the issues investors care about it, and the methods they'll employ to effect change.

It begins by asking two questions:

1. If you could only "move the needle" on one or two issue areas, what would they be and why?
2. How would each and every investment you make have an impact, whether it's in their 401(k) or investment portfolio, their consumption decisions and even where to send their kids to school?

This helps to solidify why, exactly, an investor would want to engage in impact investing.

2. Develop a Mission Statement

These answers form the basis for an impact investing mission statement, which is both similar and different from a traditional business mission statement. It's similar in that there is a stated intention, something like "I wish to eradicate poverty for one million people."

It's different in that it also contains a statement about how it will be accomplished, as well as a metric for measurement. The "why" is in any mission statement. The "how" and "what" are added to an impact investing mission statement.

3. Identify Areas of Interest

How are investor resources then allocated among different issue areas about which they're passionate? It's done through something called the "values game," a practical method for sharpening focus.

Here's how it works:

One hundred coins are distributed with instructions to allocate among nine high-level issue areas, with the coins naturally representing investable areas both in the traditional sense and from a charitable perspective. No concern is given to guilt and/or worry; it's a free and open exercise. Your blank canvas.

The investor might have 40 percent allocated to poverty alleviation and economic development, 22 percent to education, 33 percent to women's empowerment, and the remainder in energy and the environment. The game consists of multiple rounds, each with accompanying questions meant to educate and illuminate investors as to what they really feel and why.

It's about identifying how deeply, or passionately, someone feels about a particular issue area. Ultimately, it's a dialogue. It's coaching investors, rather than simply presenting important issue areas and attempting to determine their interest and capital allocation commitment.

4. Match Goals with Specific Impact Investment Opportunities

The top three issue areas are the focus of the investment opportunity, and where to concentrate assets to match values. Because impact is subjective to the individual investor, there is no right or wrong answer. It seeks a financial return equal or better, in most cases, to a traditional investment, but it's also looking to measure its impact

It's also a journey, over the course of which the investor, and their definition of impact investing, will change. Ask any impact investing veteran and they'll tell you they're far from where they started. They'll also argue that good philanthropists are good investors, and good investors are good philanthropists; they need not be separate.

Case Study 4

IMPACT INVESTOR CASE STUDY: "BEN CARTER"

Year Started Impact Investing: 2005

Primary Focus: Total Portfolio Management of all family assets

Background: In 2000, Silicon Valley entrepreneur Ben Carter emerged from the tech IPO boom with a pile of cash and the desire to make a positive impact on the world. The company that Ben had stock options in had gone public and he became a millionaire overnight.

Impact Trigger

In 2001, Ben met with a financial advisor to devise a plan for deploying his new wealth. When he asked what investment opportunities there were to put his money to work for positive impact, the advisor wasn't sure if there were such options but pointed him toward environmental social governance (ESG) mutual funds. ESG mutual funds screen out companies based on specific criteria, such as tobacco. The impact that Ben wanted to make was bigger and different than simply "screening out the bad." He didn't want to make more money with his money but wanted to invest with people he trusted and in ideas and ventures that excited him. Helping innovative social entrepreneurs, for instance, or lending money to small business owners in the community were of interest to him. The entrepreneurial spirit was part of Ben's DNA and he wanted to integrate his interests and intentions in something personal, understandable and on a human scale.

Ben continued to search for a different answer and eventually found his way into impact investing, a way of investing that seeks a financial as well as social and environmental returns.

Investment Strategy

Over time, demand from other like-minded investors helped drive the development of more investment opportunities as well as financial advisor expertise in the marketplace. With the guidance of a financial advisor versed in impact investing and in lockstep with an evolving market, Ben's portfolio is now 85 percent invested in impact investments across a well-diversified portfolio by impact strategy, impact issue and asset class. Impact strategy includes sustainable and thematic approaches. Asset classes include public equity, fixed income, hedge funds, real assets and cash equivalents. Impact issues include energy, water, financial services, community development and information technology.

Working with the right financial advisor was the catalyst for Ben to move forward in a strategic thoughtful way. The development of an Impact Investing Strategy and an Impact Investing Policy served as blueprints. The Impact Investing Strategy helped Ben think through what impact meant to him and what his impact mission, values and themes were. It also defined Ben's portfolio needs and constraints including risk, return and liquidity needs.

The Impact Investing Policy translated the strategy into a tangible investment implementation plan. One of the outcomes to the process was the determination that public markets strategies, including public equities strategies such as ESG, would play an essential role in Ben's comprehensive asset allocation. Investments into large US and global corporations derive a different source of impact relative to private market strategies. Public companies are often diversified across multiple business lines and operate globally, thus offering a unique impact opportunity to effect change on a larger and meaningful scale.

One of Ben's prominent impact issues is climate change. Despite the challenges and investment risks associated with climate change, Ben is particularly hopeful about certain initiatives such as renewable energy, green buildings and carbon pricing. Ben discovered a number of investment opportunities addressing climate change issues through a variety of asset classes, both public and private. Increasingly more investment managers are developing strategies to invest in businesses that are accelerating the transition to a low-carbon economy. These strategies vary widely and include everything from low-carbon portfolios of publicly listed companies, to venture and private equity funds that actively invest in private companies building and operating renewable energy infrastructure. In public market strategies, Ben found more than 250 equity and fixed-income mutual funds, exchange traded funds (ETFs) and separately managed accounts focused on environmental sustainability.* He also found many specialized private capital fund managers tailoring their funds on particular impact areas such as natural resource health, carbon reduction, renewable energy infrastructure, climate-smart cities, rainforest protection or waste management. These opportunities allowed him to directly fund specific projects seeking to deliver high impact. Ben has approximately 15 percent of his portfolio in diversified public and private strategies and real assets addressing climate change.

Looking ahead, Ben will continue to evolve and shape his portfolio as he learns from his experiences and understanding that it is possible to support both financial and impact goals in the same portfolio. Since inception of the portfolio some six years ago, he believes that the opportunities for impact investing have never been greater and they will continue to increase as other investors start to incorporate social and environmental values into their allocations. His goal is to have a 100 percent impact portfolio within the next few years.

* http://www.veriswp.com/investing/research/.

11

Getting to Impact

Jed Emerson

As we have stated throughout this book, impact investing is simply good, sound investment practice augmented with an impact lens—namely, consideration of how your capital may be invested with an eye toward various levels of financial return together with the generation of different types of social and environmental impact.

My expectation is as you approach the execution of your impact investing strategy you will follow a few key practices:

- Assess who you are, what type of values drive your life and where you want to be in years to come.
- Understand what your options are for investing and assess what you may already be invested in today, from cash to direct investments and everything in between.
- Educate yourself regarding the various strategies and approaches available to you within both impact and traditional investment options and then.
- Invest your capital with a goal of long-term performance and not short-term gain.

I also hope after you've taken the time to read the good words of those who contributed to this book, you will read other books on both impact investing and traditional investing practices, absorb the information in some of the papers you'll find on the various resource pages we list at the end of this book and become knowledgeable yourself about these strategies before you decide to invest for impact. This is what I tell the families I advise and this is how Mia and I try to approach our own investing.

That said, some folks will enter this discussion ready to act now—to invest today with whatever amount of capital you feel appropriate and learn about impact investing by actually *doing* impact investing. If that is true of you, then you might consider engaging in some "test cases." What I mean by that is to put your toe in the water with a smaller amount of capital to see how it goes, see how your assumptions play out and learn about the practice of impact investing through participating in a more limited way with options that could give you a chance to learn through doing. If you're working without a formal advisor to help guide your process, should you "bet the farm" on strategies you are still learning about and at a time when you're still exploring the overall field of impact investing? Of course not!

But there are still ways you can begin to participate in impact investing at the same time you continue to learn, experiment and educate yourself about the field and its promise. If that sounds appealing, perhaps some of the options we list below will be of interest to you!

First off, if you have your checking account with a major, international banking institution, consider moving your money to either your local community bank, a credit union or an entity such as Beneficial State Bank, New Resources Bank, Mighty Deposits or other entities providing not simply financial services, but advancing a community or sustainability agenda in the world. For more information on these ideas, see the *Move Your Money Project* website for articles and resources.

Once you have your own cash flow in order, explore some of these[1] additional options:[2]

Calvert Foundation (CF), through their lending fund, finances affordable housing and small business development. CF allows you to target your investment within a variety of thematic areas, such as social enterprises, community care and local development. Their community investment note can be invested in for as little as $20 and offers a range of returns and terms (0–4 percent over 1 to 15 years).

RSF Social Investment Fund (RSF), has made hundreds of loans to for-profit and nonprofit organizations ranging from sustainable agriculture to housing and community services. For a $1,000 minimum, you can invest for 90 days in a note with 0.75 percent interest rate, reset on a quarterly basis. RSF has hundreds of impact investors as a part of their community and connects investors with investees through a variety of activities and events. In 2014 alone, RSF lent nearly $14 million to 70 plus social enterprises in the United States and overseas.

Cooperative Capital Fund of New England provides financing and capacity-building support to cooperative ventures, with a preference for those cooperatives located in and serving lower income neighborhoods. Investments made out of the fund act like equity for participating cooperatives, but don't require the cooperatives to surrender control to outside investors. Investors earn 5 percent per annum.

Working Capital for Community Needs (WCCN) takes investment capital from impact investors and uses it to finance entrepreneurs throughout Latin America. Over the past 25 years, they have lent approximately $110 million and serve approximately 25,000 people per year. Two-thirds of their borrowers are women and half are from rural areas. With a $1,000 minimum, WCCN offers an easy way to learn about and participate in microfinance.

CRA Fund (retail offering) is a bond fund available to individual, retail level impact investors. Invested capital is lent to support community development and affordable housing throughout the United States. Created with a mutual fund structure, this fund offers liquidity to investors with a $2,000 minimum. Since inception, CRA Fund has placed over five billion dollars into the market.

Equal Exchange (EE), through a partnership with Eastern Bank, offers FDIC-insured certificates of deposit with a $500 minimum to investors. These deposits are used to secure a line of credit that EE then draws upon to finance its fair trade purchases from farmers and cooperatives overseas. There is a 36-month term at a guaranteed fixed rate of interest.

TriLinc Global Impact Fund lends to small and medium enterprises (SMEs) in emerging markets. SMEs are often too large to receive microfinance loans, but not big enough for major commercial banks; TriLinc seeks to fill that financing gap. Minimum investment is $2,000 and targeted returns of about 7 percent, but investors must have a net worth of at least $250,000 of investible capital (not including your home or other hard assets). TriLinc focuses upon sub-Saharan Africa and Latin America.

Greenbacker Renewable Energy is a limited liability company offering shares to investors starting at $2,000 and making distributions to shareholders as well as offering share buyback, on a quarterly basis. Funds are used to support expansion of renewable energy projects primarily in the United States.

ImpactAssets (IA)—the organization producing this book!—is a nonprofit financial services organization that manages $300 million in donor advised funds (DAFs) as well as investing its capital on an impact basis, in collaboration with its DAF clients. In 2016, IA introduced two types of investment notes (one targeting microfinance and the other sustainable agriculture) with an investor minimum of $25,000. The notes have a five-year term and targeted financial return of 3 percent.

SerenityShares launched an impact ETF, or exchange traded fund, that invests in "solutions" oriented companies but has the traditional characteristics and liquidity of a standard ETF. Many investors like ETFs for their potential transparency and ease of management.[3]

And these are just the opportunities one can find after a bit of online research. New organizations and products are being launched each week, so you would do well to subscribe (for free!) to many of the newsletters various networks and impact-oriented publications offer if you are to keep up with developments in the field. While perhaps not as easy as picking prescreened options off-the-shelf, with a bit of effort you can put together a set of investments that reflect your goals and interests. Remember: make investments only in firms and products you have fully assessed and whose strategies you understand. Good marketing should not take the place of your own good due diligence!

As you are looking for opportunities, be sure to check out the offerings of some of the larger wealth management and advisory firms. While it's probably safe to say they are not going to change the face of financial capitalism, several are working to bring the power of their institutions to the challenge of bringing retail level, impact investing products to market. For example, *Morgan Stanley* offers their Investing with Impact Access Balanced and Investing with Impact Access Equity products, each with a $10,000 minimum. And *Blackrock Impact* is offering strategies such as its BIRAX Impact US Equity Fund. Other investment groups are rolling out new offers as well, so check the firms you like best and ask what they either offer or have in the works—and if they don't offer an impact fund or retail investor option for one, let them know you want one! The reason we've gotten this far over recent years is due to client demand!

In addition to going through investment firms, you can also work with platforms offering you ways to create and execute your own strategy. For example, *OpenInvest* is an impact investing platform available to those with $3,000 to invest and helps guide you through the process with both low fee requirements and broad exposure. As one of its founders describes it, "OpenInvest (https://openinvest.co) is a Y Combinator-backed start-up offering the world's first Socially Responsible Investing (SRI) platform for retail investors, and beyond. Our team of senior technologists from the hedge fund industry and civil society leaders is mainstreaming ethical finance by making it easy, personalized, and social. Divest-invest with a swipe, vote shareholder resolutions, participate in mass campaigns, measure your impact, and claim the power that is rightfully yours in public markets." Definitely worth checking out to see if it meets your needs.

Or you might like *Swell*, an impact investment platform that aims to deliver purpose with profit. They identify high-impact, high-growth potential companies working toward progress in a number of industries. You can invest in one or all of their thematic portfolios that are based on solving important social and environmental challenges such as Green Technology, Renewable Energy, Zero Waste, Clean Water, Healthy Living and Disease Eradication. Swell says they are unapologetically selective about the companies in its portfolios, and use a double filter to optimize for impact and returns. Each company in Swell's portfolios derives revenue directly from their theme, which means they're walking the talk in terms of impact. And they are working to keep pricing simple, with a flat fee (0.75 percent) as low as the price of a daily cup of coffee per year (based on a minimum investment of $500).

If you're interested in exploring other options for retail level impact investing, the arrival of "robo" tools to help impact investors is also a promising development. These "robo" tools help individual investors search for the best offerings in exchange traded funds and other impact investment products. *Motif Impact* is described as "a values-oriented digital investing solution … and will use the platform's digital investing solution to help users determine their risk tolerance, allocate to investments and set a glide path. Trading to rebalance user accounts occurs at no cost, and subscribers can replace investments within their motifs without incurring commissions or fees."[4] Other options are in development as we go to press with this book.

And, finally, crowdfunding will have a significant impact upon how impact investors will move money over coming years. As Fast Company Magazine recently reported, across over 2,500 crowdfunding platforms active across the world in 2015 crowdfunding as a sector managed over 35 billion dollars in capital flows, of which 70 percent was in some form of charitable giving while the balance was in some form of equity investment.[5] While there are a number of platforms currently under development, a good guide to the field was recently published by Toniic and the European Crowdfunding Network.[6]

Still looking for more options to explore?

Try Credibles (https://credibles.co/) to engage in local food sourcing, Cutting Edge X (http://cuttingedgex.com/) for direct public offerings, check out the Muni Bonds at Neighborly (https://neighborly.com/) or if you're interested in leads on community investment opportunities, try ImpactUS (http://www.impactusmarketplace.com/). And, finally, there are a growing number of general resource sites such as Good With Money (http://good-with-money.com/about-us/) that bring together other resources to assist you in your research efforts!

The bottom-line is nose around, do some research, talk to folks who write blogs and traffic in impact and in a bit of time you'll find the right platform to move your money from inactive to active impact!

Notes

1 This list includes investment options included in a *Christian Science Monitor* article (many of which are well known) as well as other opportunities identified by the author, You Can Be an Impact Investor!," Published February 18, 2016, Accessed April 18, 2017, "Got $20?, http://www.csmonitor.com/Business/new-economy/2016/0218/Got-20-You-can-be-an-impact-investor.

2 All information is taken from organizational websites. You must review all placement and offering documents yourself to confirm information and receive notice of the specific terms of whatever investment you are considering!

3 "SerenityShares Launches Impact ETF," Published April 18, 2017, Accessed April 19, 2017, https://www.etfstrategy.co.uk/serenityshares-launches-impact-investing-etf-26584/.

4 Published March 8, 2017; Accessed April 19, 2017, http://www.etfa-mag.com/news/it-s-not-a-robo--motif-launches-custom-automated-impact-investing-31734.html.

5 How Will the Rise of Crowdfunding Reshape How We Give to Charity?," Published March 3, 2017, Accessed March 27, 2017, "https://www.fastcompany.com/3068534/how-will-the-rise-of-crowdfunding-reshape-how-we-give-to-charity?utm_content=buffer452f4&utm_medium=social&utm_source=twitter.com&utm_campaign=buffer.

6 "Crowdfunding for Impact," Accessed April 19, 2017, http://www.toniic.com/wp-content/uploads/2013/12/CrowdfundingForImpact.pdf

12

Concluding Thoughts on Mobilizing for Impact

Jed Emerson and Tim Freundlich

As we look back on the ground we have covered in this *The ImpactAssets Handbook for Investors*, it is clear that while impact investing has moved from the fringe toward the mainstream, the individual investor still has many moving parts and challenges to consider. Among the questions we've explored are:

- How should you define your approach?
- Where do you go for resources, support and information?
- How do you understand the nature of the impact you want to create?
- What types of returns should you expect and how do you assess the performance of your portfolio on both financial and impact terms?

All investors have before them opportunities to align capital with community and values with value creation. By thinking—and then acting!—within a Total Portfolio Management framework, you have the potential to achieve the greatest leverage and impact possible for the assets you have under management, regardless of whether you're an investor operating on your own at a retail level or a higher net worth asset owner with a team to assist you. If you're committed to impact as well as wanting to protect your financial future, you can attain various levels of financial return together with the generation of social and environmental impacts. And you can direct your resources toward not only providing for your own future, but the future of your children and community.

As we look ahead to that future, what are final words one should keep in mind when moving along the path?

Fortune Favors the Prepared Mind

Good investing involves some level of luck—that the markets move up with you; that you select the right managers at the right time and so on—but the fact is good preparation can help you increase the odds you've made the right decisions at the right times for the right reasons. Rather than attempting to "time the market" looking to take advantage of short-term ups and downs, remember to stay focused on your long-term goals and plan for those goals through creating a sound strategy. Investors need to stay on top of the latest thinking, be clear on their objectives and work to understand the investments they are making—and that is not a question of luck! If you keep in mind the suggestions in this book, as well as other guidance you can find from any number of investment advisory sources, you'll increase the odds of success and better understand the risks you may want to assume in order to create the financial and impact returns you're looking to generate.

Impact Investing Is Additive—Not Restrictive

Impact investing is not about taking away traditional investment practice and replacing it with something "flashy," new or different. Impact investing is about taking traditional, sober and conservative fundamental investing practice and augmenting it with considerations of social and environmental impact. At its best, it is taking what works about traditional investment practice and integrating it with considerations of "off balance sheet" risk and opportunity that may be identified by considering social and environmental factors that could affect your investment. And a good impact investing strategy may also include looking for opportunities to invest that optimize positive impacts for your community and our world. Ultimately, it is about *adding* considerations to an investment approach, not taking away or watering down sound investment practice.

Impact Investing Is a Lens—Not an Asset Class

Impact investing is, simply put, a lens through which one approaches the full spectrum of options and asset classes in the market and for one's portfolio. Therefore, impact investing is not an asset class; mistaking it for one does a disservice to the investor who may then be forced to compartmentalize the application of best practice. Impact investing should not be siloed, so let's not stigmatize impact investing. Rather, we should seek to let its practices and our pursuit of it flourish across the full spectrum of portfolio opportunities before us.

Define Your Process and Commit to Your Plan

Impact investing is not about chasing the latest trend or fad that promises you incredible financial returns and the ability to sleep well at night, knowing you're making the Earth a better place. It is about definition of an approach you would like to take to explore your options, research where you think the best opportunities for *you* may be and then moving deliberately to invest in those opportunities. Building upon investment practices of the mainstream and adhering to your plan while executing it in a flexible manner as you proceed, you will be able to responsibly manage your investment process and improve the possibilities of success.

Understand What Risk Means for You—Not the Investor Next to You!

One must assume some level of risk in life if one is to live—you have to leave the house and be in the world if you are to see it! But at the same time, understanding what your level of risk comfort is and how it can inform your investment approach are key to successful investing. Remember: Being a good investor is not about achieving someone else's goals and objectives; it is about assuming a level of risk that makes sense for you and where you want to go.

You may want to live on the edge or you may want to stick closer to the wall, but either way you alone must decide what is reasonable and what is the best approach for you. Don't let a "great opportunity" steer you off course. It may simply be a great opportunity for *someone else* if it is not in alignment with what you are trying to do and where you want to go. Listen to what other impact investors are talking about, understand how others are approaching their investment process—but never forget your goals, your level of risk and that your strategy is about what you want to do, not what others are promoting.

Impact Investing Is an Evolving Field—Grow with It

Though there are aspects of the "nascent" and "evolving" in impact investing and its practice, that need not be an excuse to wait on the sidelines until these developing practices are all tied up with a bow. This is the brave new world, be part of it along the way. We can learn and contribute much as the evolution takes place. Activated investors approaching impact across the full spectrum of their portfolio, demanding excellence and sustained value from the funds and companies they invest in, are well positioned to benefit from and help in the creation of greater depth in the field of impact investing.

Start with What You Know—And Learn What You Need to Know

We have found that the "personal" translates well as an on ramp into impact investing. What do you care about? Why are you specifically motivated to approach impact investing? Is there a particular impact theme you have experienced or that has touched your life as an issue? Or is a family member pushing you to engage in exploring it? Use the answers to those questions to help focus your approach. We have to start somewhere, and starting with the need or core motivation (whether life experience, issue or relationship-based) can be a grounding element as you learn about and apply an impact lens to your portfolio.

If You Don't Understand What the Investment Strategy Is—Don't Invest!

Though it might go without saying, it is worth noting the wisdom of not getting caught up in what can sometimes be the hyperbole and cool factor of "impact," any more than one should do so in the more conventional context of attempting to invest in a technology or business model one doesn't understand. Impact doesn't trump a good business model, just as a good business idea is often less important than a good management team. If you can't understand the fundamentals of why an investment is impactful, how it will make money and find its market, and which excellent people are going to be at the wheel ... you shouldn't invest!

Invest for Long Term—Not Short Term—Returns (Both Financial and Impact)

There are many reasons to take the long view. Value is well correlated to patience and the pursuit of long-term strategies. This applies to both impact and financial value creation for the investor and the world. Invest for the long term, but get going with a healthy dose of impatience in terms of putting the trains on the tracks of integrating impact as broadly as possible within your portfolio.

There is a term in finance, "Net Present Value," where we discount the expected future cash flows to come up with today's value of them. The further we go out in time, the less the value of those expected flows due to the uncertainties of time and markets. A dollar far off in the future is much less certain or more risky, with its buying power eroded by accumulating inflation. We should approach the time value of impact from a similar perspective. Positive impact is far more valuable now than later. This value of more, better impact happening as soon as possible is the accounting that needs to be accessible to investors. And to properly value such impact, we must demand impact metrics and strategies that are clearly articulated, tracked and delivered upon. Not over engineered, abstract or academic change theories, but instead, straightforward metrics that track impact that matters, and that is well integrated into the information systems and core value chains of business. The best fund managers and companies will increasingly deliver these to investors, if and as they understand them to be a "must have" requirement.

Don't Judge a Book by Its Cover

Over recent years, we've witnessed a number of new entries to the field of impact investing wherein traditional, lightly modified (sometimes preexisting!) strategies have been rebranded as "impact" and brought forward through a new marketing campaign to take advantage of the current interest in impact investing. Conversely, we've also seen some traditional, fundamental investing strategies that actually create what could be viewed as real impact overlooked by the market, simply because they were not being promoted as "impact investing." As you explore the growing array of offerings before you, don't get too wrapped up in whether or not something is called "impact." What matters is not what someone says, but rather how an investment strategy is managed, what types of companies they actually invest in, the degree of intentionally and depth to their approach and your ability to assess the types of extrafinancial, social and environmental value any given strategy advances. Remember: some folks who claim positive impact don't generate it and some who have never heard the word are actually creating real, sustainable value. Assess all those who claim to "do" impact investing and you be the judge of what they do—not what they say!

In Conclusion

In the preceding chapters, we have explored a realignment of value and values within the investment framework, to one that better reflects and reinforces our making investments in the creation of a sustainable world. We are seeing an emergent articulation of entrepreneur and company integration of values and purpose. The time when executives and companies can ignore the true costs of doing business is quickly coming to a close. Investors are coming into a clearer set of views around these same true costs, and integrating them into their investment strategy. Conversely, despite some short-term setbacks, the time when we may allow externalization of social and environmental costs off corporations' financial statements onto the world's balance sheet is also coming to an end. When we invest, we participate in a complex system of value creation that generates multiple returns with financial, social and environmental implications. Investing is far from merely the act of putting one's dollars into a financial instrument. Investing is fundamentally based on the individual's pursuit of intensely personal goals and very basic human needs expressed in financial terms. We seek to create wealth in order to have choices regarding how we live our lives, provide for our families and pursue our dreams. We seek to create wealth to build thriving economic systems to ensure we live in safe and bountiful communities that allow us, and all others, to achieve our greatest potential. Truly, the goal of creating economic wealth is seldom pursued in the abstract. Instead it is a means to an end; and the end for impact investors is the creation of a more just, sustainable economic and human system across the world.

Though investment cannot be our only tool and must compliment effective philanthropy and sound public sector policies, through directing resources away from value extracting firms, flexing shareholder power and moving capital affirmatively toward positive enterprises, impact investing may play a significant role in increasing equitability and sustainability in our own communities and around the world. Let's take these strategies and apply them, intelligently, but with urgency. Time is money and, more importantly, time is missed impact opportunities. Over the years to come, we hope you will take up this opportunity to invest with meaning!

Appendix

Impact Investing Resources*

A key point to remember when discussing resources of interest to impact investors is they are continually being updated, evolved and expanded. Your best option is to subscribe to a few magazines and newsletters in order to receive updates on the field, attend a few impact investing events to learn the latest on issues of interest to impact investors and simply keep your eyes and ears open! You'll be amazed at the number and quality of resources available to you—most of which are free.

What follows is simply a starting place with no doubt *many* additional groups we may have overlooked and could have been included in this initial list. We should also note that given the authors of this book are based in the United States, most of these resources are "US-centric." There are growing numbers of networks and resources being introduced in communities around the world, so don't forget to think globally, but act locally when looking for information and networks to inform your own good efforts. The following list is simply a starting place for you to begin your journey to impact!

Investor Networks

Toniic; www.toniic.org

Toniic is a global network of impact investors consisting of individuals and foundations investing in a variety of thematic

---

* Some descriptions are taken directly from the organization's websites.

areas. They host many annual conferences and regional networking sessions.

Investors Circle; http://www.investorscircle.net

Investors Circle (IC) is the largest and most active early stage impact investing network. Together with hundreds of angels, venture capitalists, foundations and family offices, IC has propelled over $200 million into more than 300 enterprises dedicated to improving the environment, education, health and community.

Gratitude Railroad, http://gratituderailroad.com/#welcome

Gratitude Railroad serves as a community and catalyst for investors to learn, discuss and invest across asset classes focused on delivering top tier returns and helping to solve environmental and social challenges. This community has achieved significant success as investors, operators and entrepreneurs across various sectors and stages in the traditional capital markets.

Silicon Valley Social Venture Fund; www.sv2.org/

Silicon Valley Social Venture Fund (SV2) is a community of more than 200 individuals and families who have come together to learn about effective giving and pool our resources to support innovative social ventures.

Intellecap Impact Investing Network; http://intellecap.com/our-work/initiatives/i3n

Intellecap Impact Investment Network (I³N) is India's first angel network of high net worth individuals and institutional investors seeking investments in early stage enterprises in the Intellecap Focus Sectors.

Green Impact Investing Network; https://www.switchmed.eu/en/corners/impact-investors/actions/actions/Green-Impact-Investing-Network

To stimulate the green market, to enhance a sustainable economy and to boost a real financial inclusion in the MENA region, access to finance continues to be a top priority challenge to be addressed and Green Impact Investing Network seeks to do just this. Some of the focus areas include dealing with issues such as reducing the significant number of entrepreneurs who have limited insight into financing opportunities, lack skills and capacity to make sound applications for starting up or growing their businesses.

SlowMoney; https://slowmoney.org/
An investor network that offers resources of information and collaborative support, SlowMoney organizes investors in local food systems and agriculture. Through regional meetings, annual events and a variety of resource offerings, SlowMoney supports impact investors interested in connecting their dollar with supporting the future of farming at the local/regional level.

Newsletters/Journals

Simply Google the names of these leading sources of information to subscribe to their newsletters:

- ImpactAlpha Newsletter (David Bank)
- On Impact (Cathy Clark)
- All Things Impact (Brian Walsh)

TBLI Blog (Robert Rubinstein)
http://us2.campaign-archive2.com/?e=a45b3906b7&u=af5d00fc f24bb8d0cfaaff42b&id=92209b8dd1

Responsible Investor Magazine; https://www.responsible-investor. com/
A great resource for institutional investors looking to engage in responsible and sustainable investing, as well as keep up on most recent reports and publications.

Alliance Magazine; http://www.alliancemagazine.org/
Perhaps the oldest journal focusing on strategic philanthropy, impact investing and related areas of interest to those moving money for good.

Stanford Social Innovation Review; https://ssir.org/
An excellent, consistently high-quality read for those looking to link academic level analysis with community level impact.

Industry Groups

SOCAP: http://socialcapitalmarkets.net/

Not as much an industry group as gathering of the tribes, SOCAP brings together leading impact investors for an annual meeting in San Francisco, is moving to host an expanded media platform and regional sessions, as well as having recently launched The Good Capital Project, a "cross sector" venture that seeks to bring traditional financial services actors together with leading impact investors and entrepreneurs.

Confluence; http://www.confluencephilanthropy.org/

Confluence Philanthropy advances mission-aligned investing. It supports and catalyzes a community of private, public and community foundations, families, individual donors, and their values-aligned investment managers representing more than $71 billion in philanthropic assets under management, and over $3 trillion in managed capital. Members are committed to full mission alignment when prudent and feasible. Based in the United States, Europe, Latin America, Canada and Puerto Rico, its members collectively invest around the world.

The Global Impact Investing Network (GIIN); www.thegiin.org

With one of the most comprehensive resources web page, Global Impact Investing Network (GIIN) is the go to place for information on the state of the field as well as offering a host of materials and resources of interest to the impact investor.

The Global Impact Investing Network (GIIN) conducts a comprehensive survey of impact investors each year. In the most recent edition, over 200 impact investors reported managing $114b in impact investing assets. This is not the whole universe, but this figure provides a sound estimate of the floor of the impact investing market.

USSIF: The Forum for Sustainable and Responsible Investment; http://www.ussif.org/

Perhaps the oldest network of responsible and sustainable investors, USSIF hosts events and offers information to institutional and other asset owners looking to invest engage in more than traditional investing.

The SRI Conference, http://www.sriconference.com/
An annual gathering of leading sustainable, responsible and impact investors, this conference is a solid way to get oriented to the field and meet some its leading practitioners.

Impact Capitalism Summit, http://www.impact-capitalism.com/
The Impact Capitalism Summit convenes annually in Chicago, but also holds events throughout the year across the United States and more recently in Europe. These events provide a platform to meet those from across the field of impact investing and catch-up on current practices.

TBLI Conferences, http://www.tbligroup.com/tbliconference.html
Perhaps the "granddaddy" of them all, TBLI has been bringing mission-driven investors together for over well over a decade. While many of their events are held in Europe, they have also hosted events in Asia and other regions around the world. A great network to connect with as you engage in your own global inquiry!

Guides

A Short Guide to Impact Investing, Case Foundation, 2014
http://casefoundation.org/wp-content/uploads/2014/11/ShortGuideToImpactInvesting-2014.pdf

Impact Investing: A Primer for Family Offices; World Economic Forum, 2014
https://www.weforum.org/reports/impact-investing-primer-family-offices

Navigating the Territory: A Guide to Impact Investing for Donors, The Philanthropic Initiative, 2014
http://www.tpi.org/learning-center/navigating-the-territory-a-guide-to-impact-investing-for-donors

Omidyar Network: Pioneering Impact Investment, Harvard Business Review, 2013
https://hbr.org/product/omidyar-network-pioneering-impact-investment/313090-PDF-ENG

Investing for Social and Environmental Impact, Monitor Institute, 2009
    http://monitorinstitute.com/downloads/what-we-think/impact-investing/Impact_Investing.pdf

Social Finance a Primer, Sonal Shah and Kristina Costa, Center for American Progress, 2013
    https://www.americanprogress.org/wp-content/uploads/2013/11/SocialFinance-brief.pdf

E-Guide to Early Stage Global Impact Investing, Toniic, 2013
    http://www.toniic.com/toniic-institute/early-stage-e-guide/

Academic Centers

Growing number of graduate and undergraduate institutions are now creating academic centers to support not only the work of the field, but to train future generations of leaders in impact investing and social entrepreneurship. Places to begin your search are the CASE Center at the Fuqua School (Duke University), Wharton Business School's Impact Center (University of Pennsylvania), The Sorensen Impact Center at the University of Utah, The Beeck Center at Georgetown University, and many others.

Donor Advised Funds

As outlined earlier in this book, donor advised funds can be an effective vehicle for impact investing. In addition to the organizations listed below, it is important to reach out to your local community foundation to see what they may also have to offer in the way of local impact investing opportunities.

- Impact Assets; www.impactassets.org
- RSF Social Finance; http://rsfsocialfinance.org/
- Tides Network; https://www.tides.org/

Foundations/Organizations

Led by the good work of the Mission Investors Exchange, many foundations are now coming together to learn about and engage in impact investing. A number of foundations offer newsletters of note and other information regarding the field. Here is an initial list of leading actors in the conversation:

- Mission Investors Exchange; https://www.missioninvestors.org/
- Social Impact Exchange; http://www.socialimpactexchange.org/
- F. B. Heron Foundation; http://www.heron.org/
- KL Felicitas Foundation; http://klfelicitasfoundation.org/
- Rockefeller Foundation, Impact Investing; https://www.rockefellerfoundation.org/our-work/initiatives/innovative-finance/
- W. K. Kellogg Foundation; https://www.wkkf.org/
- Ford Foundation; https://www.fordfoundation.org/

Videos

The Power of Impact Investing, Margot Brandenburg

https://ca.news.yahoo.com/video/put-markets-global-good-impact-183645464.html

Impact Investing Is the Future; Sir Ronald Cohen, Stanford Graduate Business School

https://www.youtube.com/watch?v=VgWJZiRL7BQ

Investor Resources

The ImpactAssets 50; http://www.impactassets.org/publications_insights/impact50: A free online database of impact fund managers.

ImpactBase: https://www.impactbase.org/: A database of leading impact investing funds.

The USSIF Education Center; http://www.ussif.org/education

Finally, the editor of this volume, Jed Emerson, has been active in framing and promoting concepts of Blended Value and impact investing for many years. Most of his papers, interviews and videos are available for free on the Blended Value website, www.blended-value.org, and would be worth your review as well!

Notes on Contributors

Jed Emerson

Senior Fellow
ImpactAssets

Jed Emerson has played founder roles with some of the nation's leading impact investing, venture philanthropy, community venture capital and social enterprises. Since 2010, he has served as senior strategic advisor to five family offices located around the world with over $1.4 billion in total assets, each executing 100 percent impact/sustainable investment strategies with their total net worth. Author of numerous articles and papers, Emerson is coauthor of the first book on impact investing (and winner of the 2012 Nautilus Gold Book Award), *Impact Investing: Transforming How We Make Money While Making a Difference* as well as coauthor of *The Impact Investor: Lessons in Leadership and Strategy for Collaborative Capitalism*. He has also coauthored/edited three books on social entrepreneurship. Originator of the concept of Blended Value, Emerson has presented at The World Economic Forum (Davos, Switzerland), The Clinton Global Initiative (New York City), The Skoll World Forum (Oxford, England) and professional meetings around the world. He serves as Chief Impact Strategist for ImpactAssets, a nonprofit financial services firm. He served as Associate Fellow with the Said Business School at Oxford University (2015–16), a non-resident Senior Fellow with the Center for Social Investment, Heidelberg University (Germany) and has held faculty appointments with Harvard, Stanford and Oxford business schools.

Tim Freundlich

President and Cofounder, ImpactAssets
Board Chair and Cofounder, Mission HUB
Managing Partner and Cofounder, Good Capital

Tim Freundlich is an innovator of financial instruments for impact investing. Over the past 20 years, he served 12 at Calvert Foundation (http://www.calvertfoundation.org), helping to build the $250 million Calvert Community Investment Note ($1 billion cumulatively invested into hundreds of nonprofits and for profits globally). While with The Calvert Foundation he conceived of and launched the prototype of the Giving Fund—now a $300+ million impact investment-based donor advised fund that was spun out as ImpactAssets in 2011 (http://www.impactassets.org), which he cofounded and serves as President. In addition, Freundlich cofounded and serves on the management board of Good Capital (http://www.goodcap.net), which is the General Partner of the Social Enterprise Expansion Fund LP. He is also the cofounder of two social enterprises: the SOCAP Conferences (http://www.socialcapitalmarkets.net) and ImpactHUB SF (Berkeley, NYC and DC; http://www.impacthub.net), which serve as coworking, collaboration and community spaces for more than 2,000 social entrepreneurs, and part of a global network of 85 ImpactHUBs across five continents with 20,000 members. He received a BA from Wesleyan University with a major in Film, an Executive MBA from the University of San Francisco. He lives in San Francisco with his better half Julie, and two sons, Milo and Gus.

Brad Harrison

Director
Wealth Advisory, Threshold Group

Brad Harrison is a wealth advisor at Threshold Group who works with foundations, endowments, and nonprofit organizations to align their investments with their mission. He developed the firm's scientific approach to low-carbon portfolio management and leads the environmental impact strategy focusing on clean technology, forestry, agriculture, and fisheries. In addition, he built and leads

a place-based investment platform which seeks to drive investments within the themes of sustainable environments, equitable
communities, and responsible economies to advance community-
centric outcomes. Prior to Threshold Group, Harrison worked at
Ecotrust Forest Management, a regionally focused forest investment management firm, and Green Building Services, a sustainable development consulting firm. He earned a bachelor's degree
in Applied Economics and Management from Cornell University
and master's degree in Environmental Management from Yale
University.

Amy Hartzler

Founder
Do Good Better

Amy Hartzler is the founder of Do Good Better, which provides
marketing and communications for organizations and leaders trying to do good, better. After an early chapter in academic publishing (Duke University Press) she moved to Washington, D.C.,
establishing deep roots in the local creative communications
scene. For the past five years her focus has been on translating
and marketing the many ways that capital can be used to tangibly
create the world we want. That has included campaigns focused
on positive impact investing, including work with the Calvert
Foundation, naming, launching and supporting www.OursToOwn.
org and www.AgeStrongInvest.org. Both initiatives welcome investors starting at $20 through the online platform Vested.org, and
have deployed a combined $55 million of community-directed
capital in two and a half years. More recently, she partnered with
the Business Alliance of Local Living Economies (BALLE; www.
BeALocalist.org) to help them better reflect, connect and activate its community of highly effective local and regional economic leaders—from fellows, investors and entrepreneurs to
leaders within anchor institutions and philanthropy. Her framing
drives their Local Economy Framework: that is, eight strategies to
build healthy, equitable local economies. For seven years she led
the Washington, D.C. office for Oakland-based www.FreeRange.
com, developing brand and campaign strategy services, leading

major campaigns and contributing to the book *Winning the Story Wars: Why Those Who Tell—and Live—the Best Stories Will Rule the Future* by Jonah Sachs.

Hartzler grew up in a midwestern, bipartisan, multifaith home. She is based in Washington, D.C., where she serves as Brand Director for the D.C. Department of Funk (www.FunkParade.com), and Board Chair for the sponsoring nonprofit www.AllOneCity.org. She loves to host, walk, listen, question assumptions and meet new people.

Jennifer Kenning

Co-founder
Align

Jennifer Kenning is co-founder of Align, which serves as an independent impact advisor to asset owners. In collaboration with advisors, Align aims to increase the effectiveness and alignment of philanthropic grants, impact investments and mission-related investments. Kenning was named "40 under 40" for InvestmentNews in 2014, a finalist for "Rising Star for Family Wealth" report and selected for Private Asset Management's "50 Most Influential Women in Private Wealth" 2016. Kenning sits on the industry advisory board for the Center for High Impact Philanthropy, Wharton Social Impact Initiative and Tara Health Foundation joint project aligning investors interests in improving the lives of women. She has a BBA degree in finance and BA in economics from the Southern Methodist University and graduated cum laude. She finished her accounting certificate at UCLA and holds a Series 65 license.

Sara Olsen

Founder
SVT Group

Sara Olsen is the founder of SVT Group, "your outsourced Chief Impact Officer," an impact management firm that provides investors, companies and social enterprises support to measure, manage and communicate their social and environmental impact (e.g., theory of change, impact metrics, impact IT systems onboarding and support, retrospective impact analyses and more). A pioneer in the social capital markets, Olsen and SVT's team of subject-matter experts have measured the social and environmental value of approximately $9.08 billion in private equity, debt and grants in dozens of countries and issue areas. Recent clients include Yo Yo Ma, Restore the Earth Foundation, Fair Trade USA, Global Fund for Women, Beneficial State Bank, and CalPERS' Environmental Investment Advisor.

Olsen has been recognized twice as one of America's Most Promising Social Entrepreneurs by *Bloomberg Businessweek* for her work defining the impact management discipline. She is a founding board member of Social Value United States, and an adjunct faculty member at Middlebury Institute of International Studies and Hult International Business School. There and in collaboration with SVT clients, she has educated over 5,000 people in-person on impact management.

Sandra Osborne

Director, Investments
ImpactAssets

Sandra Osborne, CFA, is Director of the ImpactAssets Investments team, managing investment management for the Giving Fund and ImpactAssets' Impact Notes. She also supports ImpactAssets' product development and field building. Prior to joining ImpactAssets, she served as a risk officer at Developing World Markets, an impact investment asset manager focused on linking the capital markets and financial institutions serving the bottom of the pyramid in emerging and frontier economies. Osborne also worked at Keefe Bruyette & Woods, a boutique investment bank where she worked in sell-side equity research covering the US banking industry. She holds an MA in Economics from New York University and a BS in Economics from Louisiana State University. She is a Chartered Financial Analyst and speaks Spanish.

Kris Putnam-Walkerly

Founder
Putnam Consulting Group

Kris Putnam-Walkerly is a trusted advisor to high-wealth donors and foundation leaders across the globe, helping them transform their giving and catapult their impact. She's advised over 60 foundations and philanthropists to strategically allocate and assess over $350 million in grants and gifts, including leading funders such as the Charles and Helen Schwab Foundation, David and Lucile Packard Foundation, Robert Wood Johnson Foundation, and Annie E. Casey Foundation.

Putnam is the author of *Confident Giving: Sage Advice for Funders*, which was named one of the 10 Best Corporate Social Responsibility Books. She was named one of America's Top 25 Philanthropy Speakers, and regularly gives keynotes and work-shops at private donor meetings and leading philanthropy asso-ciations. As a thought leader in transformative giving[SM] and delusional altruism[SM], Kris was one of six global consultants inducted into the 2017 Million Dollar Consulting™ Hall of Fame.

Putnam is a frequent contributor in the publications of organ-izations such as the National Center for Family Philanthropy, Exponent Philanthropy, AsianNGO, Learn Philanthropy, Foundation Center, and Southeastern Council on Foundations. She provides expert commentary about philanthropy in the *Wall Street Journal*, *Washington Post*, *Seattle Times*, *Washington Examiner*, Entepreneur.com, BusinessWeek.com, and others. Learn more at putnam-consulting.com.

Stephanie Cohn-Rupp

Managing Director
Threshold Group

Stephanie Cohn-Rupp is Head of Impact Investing, Threshold Group, a multifamily office offering wealth management and family office services to clients throughout the United States. She oversees all aspects of impact investing strategy and crafts mission-aligned portfolios for clients. Stephanie's extensive experience spanning the global ecosystem of impact brings with it a multi-faceted toolkit of skills in sourcing, evaluating and measuring opportunities from both investment and impact perspectives. She is also the Head of the San Francisco Threshold Group Office, growing its local presence in the Bay Area.

Most recently, Cohn-Rupp served as CEO of Toniic, a glo-bal action community of impact investors, who seek social and environmental impact through investment in all asset classes.

She led all aspects of strategy, growth and operations for the San Francisco–based organization. She scaled the organization from 35 to over 300 families and foundations worldwide–growing its presence in the United States, Canada, Mexico, India, Europe, Middle East, Australia and South Africa. She also helped develop the 100%IMPACT network, within Toniic, which is a subgroup of families and foundations dedicated to "total portfolio activation" and peer learning by sharing portfolios, theories of change and how best to overcome obstacles to mission alignment. Prior to Toniic, at Omidyar Network, an impact investment firm created by eBay Founder, Pierre Omidyar, she managed a $70 million portfolio of early stage investments and grants in the United States, Europe, South Asia, West Africa and Latin America focused on property rights and microfinance. She also held positions at Planet Finance originating microfinance loans in Central Asia and Mexico for socially responsible investors and in the public finance group at UBS Investment Bank, where she held a Series 7 license. She has also served as a consultant to the World Bank and UNESCO focused on education finance in Sub-Saharan Africa.

Lindsay Smalling

Producer Curator, SOCAP

Lindsay Smalling is Producer and Curator of the Social Capital Markets Conference (SOCAP), convening impact investors and social entrepreneurs at the intersection of money and meaning. The annual flagship event in San Francisco is the largest conference for impact investors and social entrepreneurs and has drawn more than 12,000 people since 2008. Smalling was previously Strategic Initiatives Officer at ImpactAssets where she was focused on building knowledge resources that advance the field of impact investing, authoring multiple issue briefs and producing the annual ImpactAssets 50.

Prior to receiving an MBA at Columbia Business School, Smalling worked at Entrepreneurs Foundation, consulting with venture-backed, pre-IPO companies on corporate social responsibility programs. She spent the first four years of her career in financial services at Wellington Management and Lord Abbett.

Smalling graduated from Pomona College, where she was a
Division III National Champion in water polo.

Matthew Weatherly-White

Partner
The CAPROCK Group

Shaping The CAPROCK Group's initiative in impact investing,
Matthew Weatherly-White is a sought-after speaker and thought
leader. In addition to keynoting the 2013 European Commission's
Annual Award for Social Innovation, Weatherly-White has guest-
lectured on sustainable business management and nonfinancial value creation at such business schools as Stanford, Oxford,
Dartmouth, Northwestern, University of Chicago and the
American University in Paris, has presented at global conferences,
serves as a strategic advisor to several impact investing funds, and
has been quoted widely in the media, including *Barron's*, *NPR*,
International Business Daily, *Bloomberg Business Week*, *Kipinger's*, *Forbes*
and *The New York Times*. More recently, he successfully shepherded
two pieces of legislation through the Idaho Statehouse: the first
authorizing Pay For Success Contracting and the second awarding
legal status to businesses structured as Benefit Corporations.

Weatherly-White graduated from Dartmouth College, has
competed internationally in five different sports and continues to
serve as a Director for the Lee Pesky Learning Center, an organization he helped launch nearly 20 years ago. When not working,
he can usually be found outside, running, skiing, mountaineer-
ing, cycling ... and generally encouraging his daughter to enjoy
wilderness with the same irrational exuberance as her father.

Special thanks go to the ImpactAssets team for their contributions to this volume. In particular, Amy Bennett contributed
significantly to the profiles as well as resource sections and Mo
Shaffroth also contributed to our vision and marketing for this
edition. Many thanks to you both!

Index